Also by Paula Martinac

Chicken

Home Movies

Out of Time

THE

QUEEREST

PLACES

THE

QUEEREST

PLACES

A National Guide
to Gay and Lesbian
Historic Sites

PAULA MARTINAC

AN OWL BOOK
HENRY HOLT AND COMPANY
NEW YORK

Henry Holt and Company, Inc.
Publishers since 1866
115 West 18th Street
New York, New York 10011

Henry Holt® is a registered
trademark of Henry Holt and Company, Inc.

Library of Congress Cataloging-in-Publication Data

Martinac, Paula, date.
The queerest places: a national guide to gay and lesbian historic
sites / Paula Martinac.—1st ed.
p.   cm.
"An owl book."
Includes bibliographical references and index.
ISBN 0-8050-4480-9 (alk. paper)
1. Gay Men—Travel—United States—Guidebooks.   2. Lesbians—
Travel—United States—Guidebooks.   3. Gay men—United States—
History—Guidebooks.   4. Lesbians—United States—History—
Guidebooks.   I. Title.
HQ75.26.U6M37   1997   97-1707
917.304'929'08664—dc21   CIP

Henry Holt books are available for special promotions and
premiums. For details contact: Director, Special Markets.

First Edition 1997

Designed by Brian Mulligan

Printed in the United States of America
All first editions are printed on acid-free paper. ∞

1   3   5   7   9   10   8   6   4   2

For Katie

my true love and traveling companion through life

A past lacking tangible relics seems too tenuous to be credible.

—David Lowenthal,
The Past Is a Foreign Country

Even today, the public space in which I can be queer
is small, contested, and far from "free."

—Urvashi Vaid,
Virtual Equality: The Mainstreaming of Gay and Lesbian Liberation

CONTENTS

V. MIDWEST

V. WEST

PREFACE

Every morning on my walk to my office, I pass a plaque that marks the address where writer Herman Melville lived while he was writing *Billy Budd*. The actual house is gone, like so many New York landmarks, and a pre–World War II office building stands in its place. But if you look around the neighborhood and notice the other nineteenth-century row houses, you can almost imagine Melville in his later years, beaten down as a writer but still plodding on, penning his homoerotic sailor odyssey.

I can't remember a time when I wasn't attracted to historic places. When I was a child, my parents didn't have to drag me to Civil War battlefields and historic house museums; I went willingly. As an adult, my first professional job was at a restored historic village. I still think a vacation is incomplete unless I've taken in at least one town that time has forgotten. Recently asked about my favorite magazines, I named *Preservation* at the top of my list.

But one thing that historic sites and travel guides never taught me was about a most important part of myself—my heritage as a gay person in this country. If it weren't for the work of lesbian and gay historians in the past few decades, queer history would be buried. I found in compiling this guide that, even in the late 1990s, many gay people I spoke to were unaware that they had any significant collective history at all. "That'll be a short book!" one lesbian said to me when I told her about this project. On the contrary, I found an abundance of "queer" historic sites relating to lesbian, gay, bisexual, and transgender history. Some were popular tourist attractions that had never been written about from a queer perspective. Others were sites that had not been written about at all. Still others no longer existed, victims of time or urban renewal projects.

For my purposes, I defined a "historic site" as any house, structure, or geographic location with an association to a historic queer person or event. A site did not need to be listed on the National Register of Historic Places, nor did a structure need to be still standing to be included in this study. By "queer" I meant individuals of gay, lesbian, or bisexual orientation, either of an affectional or sexual nature, and also transgendered people.

Some people will undoubtedly pick up this book, open to a certain page, and snort, "Hmph! Herman Melville was gay? Where's her proof?" I didn't always have the kind of evidence that would hold up in a court of law or that traditional scholars would accept. In fact, I don't actually believe that "proof" of gay or lesbian sexual relations is required to reclaim a historical figure as queer, any more than "proof" of heterosexual intercourse is required to name a person straight. The very idea that we need "proof" assumes that being queer is "wrong" and that to "accuse" someone of homosexuality is a terrible thing to do.

Like others investigating the queer past, I had to devise an alternate detective system. Because lesbians and gay men have had to hide for such a long time (their sexual relations in almost half the United States are still criminal), many of the rules of evidence simply don't apply. Something as seemingly cut-and-dried as heterosexual marriage and children, for example, can't rule out that someone was gay—how many of your gay friends were married once, too? In claiming people as gay, I was more interested in looking for how people lived their lives—their friends and community, their work, their relationships. And yes, I sometimes relied on rumor and gossip, which has been called the "oral history" of queer people.

In this book, I have also included what will seem to many to be current events more than history, listing sites from as recent a time as the mid-1980s. But since many of the sites associated with the lesbian-feminist movement of the 1970s, for example, have already faded from view, they need to be documented for future queer generations.

Of course, the research for this book could have gone on for years and the finished product could have been two or three times larger than it is. The book is not meant to be exhaustive, merely a subjective sample of sites. While historians in some places have begun to document their region's queer geography (for example, New York City, Boston, Los Angeles, San Francisco, Portland, Chicago), I hope other queer communities will begin to preserve their physical past and dig up all the sites that have been missed.

Because this was an enormous undertaking, I'd like to thank the dozens of people and organizations that provided leads, information, location tips, research help, and outstanding generosity, in particular: Arlene Avakian and Martha Ayres; Fred Bachman, of the Quatrefoil Library; Alison Bechdel; Leo Blackman; Gayl Bowser; Richard Burns, of the Lesbian and Gay Community Services Center, New York; Martha Cabrera; Tom Cook, of the Gay and Lesbian Archives of the Pacific Northwest; John Cooper, of the Cathedral of Hope; Tee A. Corinne; Terri de la Peña; Susannah Driver; Martin Duberman; Gene Elder, of The Happy Foundation; Carol Fitzgerald; Marcia L.

Foster; Trisha Franzen; Fran Goldstein and Tracey Lind; Larry Hanks; Win-
nie Hough and Diana Dawson; Tom Jevec, of the Gerber/Hart Library and
Archives; the Lesbian History Archives; Lee Lynch; Deacon MacCubbin;
Billie Miracle; Ruth Mountaingrove; Ben Munisteri; the Ohio Lesbian
Archives; Penny Perkins and Debra Raftery; Flavia Rando; Yolanda Retter, of
the Lesbian History Project/University of Southern California; Stacy Sulli-
van; Rich Wandel, of the National Museum and Archive of Lesbian and Gay
History; David Williams, of the Williams-Nichols Institute; Barbara Wilson;
Robert Woodworth; and many anonymous friends from the Gay and Lesbian
Forum of America Online.

I've relied heavily on the work of lesbian and gay historians, who have
been diligently unearthing the queer past for the last few decades. I'd especially like to acknowledge the pioneering work of Allan Bérubé, George
Chauncey, Martin Duberman, Lisa Duggan, Lillian Faderman, Jonathan
Ned Katz, Elizabeth Lapovsky Kennedy and Madeline Davis, Eric Marcus,
Joan Nestle, Esther Newton, Judith Schwartz, and Barbara Smith. For this
project, I read dozens of biographies of famous people, many of which never
mentioned their subjects' sexuality or else actively tried to refute the possibility of homosexuality. I began to cherish the biographers who dealt openly
with sexual orientation, in particular Blanche Wiesen Cook, David Hadju,
Helen Lefkowitz Horowitz, Judith Mayne, Patrick McGilligan, and Sharon
O'Brien.

Thanks to Nancy Kraybill and Joan Blair for their heroic investigating of
the Hollywood sites, which, they tell me, required scaling cliffs, trespassing
on private property, and other feats of derring-do.

Thanks also to my agent, Neeti Madan of the Charlotte Sheedy Agency,
and to my editor at Holt, Tracy Sherrod, for believing in this project and for
their faith in me.

And finally, my greatest thanks to my love, Katie Hogan—writer, teacher,
activist—who shared so many of these sites with me and understood from
the beginning why I wanted to do this project. Her unwavering belief in me
and in my work, even while bravely pushing forward with her own, keeps me
going.

—*Paula Martinac*
New York City
February 1997

I

NEW ENGLAND

CONNECTICUT

BRIDGEPORT

Bloodroot
85 Ferris Street
In the late 1970s, Bloodroot opened as a "feminist restaurant/bookstore with a seasonal vegetarian menu," and it is still in operation. The name derived from a native Connecticut wildflower used by local Indians as a dye and for war paint. At its waterfront site, Bloodroot consists of a large white room furnished with tag-sale tables and chairs, none of which match, and one wall covered in her-storic photos of women. Off the restaurant is a small bookstore crammed with books by women. Special weekend and evening events at Bloodroot have included readings and tarot workshops.

Meals at the restaurant are strictly self-service—ordering, picking up food, bussing tables. The veggie menu—printed daily on a chalkboard—includes exotic soups and salads, crusty breads, and rich desserts. The Bloodroot Collective has also published two cookbooks, *The Political Palate* and *The Political Palate II*, which include not only recipes but the most appropriate seasons in which to make the various dishes.

CORNWALL

New England Women's Musical Retreat (NEWMR)
Mohawk Mountain Ski Area
Route 4
This Berkshire ski retreat was the site of the first NEWMR festival on Labor Day weekend in 1981, which the organizers billed as "a three-day retreat into an all-female, women-identified environment filled with workshops, poetry, politics, jam sessions, theater, dance, spirituality, AND

MUSIC." Based on the model of the Michigan Womyn's Music Festival, NEWMR's setup featured sites for "Amazon camping," "slightly ambitious Amazon camping," and "absurdly ambitious Amazon camping." Performers at the first festival included Margie Adam, Latteta Theresa, Alix Dobkin, Maxine Feldman, and Judy Sloan. Festival-goers were expected to share work responsibilities and to bring their own plates and silverware for the vegetarian meals. NEWMR is still going strong today, though in a different location from its original site.

HAMDEN

Thornton Wilder home
50 Deepwood Drive
Though he spent the early part of his life in Wisconsin, California, and Shanghai, playwright Thornton Wilder (1897–1975) called this Hamden address home from 1929 on, and it was here that he died. Wilder won the Pulitzer Prize for drama three times, for *The Bridge of San Luis Rey* (1927), *Our Town* (1938), and *The Skin of Our Teeth* (1942). A lifelong bachelor who as a young man described his own walk and mannerisms as "queer," Wilder was intensely homophobic. He commented to Gore Vidal that "a writer ought not to commit himself to a homosexual situation of the domestic sort" because it would damage his career. As a result, Wilder experienced only arm's-length infatuations, often with actors (including Montgomery Clift), and brief, clandestine sexual encounters. He would have hated this book, believing that to speculate on the sexuality of famous writers was simply to "whip up a prurient oh-ha! in millions of people." (*See also* Berkeley, California; Princeton, New Jersey; and Madison, Wisconsin.)

∧　∧　∧

HARTFORD

Gay pride march

Connecticut's first lesbian and gay pride rally occurred the year following the Stonewall Rebellion in New York City. Organized in the capital city of Hartford, the march stepped off on October 1, 1970, at *Elizabeth Park*, continuing to *Farmington Avenue*, from there to *Ford* and *Trinity Streets*, and finally onto the *south lawn of the state capitol*. Only ninety people participated in this small but historic event.

Rebecca Primus home
20 Wadsworth Street

Much information has already been unearthed about romantic friendships between white women of the last few centuries. But in a compelling recent essay in the journal *Feminist Studies*, Karen V. Hansen writes about a passionate relationship between two African-American women, preserved through correspondence they exchanged before and during the Civil War. One of those women, Rebecca Primus, was born at this address in 1836 and lived here for much of her life.

Rebecca's parents were prominent in the African-American community of Hartford, her father a grocer and her mother a self-employed dressmaker who founded the Talcott Street Church for blacks in 1833. Rebecca received a high school education and became a schoolteacher. Immediately after the Civil War, she went south to Royal Oak, Maryland, where she established a school for those formerly enslaved, which the local community named the Primus Institute in her honor.

Born around 1832, Addie Brown was an orphan, a free black woman who worked at various jobs to support herself—domestic worker, seamstress, cook. She and Rebecca attended the same church in Hartford and became intimate friends. Today, Addie's letters to Rebecca during their various separations are located in the Primus family records at the state historical society. They reveal a passionate relationship between the two women that in all likelihood was sexual. "I turn Mr. Games [her boss, a black man] away this morning," Addie wrote to Rebecca. "No *kisses* is like youres [*sic*]."

The relationship between Addie and Rebecca was accepted by their families—as long as it didn't interfere with their entering heterosexual marriages, which both eventually did. "I do love him," Addie wrote of her soon-to-be-spouse, Joseph Tines, "but not passinately [*sic*] and never will." After Addie's marriage and move to Philadelphia, the women's correspondence dropped off, and Addie died of tuberculosis at age twenty-nine. After her own husband died in 1891, Rebecca returned to Wadsworth Street to live with her mother.

> If you was a man, what would things come to? They would come to something very quick.
> —Addie Brown to Rebecca Primus, ca. 1865

NEW CANAAN

Glass House

Philip Johnson (b. 1906)—the celebrated architect who designed the sculpture garden and East Wing of the Museum of Modern Art, among numerous other structures (*see box below*)—built this home in 1949 in one of the wealthiest areas of Connecticut. The idea for a "glass house" came from an argument with his mentor, Ludwig Mies van der Rohe. Mies van der Rohe said it could be done; Johnson maintained it could not. The two competed to prove each other wrong, with Johnson finishing his house first. Van der Rohe's, located in Plano, Illinois, was not completed until 1950.

Johnson's Glass House is located in a thickly wooded area on a knoll overlooking a pond. "I learned from the Japanese . . . [that] a shelf keeps good spirits from straying, and the evil spirits will be unable to climb up to you," Johnson has noted about the location. The Glass House is a simple, modern structure, a thirty-two by fifty-six foot rectangle with one door centered on each side. Eight black steel columns form the framework, holding sheets of clear glass between them. From the center of the house rises a brick cylinder, which contains a bathroom and fireplace. When Frank Lloyd Wright visited the completed house, he reportedly asked, "Am I indoors or am I out?" Says Johnson, "With the lights out and the snow falling, it is almost like a celestial elevator."

Over the next thirty years, Johnson added other structures to his thirty-three acres of land—a solid brick guest house to contrast with the glass structure; an arched pavilion in the pond; an underground art gallery; and a climbable tower in the woods, built to honor his friend Lincoln Kirstein, cofounder of the New York City Ballet. One critic calls the compound Johnson's "architectural autobiography"; he himself has labeled it "the diary of an eccentric architect." Johnson—whose recent biography revealed him to be gay—has willed the property and all the buildings to the National Trust for Historic Preservation. The compound—complete with a visitors' center designed by Johnson—will remain closed to the public until after the architect's death. Johnson spends long weekends there; remarkably, at age ninety he only recently stopped practicing architecture in New York City.

SELECTED PHILIP JOHNSON DESIGNS

> Sheldon Memorial Art Museum (Lincoln, Nebraska)
> East Wing and Sculpture Garden, Museum of Modern Art (New York City)
> Four Seasons Restaurant (New York City)
> New York State Theater at Lincoln Center (New York City)
> International Place (Boston)
> Transco Tower (Houston)
> PPG Building (Pittsburgh)
> AT&T Building (New York City)
> 580 California (San Francisco)
> RepublicBank Center (Houston)
> Cathedral of Hope (forthcoming; Dallas)

New Haven

Cole Porter residence
242 York Street
While an undergraduate at Yale, Cole Porter (1891–1964) lived at Garland's Rooming House at this location. From his home in Indiana, young Cole arrived in New Haven with a wardrobe of checked suits, pink and yellow shirts, and salmon-colored ties, which he thought were appropriate Ivy League wear but which really made him stand out like a sore thumb. Luckily, he also brought with him a battered upright piano. To win over his more genteel, upper-crust classmates, Porter composed and performed songs with droll, uniquely rhymed lyrics that included the names of the young men whose companionship he craved. His close and longtime friendship with actor Monty Woolley dated from their Yale days. (*See also* Marion and Peru, Indiana; and Williamstown, Massachusetts.)

Southbury

Gladys Taber house
Stillmeadow
Stillmeadow, a house near Southbury dating back to 1690, was the home of Gladys Bass Taber (1899–1980), a syndicated columnist, fiction writer, and memoirist whose work has since passed into obscurity. Taber was known in the 1930s through the 1960s for her down-to-earth books and articles about home, children, gardening, and cooking. In addition to a monthly column in *Ladies' Home Journal* called "The Diary of Domesticity" and a later one in *Family Circle* called "Butternut Wisdom," Taber penned light "women's" novels about frustrated middle-aged housewives and also memoirs of her daily life at Stillmeadow.

What we would never know from her official obituary is that Taber enjoyed a long-term romantic friendship with a woman she called "Jill" in her memoirs. Taber and "Jill" (her real name was Eleanor Mayer) met at summer camp when they were fourteen years old and were later roommates at

Wellesley. Though both married men, they became neighbors in Connecticut, and Taber's memoirs form an unabashed tribute to her "beloved companion." According to Barbara Grier, in *Stillmeadow Daybrook* (1946) Taber neglects to call either Jill's or her own husband by name, though she gives the names of neighbors and even pets! After Jill died in 1960, Taber wrote a book on coping with grief called *Another Path*, in which she asserted that "for me, the world had ended" with her dear Jill's death. Taber's published works also include what Grier calls "variant poetry," which is subtly lesbian and very much open to interpretation.

WESTPORT

Lillian D. Wald house
"House on the Pond"
4 Round Pond Road
Lillian D. Wald (1867–1940), one of the pioneers of the settlement house movement in this country, bought this charming white "house on the pond" in 1917. Between her work at the Henry Street Settlement (*see* New York City, New York) and trips abroad on behalf of the peace movement, Wald entertained friends such as Eleanor Roosevelt and Jane Addams at her quiet country retreat surrounded by willow trees. In the winter, Wald delighted in having local children ice-skate on the pond in front of her home. She retired here in 1933, and on her seventieth birthday, the citizens of Westport presented her with a commemorative photo album, thanking her for making their town "a better and happier place." (*See also* Cincinnati, Ohio.)

Maine

Camden

Edna St. Vincent Millay memorial
Whitehall Inn
52 High Street

A local girl born at *200 Broadway* in Rockland, Edna St. Vincent Millay (1892–1950) used to work at this tourists' inn during the busy summer season. In 1912, "Vincent," as she preferred to be called, did her first public reading here for guests and employees at the inn's end-of-summer party. The first lines of the poem she read, "Renascence," described the view of the Maine countryside from nearby Mount Battle, which Vincent loved to climb. "All I could see from where I stood," the poem began, "was three long mountains and a wood."

Fortuitously, a professor who was vacationing at Whitehall Inn was so impressed by Vincent's poem that he arranged to have one of his wealthy friends pay for the girl to study at Vassar College, from which she graduated in 1917 and where she wrote her play "The Lamp and the Bell," the most overtly lesbian of all her works.

The "Millay Room" of the Whitehall Inn contains a corner display of Millay's books, an unpublished manuscript, and a facsimile of the original draft of "Renascence," which was published in 1912. The exhibit also holds a scrapbook of articles about the poet and photographs of her at various ages. Just north of Camden, on top of the inspirational Mount Battle, an eight-hundred-foot tower bears a plaque honoring Millay. Though Millay lived most of her adult life in New York City and upstate New York, Maine remained a second home to her.

ASIDE-STEP

Cushing Mansion, 31 Chestnut Street, in Camden, is a two-story frame house that belonged to Edna St. Vincent Millay (1892–1950) and her husband, Eugen Boissevain. It was their Maine retreat before they purchased Ragged Island, a deserted hideaway off the Maine coast.

NORTH BROOKLIN

Helen Hull/Mabel Robinson home
Bayberry Farm

Novelist and teacher Helen R. Hull (1888–1971) met her life partner, Mabel Louise Robinson, in 1912 while both were English instructors at Wellesley College. Two years later, the two began renting a summerhouse together on the coast of Maine in the tiny town of North Brooklin. In 1920, they bought the property, which was called Bayberry Farm.

In addition to the white frame main house, the farm had two small outbuildings, where Helen and Mabel had their own writing studios. Friends occasionally joined them for vacations, and one, Eleanor Wheeler, bought the house across the road from them. Other women writers and artists began flocking to North Brooklin in the summers, forming a small, supportive community. As one year-round resident described them to Hull's biographer, Patricia McClelland Miller: "They used to go flying down the roads on their bicycles in their khaki knickers and middy blouses, their hair flying out behind them. They were very strong minded." Locals began calling them "the Bicycle Girls."

Hull and Robinson relocated from Massachusetts to New York in 1915 to teach and study at Columbia University, where they were instrumental in forming the university's creative writing program for adults. One of Hull's most famous students was the young Carson McCullers, whom she called "a nice little girl." (*See also* New York City, New York.)

South Berwick

Haggens House
Portland Street

What is now called Haggens House and serves as the town library was the childhood home of Sarah Orne Jewett (1849–1909). Her grandfather, Captain Theodore Jewett, a wealthy sea captain and trader, purchased the larger house next door at 5 Portland Street in 1839 (*see below*). When his son Thomas married, the captain built this small house for him adjoining his own residence. At his father's death, Thomas, a country doctor, and his family moved to the captain's house, which Sarah eventually inherited and lived in until her own death.

It's fitting that the home where Jewett grew up is now a library, since her early years were spent delving into her family's extensive collection of books. Besides being an avid reader as a child, Jewett also began writing, filling her stories with local characters and idiomatic expressions. She published her first story in *The Atlantic Monthly* when she was just eighteen years old. In 1877, her first book-length work appeared, a collection of stories all focused on Deephaven, a town that very much resembled South Berwick.

Sarah Orne Jewett house
5 Portland Street

Sarah Orne Jewett was born in 1849 and lived much of her adult life in this comfortable frame house belonging to her paternal grandparents. Her friend Willa Cather once wrote that Jewett was "born within the scent of the sea but not within sight of it, in a beautiful old house full of strange and lovely things brought home from all over the globe by seafaring ancestors." Today, the house still contains the Jewett family furnishings, including many items Captain Theodore Jewett brought back from his extensive sea travels, and it looks much as it did when its famous resident lived there.

In the downstairs library hangs a portrait of Annie Fields, Jewett's companion of over twenty-five years, with whom she lived seven months of each year in Boston (*see* Boston, Massachusetts). The months Jewett spent alone in South Berwick were her time for writing and contemplation. "Here I am at my desk again," reads one forlorn letter to Annie, "remembering that this is the first morning in more than seven months that I haven't waked up to hear your dear voice and see your dear face."

Upstairs in the writer's combination bedroom and study is another picture of Fields, as well as a portrait of George Sand, given to Jewett by Willa Cather. Next to her bed Jewett kept a container of pens and pencils so that she would have them at the ready in case she woke up with the desire to write. In this house, Jewett penned such novels as *A Country Doctor* (1884) and *The Country of the Pointed Firs* (1896), which abound in local color. Inspired by the Maine landscape, her fiction focused on "the people who grew out of the soil and the life of the country near her heart," as Cather phrased it.

> When one really knows a village like this and its surroundings, it is like becoming acquainted with a single person. The process of falling in love at first sight is as final as it is swift . . . , but the growth of true friendship may be a lifelong affair.
> —Sarah Orne Jewett, *The Country of the Pointed Firs*

WELLS

Rachel Carson National Wildlife Refuge
Route 2
Beginning in the early 1950s, the eminent scientist Rachel Carson (1907–1964) spent summers in a cottage on Southport Island off the Maine coast, studying local ecology and wildlife. It was there that in 1953 she met Dorothy Freeman, a Massachusetts native who vacationed on the

island with her husband and who was a fan of Carson's *The Sea Around Us.* Both women were intensely interested in sea life and the environment. Carson and Freeman became intimate friends who exchanged voluminous correspondence during the three seasons of the year they were not together, right up until Carson's death. As Rachel Carson wrote to her friend early in their relationship, "I think that the rapid flowering of our friendship, the head-long pace of our correspondence, reflects a feeling, whether consciously recognized or not, for the 'lost' years and a desire to make up for all the time we might have enjoyed this, had something brought us together earlier." Those are pretty strong emotions for "friends."

Freeman's granddaughter was the recipient of the women's correspondence, and she published it (hesitantly) in 1995. She explained that on one of Freeman's visits to Carson's home in Maryland, the two women together burned packets of Freeman's letters in the fireplace. In addition, each independently destroyed some of the other's letters. They were concerned how the intensity of their relationship might look from the outside. The "lesbian question," however, was never raised by Freeman's granddaughter.

In Wells, a wildlife refuge was dedicated to Carson's memory in 1970, six years after her death. In her best-selling *Silent Spring* (1962), the book that helped launch the environmental movement, Carson decried the "senseless destruction" of Maine's natural beauty, its "evergreen forests, roads lined with bayberry and sweet fern, alder and huckleberry." (*See also* White Oak, Maryland; Pittsburgh, Pennsylvania; and Springdale, Pennsylvania.)

Massachusetts

Amherst

Emily Dickinson home
280 Main Street

Emily Dickinson (1830–1886), preeminent nineteenth-century American poet, rarely left her stately yellow clapboard house in the sleepy town of Amherst. Literary history has portrayed her as a recluse, a pathologically shy spinster, when, in fact, she suffered from Graves' disease, which caused frequent urination and quite possibly the need to stay close to home. A dedicated artist, she enjoyed a full life writing in her second-floor bedroom, where she composed reams of poems that she sewed together into handmade books. When Dickinson died, her sister discovered the books in a bureau drawer and unwittingly took apart the stitching, so the poet's original intent in ordering her manuscripts has been lost.

Dickinson's home is now owned by Amherst College and is open only by appointment. The caretakers of the Dickinson Homestead seem a tad nervous about the suggestion that the great poet was a lesbian—in affectional orientation, if not in actual sexual practice. During the tour, visitors are shown the famous photograph of Emily at age eighteen (the only one in existence), in which she looks every inch the serious poet. But they also see a retouched photo, in which Emily is burdened with elaborately curled hair and a frilly lace color—a painstaking attempt on the part of the curators to "femme" her up. This is probably how she looked in later life, the guide contends, not as "plain" as in the early photo.

On the tour, there is much discussion about the men in Emily's life—her alleged "gentlemen callers"—and almost nothing about Sue Gilbert, the sister-in-law with whom she shared an ardent daily correspondence via a clothesline connecting their adjacent homes. "If you were here—and Oh that you were, my Susie, we need not talk at all, our eyes would whisper for us, and your hand fast in mine, we would not ask for language." Beloved "Susie" may also have been the subject of some of Emily's passionate poetry. One of Emily's bedroom windows wistfully faces the home Sue shared with Austin Dickinson. Describing Emily's room, your guide will tell you, "There were no closets in the nineteenth century"—ironic, considering how careful the Dickinson caretakers are to "straighten out" Emily!

> Susie, will you indeed come home next Saturday, and be my own again, and kiss me as you used to? . . . I hope for you so much and I feel so eager for you, feel that I cannot wait, feel that now I must have you—that the expectation once more to see your face again, makes me hot and feverish.
> —Emily Dickinson to her sister-in-law, Sue Gilbert Dickinson

BOSTON

For a more detailed look at lesbian and gay Boston and Cambridge, see "Location: A Historical Map of Lesbian and Gay Boston," available from the Boston Area Gay and Lesbian History Project.

Denison House
93 Tyler Street

Originally located here, Denison House was a settlement house founded in 1892 by Wellesley College professors Vida Scudder, Emily Balch, and Katharine Coman. Like other settlements that had sprouted up across the country, Denison House was designed to ease the transition of the large immigrant population into American society, offering education, medical attention, and child care to the newly arrived. A dedicated activist and radical socialist, Scudder later wrote, "The center of my social living was at that dear House . . . where fifteen hundred people a week were presently passing through our pretty Green Room." At Wellesley, Scudder lived in a "Wellesley marriage" with another professor, writer Florence Converse. Coman was the life partner of Katharine Lee Bates, author of "America the Beautiful" (*see* Wellesley, Massachusetts). Denison House is still in operation, but its present-day location is at 584 *Columbia Road, Dorchester.*

Annie Fields/Sarah Orne Jewett home
148 Charles Street

In December 1879, Sarah Orne Jewett, a young writer, attended an *Atlantic Monthly* reception in Boston in honor of Oliver Wendell Holmes. At that party she met Annie Adams Fields, the wife of James Fields, cofounder of the publishing company Ticknor & Fields and editor of the *Atlantic Monthly.* Annie Fields was a vivacious hostess who ran a salon attended by such prominent cultural figures as Charles Dickens, Winslow Homer, Ralph Waldo Emerson, and Henry Wadsworth Longfellow. When her husband died in 1881, Annie quickly published a biography to honor his memory.

But prior to James Fields's death, Annie Fields and Sarah Orne Jewett had already become intimate companions. One of Jewett's 1880 poems, originally titled "Love and Friendship," recalled in romantic detail a visit to Fields at her summer home in Manchester-by-the-Sea. Their schedule of living together in Boston for about seven months of each year began in 1882, after a trip they made to Europe together, and continued until Jewett's death. The remaining months of the year Jewett spent writing at her home in Maine (*see* South Berwick, Maine).

Jewett's presence at 148 Charles Street was taken for granted by Fields's friends, whose invitations and letters included both women, in recognition of their status as a couple. A large drawing room that ran the length of the house and enjoyed a view of the Charles River was the site of Annie's famous salon. With bookcases to the ceiling and every corner filled with literary and art treasures, it was no wonder Henry James once christened Fields's home "the waterside museum." Its atmosphere, James went on, fostered "the cultivation of talk and wit." Today, a parking garage stands where "Mrs. Fields and Miss Jewett" once held court.

Angelina Weld Grimké home
61 Temple Street

Angelina Weld Grimké (1880–1958) was born at this address in Boston and was named for her white great-aunt, Angelina Grimké. Aunt Angelina was from an aristocratic South Carolina family but rebelled and immigrated north with her sister, Sarah. The two famous sisters were both ardent abolitionists and women's rights activists. In their old age, they discovered the existence of two black nephews, sons of their brother by one of his slaves, and they helped the young men with their education and careers. One of these nephews, Archibald, became a distinguished lawyer, married a white woman, and fathered the poet Angelina Weld Grimké.

Angelina's mother left when she was small, and her father raised his daughter in the lap of luxury. She attended private schools and had many opportunities that other young black women did not have. But her father was a busy man who traveled often, and Angelina filled her time by writing poetry. For a while, she lived with her uncle and was inspired by the example of his wife, Charlotte Forten Grimké, a poet who had also been the first black teacher with the Port Royal Experiment during the Civil War. (*See* St. Helena's Island, South Carolina.)

> *How little we knew my Darling,*
> *All that the year would bring!*
> *Did I think of the wretched mornings*
> *When I should kiss my ring*
> *And long with all my heart to see*
> *The girl who gave the ring to me?*
> —Sarah Orne Jewett, "Love and Friendship," 1880

Angelina was also trained as a teacher and worked for a number of years at Dunbar High School, a black college preparatory school in Washington, D.C. During the Harlem Renaissance, her poems frequently appeared in such magazines as *The Crisis* and *Opportunity* and in anthologies by Alain Locke and Countee Cullen. Gloria T. Hull has characterized Grimké's published poetry as "delicate, musical, romantic, and pensive," often expressing a sad wish for the "peace" of death. In addition to her poetry, Grimké authored a well-known play about lynching, *Rachel*, which she wrote "to enlighten the American people relative to the lamentable condition of ten millions of Colored citizens in this free republic."

Gloria Hull has discovered numerous unpublished love poems by Grimké—with titles such as "Rosalie," "If," and "To Her of the Cruel Lips"—that dealt with painful, unrequited, or secret lesbian love. In contrast, Grimké's published love poems were more circumspect and closety, carefully avoiding references to gender. Not surprisingly, most studies of Grimké's work other than Hull's fail to mention her lesbian work.

Elizabeth Peabody home
15 West Street

Social and educational reformer Elizabeth Peabody (1804–1894) was the model for the lesbian character Miss Birdseye in Henry James's *The Bostonians*. The book-filled parlor of Peabody's home on West Street served as a bookstore and literary center, where she sold the works of writers such as Thoreau and Hawthorne and where the Transcendental Club routinely met. The journal of the Transcendentalists, *The Dial*, was copublished by Peabody. Committed to education, she is also remembered as the founder of the first public kindergarten in the United States.

Every Wednesday afternoon from 1839 to 1844 in Peabody's parlor, writer Margaret Fuller (1810–1850) led a few dozen young women in "conversations." From these talks came the ideas that Fuller eventually published as *Woman in the Nineteenth Century* (1845), now a classic feminist text. Though she married and had a child, Fuller admitted only a few years before her early death to being a woman-loving woman and wrote in defense of same-sex passion: "It is so true that a woman may be in love with a woman, and a man with a man."

Pinckney Street

A number of famous queer folk lived along Pinckney Street in the past. Some of them are:

George Middleton, 5 Pinckney Street: This was the first house on the street, built in 1786 by two African-American men—George Middleton, a coachman who had led an all-black regiment during the Revolutionary War, and Louis Clapion, a barber. Middleton, a confirmed bachelor, died in 1815, willing all his house and his possessions to "my good friend Trustom Babcock."

F. Holland Day, 9 Pinckney Street: F. Holland Day (1864–1933), a photographer who concentrated his work primarily on the male form as art, located his studio here beginning in 1894. Six years later, a horrible fire destroyed most of his prints and negatives, and Day's fame subsequently declined.

Louisa May Alcott, 20 Pinckney Street: The creator of the indomitable Jo March lived at this location in the late 1860s at the time *Little Women* was published, though the book was actually written at a rooming house at 6 *Hayward Place*. A strong, career-minded woman, Alcott counted among her close friends actress Charlotte Cushman and her lover, sculptor Emma Stebbins. (*See also* District of Columbia, and Concord, Massachusetts.)

ASIDE-STEP

One of Boston-born Charlotte Cushman's (1816–1876) most famous theatrical roles was played in drag—as Romeo in the Shakespearean tragedy.

^ ^ ^

Pre-Stonewall gay hangouts

The following lesbian and gay venues were in existence decades before the Stonewall Rebellion of 1969, and a few are still going strong:

The Block, Marlborough Street (near the Public Gardens): Famous as a gay cruising area in the 1950s, this block was nicknamed "Vaseline Alley."

Cavana's, 335 Tremont Street: This was a "rough" lesbian bar in the 1950s and early 1960s. As in many early bars catering to queers, there was one room for straight people and another for lesbians.

The Empty Barrel, 99½ Broadway: One of the earliest-known lesbian bars in the Boston area, it was popular in the 1930s. Tables and chairs were made of barrels, hence the name.

The Napoleon Club, 52 Piedmont Street: Though this piano bar has been a haven for queer Bostonians since the 1940s, The Napoleon Club became exclusively gay in 1952. Celebrities such as Judy Garland (*see also* Grand Rapids, Minnesota) and Liberace paid visits here.

Playland, 21 Essex Street: This is the oldest gay bar still in operation in the city, opening in 1937 and exclusively gay since the 1940s. Notably, the bar has served Thanksgiving and Christmas dinners to the homeless since 1950.

22 Bromfield Street

This building acted as an ad hoc lesbian and gay community center during the mid-1970s and early 1980s. Groups that rented the space here on the second floor included the publications *Gay Community News* (*GCN*), *Fag Rag*, and *Boston Gay Review*, as well as Glad Day Bookshop (now at 673 Boylston Street). The Boston Area Lesbian and Gay History Project—part of a national move to recover our lost history—held its first meeting here in 1980. After numerous threats and break-ins—"Some years our offices were broken into and ransacked three or four times in a single year," says former *GCN* editor Richard Burns—arson finally destroyed 22 Bromfield in 1982.

^   ^   ^

BROOKLINE

Amy Lowell home
"Sevenels"
Heath Street

Amy Lowell (1874–1925) was born in Brookline to a wealthy and prominent New England family. Her father, Augustus, was, among other things, one of the founders of the Massachusetts Institute of Technology. Here at the Lowells' ten-acre estate, young Amy—who was born late in her parents' lives and was much younger than her siblings—led a lonely childhood, roaming beautiful gardens landscaped by her father. She lived in the elegant mansion all her life, redecorating many of the rooms according to her own taste after the death of her parents. For example, she combined the front and back parlors to create a magnificent library with built-in bookshelves and imported carved paneling. There in a plush leather chair with matching hassock she would spend hours reading and thinking.

Lowell has been painted by critics as a homely, obese, cigar-smoking spinster who never knew real passion. But, in fact, she met the love of her life, Ada Dwyer Russell (*see* Salt Lake City, Utah) in 1912, and the two were constant companions for a dozen years. It took Lowell two years to convince Russell (whom she called her "very intimate friend") to come and live with her at Sevenels, which Russell finally did in 1914. Forsaking her own career, Russell concentrated instead on Lowell's—she read the proofs for all of Lowell's books and listened to all of her compositions in the evenings, serving as both audience and critic. Lowell often stated that she wanted to put a sign over the doorway at Sevenels that would read: "Lowell & Russell, Makers of Fine Poems." Russell was not only Lowell's critic,

When you came, you were like red wine and honey,
And the taste of you burnt my mouth with its sweetness.
—Amy Lowell, "A Decade"

she was also the inspiration for much of her poetry. Lowell was always careful, though, to make her poems gender-neutral, as in the above excerpt from "A Decade." Only those who knew both of the women suspected the identity of Lowell's "muse."

CAMBRIDGE

Alice James home
20 Quincy Street

No longer standing, this was the home of the celebrated James family in the 1860s. A brilliant and talented woman completely eclipsed by her older brothers Henry and William, Alice James (1848–1892) understandably suffered from a severe depression that kept her in bed during the last years of her life. (Susan Sontag has written a play about her called "Alice in Bed.") Alice's only published work, her diary, appeared posthumously to great critical acclaim.

The most important relationship of Alice's life was with Katharine Loring, whom she met around 1880, shortly after suffering a nervous breakdown. Katharine, healthy and energetic, had an enormous and positive impact on Alice's outlook. Henry James—who pictured a Boston marriage in his novel *The Bostonians*—wrote that Katharine's love for Alice was "a devotion so perfect and generous . . . that to brush it aside would be almost an act of impiety." The two women traveled to England together in 1884 and lived there until Alice's death, though they did not occupy the same house until 1891, when Alice became seriously ill and Katharine cared for her.

Lesbian-feminist Cambridge

Here are a few Cambridge sites associated with the women's movement of the 1970s, some of which are still in operation and going strong:

Bread and Roses, 134 Hampshire Street: During the mid-1970s, Bread and Roses was a women's café and an ad hoc community center. Such lesbian and bisexual celebrities as Audre Lorde, Kate Millett, and Alice

Walker read here during its heyday. Bread and Roses was succeeded by a similar women's space called Amaranth, run by the Ducky Haven Cafe Collective, which closed in 1979.

Cambridge Women's Center, 46 Pleasant Street: Founded in 1971 and still active today, the Center offers meeting space to a variety of lesbian groups. Lesbian Liberation has been meeting there since the first year. The Center was the site of the meetings of the Combahee River Collective, the famous women of color activist group founded in 1974, whose leadership included many well-known lesbians, such as writer-publisher Barbara Smith.

New Words, 186 Hampshire Street: Originally located in Somerville, New Words has been the metropolitan area's major women's bookstore since 1974.

Old Cambridge Baptist Church, 1151 Massachusetts Avenue: The last remaining chapter of the pioneering lesbian organization the Daughters of Bilitis (*see* San Francisco, California) has met at this location since the late 1970s.

Mt. Auburn Cemetery
580 Mount Auburn Street

A guide map is available at the entrance to this historic cemetery, which will steer you to the famous lesbians and woman-identified women buried in this beautiful spot—as long as you know who to look for. You can visit the graves of actress Charlotte Cushman, writer Margaret Fuller (*see* Boston, Massachusetts), sculptor Harriet Hosmer (*see* St. Louis, Missouri), and poet Amy Lowell (*see* Brookline, Massachusetts). Also in the park is a statue by lesbian sculptor Edmonia Lewis (*see* Oberlin, Ohio) of Hygeia, the Greek goddess of health, which was commissioned in 1875 for the grave of pioneering physician Harriot K. Hunt.

∧   ∧   ∧

CONCORD

Louisa May Alcott home
"Orchard House"
399 Lexington Road

Louisa May Alcott (1832–1888), who immortalized her girlhood in the novel *Little Women* (1868) moved to Orchard House with her parents, Bronson and Abby, and her sister May (Amy in the novel) in 1858. An older sister, Anna (Meg), was about to be married and leave home, and a third sister, Lizzie (Beth), died of complications from scarlet fever just a few months before the family moved here. Though this is the classic New England house depicted in the movie version of *Little Women*, the Alcott girls' home during their adolescence was in fact located just down the road.

Louisa did much of her writing at a semicircular shelf desk in her second-floor bedroom, but *Little Women* was not written here, as legend has it, but in a rooming house in Boston. The flowers painted on Louisa's bedroom floor were done by May, and the bookshelves were built by Bronson himself. In fact, over half of the furnishings in the house today belonged to the Alcott family. The small trunk in May's room preserves the costumes that the young Alcott girls wore in the amateur theatricals that Louisa (the model for Jo) wrote and in which she preferred to take the male roles.

In *Little Women*, Louisa married off Jo to the Professor, giving in to the social mores of her age. But, in fact, Louisa May Alcott never married and thought that Jo "should have remained a literary spinster," as she later wrote to a friend. Louisa was an ardent feminist who believed the "Boston marriage" to be the answer for independent and strong-willed women, though she never seemed to have one intimate companion of her own. Her active life took her to Washington, D.C., as a nurse during the Civil War. Here, she produced over three dozen books, some of which were gory, "unladylike" thrillers written under the pseudonym A. M. Barnard. One of the best-paid writers of her day, the self-sacrificing Louisa (who really yearned to be an actress) supported her parents financially for years and also paid for May's artistic training. (*See also* District of Columbia, and Boston, Massachusetts.)

Walden Pond
Route 126 (near intersection Route 2)

The sexuality of Henry David Thoreau (1817–1862) has been a subject of considerable discussion. Was he asexual? Homosexual? Thoreau wrote very little about women except to complain that they "lacked brains" and were "feeble." His writings abound, however, in longing references to love and companionship between men. "What if we feel a yearning to which no breast answers," Thoreau wondered, sounding like so many other isolated gay people. "I walk alone. My heart is full. . . . I knock on the earth for my friend. I expect to meet him at every turn." Thoreau also devoted much space in his writings to Alek Therien, a handsome though "boorish" French-Canadian woodchopper whose acquaintance he made, and to Tom Fowler, his rugged guide on a trip to Maine. Like his contemporaries Walt Whitman and Herman Melville, Thoreau was attracted to strong, "simple" laborers who "represent the bodies of men."

Thoreau is perhaps best remembered as the author of *Walden, or Life in the Woods* (1854), a reflection on the two years that he enjoyed a rustic life of self-imposed solitude in a cabin on the northern shore of Walden Pond, "a mile from any neighbor." He earned his living entirely by his hands, taking on odd carpentry and surveying jobs. "I have . . . a tight shingled and plastered house," Thoreau wrote, "ten feet wide by fifteen long, and eight-feet posts, with a garret and a closet, a large window on each side, two trap doors, one door at the end, and a brick fireplace opposite." Built by its occupant from local pine trees and secondhand materials, Thoreau's cabin cost a total of twenty-eight dollars in 1845, less than a year's lodging at nearby Harvard, his alma mater. In the book *Discovery at Walden*, Roland Robbins reveals how he pinpointed the exact location of the cabin, which is no longer standing but which has markers outlining its placement.

FALL RIVER

Lizzie Borden house
92 Second Street (formerly 234 Second Street)

> *Lizzie Borden took an axe,*
> *Gave her mother forty whacks.*
> *When she saw what she had done,*
> *Gave her father forty-one.*

The gruesome August 1892 murders of Andrew and Abbey Borden, a wealthy Fall River businessman and his second wife, have haunted American legend, literature, and song. Borden's youngest daughter, Lizzie, a thirty-two-year-old spinster who lived with her father and stepmother, was tried for and acquitted of the bloody murders. Though evidence strongly pointed to Lizzie's guilt, proper Fall River society considered it "unseemly" to incarcerate a lady. With their hefty inheritance, Lizzie and her older sister Emma (also unmarried) purchased an elegant mansion on a hill overlooking the town, where their many guests included Lizzie's intimate companion, actress Nance O'Neill.

The Second Street house where the murders were committed still stands, looking much as it did in Lizzie's day. In August of 1996, it opened as a bed and breakfast, and intrepid guests can now actually stay in the murder room. The owners also have on view a collection of Borden memorabilia. Lizzie's story is also preserved across town at the *Fall River Historical Society Museum, 451 Rock Street*, a venerable 1840s mansion where the tour guides revel in the gory details of the murders. If you have the stomach for it, you can view on display the axe that whacked the Bordens, as well as photos of the crime scene and the Bordens' cleft skulls. But be prepared for your guide to pooh-pooh the rumors of Lizzie's same-sex affectional orientation and her relationship with Nance O'Neill.

The house that the Borden sisters bought with their inheritance is also still standing at *306 French Street*. A much grander home than their father's, Lizzie and Emma's house had fourteen rooms in all, with four bathrooms, a carriage house, a garden, and a staff of servants. Though the wealthy of Fall River frowned on naming their residences (too "common"), Lizzie called the new home "Maplecroft" and had the name chiseled into the top step of the front entrance, where you can still see it if you pass by.

FALMOUTH

Katharine Lee Bates birthplace
16 Main Street

Best known as the author of "America the Beautiful," Katharine Lee Bates (1859–1929) was born at this address. Bates's mother was a teacher who instructed her children at home. From childhood, the precocious Katharine kept a journal, in which at age nine she wrote: "I like women better than men. . . . Girls are a very necessary portion of creation. They are full as necessary as boys."

After attending Wellesley College, Bates was invited to teach English there in 1885, which she did until her retirement in 1920. At Wellesley, she moved in a circle of "Wellesley marriages" and enjoyed a twenty-year relationship with history and economics professor Katharine Coman. (See Wellesley, Massachusetts.)

Other sites in Falmouth associated with Bates include a bronze statue of the author on the grounds of the *Falmouth Public Library, Main Street*, which portrays Bates at the summit of Pikes Peak, where she was inspired to write the poem that won her fame (*see also* Colorado Springs, Colorado.) Bates is buried at *Oak Grove Cemetery*, and at her gravesite a stone with the text of "America the Beautiful" commemorates her contribution to the American patriotic spirit.

^   ^   ^

LEE

Jacob's Pillow Dance Festival
Ted Shawn Theater
Route 20 (about eight miles east of Lee)

In 1915, modern dance pioneers Ted Shawn and Ruth St. Denis founded the Denishawn School of Dancing and the Denishawn Company in Los Angeles, whose most illustrious student was Martha Graham. In her autobiography, Graham wrote that Shawn was prone to auditioning men for Denishawn by requiring that they send nude photos of themselves. Shawn and St. Denis (who was fourteen years older than Shawn) were legally husband and wife for fifty years, though each enjoyed outside affairs. In 1927, they unfortunately fell in love with the same man, Fred Beckman, whom they made their "personal representative." Having the same taste in men caused an irreparable split in their marriage, and four years later, they began living separately and closed Denishawn.

Shawn (1891–1972) bought a colonial-era farm at this location in the Berkshires after his marriage collapsed. He called the site Jacob's Pillow after a big, sloping rock near the main house. In 1933, he founded an all-male troupe called the "Men Dancers," designed to showcase men's contributions to the field of modern dance. Shawn and his young male dancers lived on the property in a rustic setting without heat or running water. (Shawn had a private shower and toilet, but the other dancers used an outhouse papered with covers from the *New Yorker*.) At lunchtime, on the terrace, Shawn would read aloud to the dancers, who were all nude, from books on art, physics, and history.

The Men Dancers gave their first performance at Jacob's Pillow in the summer of 1933. It was held in the barn/studio and attended by fifty people, who paid seventy-five cents each. After that, the company held dance performances yearly, though they were then called "teas" and not a festival. Shawn's company lasted until 1940, when he disbanded it and gave each member either a cash settlement or a parcel of land at Jacob's Pillow. The rest of the land he sold the following year to a group who founded the

Jacob's Pillow Dance Festival, which continues today as one of the world's preeminent performance festivals. In 1942, the festival converted the old barn into the Ted Shawn Theater, which retained the rustic charm of the early days of Shawn's endeavor while being the first theater designed specifically for dance.

LOWELL

Jack Kerouac Commemorative
Eastern Canal Park

Writer Jack Kerouac (1922–1969) was born in this old mill town to French-Canadian parents, and he did not learn to speak English until he went to school. Kerouac left Lowell at age seventeen for New York, where he briefly attended Columbia University. In 1944, his first wife, Edie Parker, introduced him to Allen Ginsberg and William Burroughs, and the triumvirate formed the core of the disaffected Beat Generation of the 1950s and 1960s. ("Beat" referred to being tired and downtrodden, not to poetic rhythm.) Kerouac's most famous novel, *On the Road* (1957), was written in three weeks and became a bible for the Beats.

Kerouac married three times and had one daughter, whom he never acknowledged. (Jan Kerouac, also a writer, committed suicide in 1996.) He also had a variety of male lovers, among them Ginsberg, Burroughs, and writer Gore Vidal. Ambivalent about his sexuality, Kerouac never included homosexuality as a theme in his writing. An alcoholic, he died young of complications of the disease.

Lowell erected this sculpture to its native son in 1988, after several years of dispute over whether the town should memorialize an alcoholic. Citing his literary contributions, Kerouac supporters won out, and Ginsberg read some of his early poems at the June dedication. "Kerouac is the heart and spirit of what has brought us together!" Ginsberg proclaimed. The series of commemorative panels is inscribed with excerpts from Kerouac's works, including the opening paragraph of *On the Road*.

NANTUCKET

Tennessee Williams retreat
31 Pine Street
In the summer of 1946, playwright Tennessee Williams and his lover at the time, Pancho Rodriguez y Gonzalez, were renting a "wind-battered, gray two-story house" at this address on the island of Nantucket. Williams had been ailing on and off all year and was having difficulty with the play he was trying to write, which was then called *Chart of Anatomy.*

Earlier that year, Williams had read Carson McCullers's new novel, *The Member of the Wedding*, and wrote her a fan letter. A mutual friend arranged for McCullers to visit Williams on Nantucket for a weekend. The two writers had an immediate rapport, and the "weekend" quickly turned into half the summer. Together they swam, rode bicycles around the island, and enjoyed candlelit dinners. Stationed at opposite ends of the cottage's long dining room table, Williams worked on the first draft of *Chart of Anatomy* while McCullers began transforming *The Member of the Wedding* into a play, using the model of *The Glass Menagerie.*

At the end of his new friend's visit, Williams presented McCullers with a jade ring that had belonged to his beloved sister, Rose, who like McCullers had suffered from depression and ill health. And when completed, Williams's play—with the revised title, *Summer and Smoke*—was dedicated to Carson McCullers.

PITTSFIELD

Herman Melville home
"Arrowhead"
780 Holmes Road
There's a marked difference between the way that Emily Dickinson's home and Herman Melville's home are interpreted for the public. Both were prominent nineteenth-century writers, but at the Dickinson homestead, guides focus on Emily's "petite figure" and the number of her "suit-

ors." By contrast, at Arrowhead Melville's writing is of foremost importance, his study the centerpiece of the house.

At Arrowhead, where he lived from 1850 to 1863, Herman Melville (1819–1891) wrote what is considered his masterpiece, *Moby-Dick* (1851), reportedly inspired by the view from the window of his study of Mount Greylock, a rolling mountain with the vague shape of a giant whale. Melville would rise early to feed the farm animals, and then after breakfast he would light the fire in his study and work on his writing until late afternoon.

It was also here in the Berkshires that his friendship and fascination with Nathaniel Hawthorne, who lived nearby, blossomed, though there is no evidence that the relationship between the two writers was anything but platonic. Melville held a lifelong attraction for sailors, filling his sea tales with homoerotic undertones. If you carefully examine the document displayed on his desk at Arrowhead, you will smile at a line in a letter to his seafaring brother, who had complained about the laziness of his fellow sailors. "For my part I love sleepy fellows," Herman Melville wrote, "and the more ignorant the better."

Melville wrote many other works at Arrowhead, including the humorous short story "I and My Chimney," in which he extolled the virtues of his large stone chimney. Later, Melville's brother Allan lived at Arrowhead and had the opening sentences of the story inscribed around the fireplace in honor of his famous brother. At this location, Melville also penned the six stories known as *The Piazza Tales*, named for the piazza that

I have been building some shanties of houses (connected with the old one) and likewise some shanties of chapters & essays. I have been ploughing & sowing & raising & printing & praying, and now begin to come out upon a less bristling time, and to enjoy the calm prospect of things from a fair piazza at the north of the old farmhouse here.

—Herman Melville

ran the width of the house, which he added to Arrowhead during his years there.

When he purchased Arrowhead with the help of his wife's father, Melville had the idea that he would write part-time and farm the rest. But he was unprepared for the strenuous life of a farmer, and his experiment finally ended after more than a decade, when he and his family moved to New York City and Melville became a customs office inspector (*see also* New York City, New York). Arrowhead is now operated by the Berkshire County Historical Society and is open for tours daily.

PROVINCETOWN

A resort that draws gay people like flies, Provincetown started off as a quiet Portuguese fishing village. In the late nineteenth century with the arrival of rail transportation, Provincetown became a popular artists' retreat, best known as the site of the founding of the little theater group, the Provincetown Players, in 1915. Where there are arts, you're bound to find gay people, and Charles Demuth, Marsden Hartley, Katharine Lee Bates, Edna St. Vincent Millay, Mabel Dodge, and Edna Ferber were just a few of the queers flocking to P-town in the early part of the century. (When Bates first arrived, she described P-town's narrow streets as "queer, irregular crossways.") Later came Robert Duncan and Tennessee Williams, who called the town the "frolicsome tip of the Cape." Gradually, Provincetown gained a reputation as a queer haven, and it now boasts numerous gay and lesbian guest houses, bars, bookstores, and restaurants, as well as contemporary celebrities-in-residence.

A few queer historic sites in P-town are:

Ace of Spades
193-A Commercial Street
Currently the location of a popular women's bar, the Pied Piper, the Ace of Spades was its lesbian predecessor, which opened about 1950 and continued in operation through the 1960s.

Atlantic House
8 Masonic Place

Now home to a popular gay bar, this was probably the rooming house where Tennessee Williams first stayed in the summer of 1940, which he called a "charmingly casual old frame building with a swing on the verandah." On his first evening in town, Williams wrote in his memoirs, he encountered at the rooming house "a blond youth who succumbed to my precipitate courtship." After a short stay, Williams rented an apartment at *30 Commercial Street.*

Captain Jack's Wharf

"Some casual acquaintance took me to the wharf one noonday," Tennessee Williams recalled of his 1940 summer in Provincetown. At the stove of a two-story shack on the wharf, Kip Kiernan—"the youth to whom I dedicated my first collection of stories"—was cooking clam chowder, and Williams was instantly smitten. Within a short time, he had moved into Kiernan's second-floor room with him and wrote to his friend Donald Windham that he could hear "the tide lapping under the wharf. The wind blows the door wide open, the gulls are crying." The affair lasted only the summer. Within a few years, Kiernan married and died at age twenty-six of a brain tumor.

On a return to Provincetown in 1944, Williams rented a one-room studio on this wharf close to the place where he had cohabited with Kiernan.

Robert Duncan cottage
42 Pearl Street

The noted Robert Duncan (1919–1988) rented a cottage here in the summer and fall of 1944 for a grand total of one hundred and fifty dollars. That was still pricey for Duncan, who washed dishes in a local restaurant to support himself. He set up a work space and library for himself in the cottage's L-shaped living room. But Duncan was lonely without someone to share it with: "This house is so desolate," he wrote. He found the P-town landscape and weather "grey and foggy with weird lights."

Flagship Restaurant
463 Commercial Street (at Bangs)
The oldest restaurant in town, the Flagship opened in 1933, and in its
early days reputedly served such famous queer folk as Gertrude Stein and
Anaïs Nin.

Peaked Hill dune shacks
Snail Road
These beach shacks have stood on the dunes since the early twentieth
century. Many others were destroyed by hurricanes over the years, including the one that Mabel Dodge restored and that later belonged to Eugene
O'Neill. Since 1988, the shacks have been listed on the National Register
of Historic Places and are available for rental by lottery. Tours of the dune

ASIDE-STEP

In the early twentieth century, John A. Francis was a local grocer and
East End real estate broker who found housing and negotiated deals for
many P-town celebrities, including Mabel Dodge and Eugene O'Neill.
He also rented out rooms above his grocery store on Commercial Street
(near Conway), and in the summer of 1916, Marsden Hartley and
Charles Demuth stayed at Francis's Flats, as did O'Neill and his wife.
Demuth, a close friend of O'Neill's (the playwright based his *Strange
Interlude* character Charles Marsden on the painter—*see also* Lancaster, Pennsylvania), was reportedly the one who inscribed part of a
favorite poem on the rafters of O'Neill's apartment, the lines of which
are still visible.

A real dandy, Demuth habitually dressed in white trousers, a black
shirt, and highly polished black shoes, with a plum-colored scarf
draped around his waist. Reportedly, he liked to ride the town bus from
one end of town to the other, waving to his friends.

shacks are given by reservation (518-487-1950). Reportedly, Tennessee Williams and Jack Kerouac, among others, once stayed in the cottages, but there isn't any reference to them in any of the literature about Williams.

SALEM

The entire town of Salem is included here, because its name is indelibly linked with witchcraft. Salem's persecution and execution of innocent citizens in the late 1600s—most of whom were, in one way or another "misfits," and several of whom were suspiciously unmarried women—is notorious. The word "witch-hunt" is now synonymous with any institutionalized scapegoating of individuals—such as of Communists and homosexuals during the McCarthy era. Today, Salem capitalizes on its gruesome past with several campy museums, among them the *Salem Witch Museum, 19-1/2 Washington Square*, and the *Witch Dungeon Museum, 16 Lynde Street*, which features a live reenactment of a witch trial. *Judge Jonathan Corwin's home, 310-1/2 Essex Street*, was the site of many witch "examinations."

WELLESLEY

Katharine Lee Bates–Katharine Coman home
"The Scarab"
70 Curve Street
In 1887, while a young English instructor at Wellesley, Katharine Lee Bates, the author of the poem "America the Beautiful," met the woman who would become her life partner, Katharine Coman, a history and economics teacher at the college. Bates and Coman became part of a community of "Wellesley marriages," which included, among others, Vida Scudder and Florence Converse. Susan B. Anthony called the late nineteenth century the "epoch of the single woman," when it was commonplace for unmarried female teachers to live together and be treated much

as married couples were. It was not until the 1930s that single women on the faculty of Wellesley came under attack as "abnormal" and that same-sex colleges were criticized for promoting a "homosexual atmosphere."

Bates and Coman first began living together in 1894, sharing a house near campus with a female chemistry professor. Finally, in 1907 Bates had "The Scarab" built to order for her and Coman (whom she affectionately called "Joy-of-Life") with royalties from "America the Beautiful." The house was named for a carved amulet that Bates had brought back from a trip to Egypt. Construction put her heavily in debt, and the two women decorated their home with secondhand furniture and books. Historian Judith Schwartz paints a portrait of "The Scarab" as large and sunny with "cozy corners, fireplaces, and bookcases everywhere." Bates herself described it as "simple in its appointments . . . a dear little house . . . all furnished with nothing but books."

On the third floor was a spacious room nicknamed "Bohemia," which served as Katharine Coman's study. When Coman became ill with breast cancer in 1914, Bates had a hole cut through the three floors of the house to accommodate an elevator, so that her beloved could still come downstairs to enjoy evenings with friends. After Coman's death a year later, Bates used "Bohemia" as her own study but kept all of Coman's things as they had been in her life. Bates retired from teaching in 1920 and devoted her remaining years to writing. In 1922, she published a memoir of her re-

ASIDE-STEP

One of the earliest recorded references to lesbianism in the American colonies was a court hearing against Sara Norman and Mary Hammond in Plymouth in 1649. Both women were married to men and living in Yarmouth when they were charged with "leude behauior each with [the] other upon a bed." Mary Hammond, who was fifteen years old, was pardoned, but Sara Norman, who was older, was forced to publicly declare her "unchaste behavior" with Hammond.

lationship with Coman called *Yellow Clover: A Book of Remembrance,* in which she called them "one soul together." "The Scarab," Bates wrote, "was a house where rich memories were cherished lovingly. . . . it was always 'our laurel,' 'our home.'" (*See also* Colorado Springs, Colorado, and Falmouth, Massachusetts.)

WILLIAMSTOWN

Cole Porter home
"Buxton Hill" (off Route 7)
In 1919, composer Cole Porter (1891–1964) married sophisticated divorcée Linda Lee Thomas, a woman eight years his senior who may have been a lesbian. Whatever her sexual orientation, Linda proved a perfect "beard" for her husband, agreeing to separate bedrooms early in the marriage and tolerating his frequent, though always brief, sexual encounters with men.

The Porters had homes in Los Angeles and New York City before purchasing this two-hundred-acre estate in the northwest corner of Massachusetts. Cole hated the place at first, complaining that it was too far removed from the active social life he was accustomed to in Manhattan. Later, he grew to love the sprawling estate, when he discovered he could entertain in the style he enjoyed and accommodate numerous guests in the spacious main house and the separate guest cottage. Prospective weekend visitors received copies of a detailed map directing them to Buxton Hill ("down dirt road & up over hill"), complete with a schedule of the best train service from Grand Central Terminal (the "Green Mountain Flyer" to North Bennington, departing New York at 10:15 A.M.).

As his private workplace, Cole used the gatekeeper's cottage, posting a warning sign saying "No Trespassing." Here he could work any hour of the day or night without disturbance. Linda Porter died in 1954, and during the remaining years of his life, Porter became a virtual recluse at Buxton Hill. He was embarrassed and incapacitated by the amputation of one of his legs, which had been crushed in a riding accident in the 1930s. According to one of his biographers, visitors to Buxton Hill became fewer and fewer because most weekends Porter was drunk and ignored his guests, some of whom dubbed the farm "the torture chamber."

At Porter's death in 1964, Buxton Hill was deeded to Williams College.

A Few More Famous Queers and Their Massachusetts Birthplaces

Leonard Bernstein (1918–1990), Roxbury

Elizabeth Bishop (1911–1979), Worcester

John Horne Burns (1916–1953), Andover

John Cheever (1912–1982), Quincy

Mary E. Wilkins Freeman (1852–1930), Randolph

Harriet Hosmer (1830–1908), Watertown

Paul Monette (1945–1995), Lawrence

New Hampshire

Jaffrey

Willa Cather retreat
Shattuck Inn
Dublin Road

Every fall during the early 1900s, novelist Willa Cather (1873–1947) came to this quiet country inn (torn down in 1996) to write and escape the hectic pace of New York City. Cather never had to sign the hotel guest register and always had two small rooms on the third floor, which looked out onto nearby Mount Monadnock, reserved for her arrival. By day, Cather worked in a tent-studio in the woods, writing parts of the novels *My Ántonia* (1918) and *One of Ours* (1922). At night, she often joined other hotel guests at the fireplace in the common room. Cather's intimate companion, Edith Lewis, called the Jaffrey studio the place Cather "found best to work in." When Cather's work space was destroyed by a hurricane in 1938, she stopped coming to Jaffrey. But because the spot was so beloved to her, Cather chose to be buried in town at the *Old Town Burial Ground*. Her gravestone is inscribed with a quote from *My Ántonia*: "That is happiness, to be dissolved into something complete and great." Lewis is buried beside her.

Peterborough

MacDowell Colony
MacDowell Road

Once the home of composer Edward MacDowell and his wife, Marian Nevins MacDowell, this site has been a favorite retreat of writers, artists, and musicians since 1908. MacDowell purchased the secluded five-hundred-acre farm for his own work, and his wife turned it into the cultural mecca it is today. Doris Grumbach based her novel *Chamber Music* (1979) on the founding of the colony; in it, both husband and wife are queer.

Besides the main building, Colony Hall (open to visitors in the afternoons), there are a number of private studios and cottages set in the woods for artists. MacDowell continues to be a haven for queer writers. Some of the Pulitzer Prize–winning works by queer authors from the past that were started or finished here include Willa Cather's novel *One of Ours* and Thornton Wilder's plays *Bridge of San Luis Rey, Our Town,* and *The Skin of Our Teeth.*

STRATFORD

Paul Goodman grave
Stratford Center Cemetery
Paul Goodman (1911–1972) was an outspoken, socially committed writer who frankly admitted and accepted his sexual orientation. "I have been fired three times because of my queer behavior or my claim to the right of it," he acknowledged. One firing was from the experimental Black Mountain College, where even gay faculty members voted to deny Goodman a full-time position, fearing that he might be a child molester (*see* Black Mountain, North Carolina).

Though he authored several novels, Goodman is best remembered for his innovative nonfiction works. *Communitas* (1947), written with his brother Percival, was a pioneering text on rethinking urban design and city planning. His *Growing Up Absurd* (1960), an attack on the "phony" nature of American culture and its effect on the country's youth, became the bible of the New Left in the 1960s.

One dishy anecdote: In 1949, Goodman was the cause of the breakup of poet Robert Duncan and his boyfriend, Gerald Ackerman. Duncan and Ackerman shared a spacious room in a Berkeley, California, household that also included the novelist Philip K. Dick. Duncan came home unexpectedly and found Ackerman in bed with Goodman. Instead of confronting his unfaithful lover, Duncan merely ran away in horror.

RHODE ISLAND

NEWPORT

Army and Navy YMCA
50 Washington Square

Since the early twentieth century, YMCAs have been gathering places for gay men. Newport's Army and Navy YMCA opened in 1911, and when the fleet was in—Newport was home to an important naval training station—the building was often filled beyond capacity. Here soldiers and sailors could bank, shop at the canteen, and eat a homestyle meal. Activities included swimming, bowling, and jogging (and surely numerous other "indoor sports"). The administrators also showed movies and sponsored cabaret evenings of song and performances.

In his article "Christian Brotherhood or Sexual Perversion? Homosexual Identities and the Construction of Sexual Boundaries in the World War I Era," historian George Chauncey relates the story of an official navy investigation in 1919–1920 of homosexuality in Newport. Under orders from then Assistant Secretary of the Navy Franklin Roosevelt, young enlisted men acted as decoys to entrap homosexuals, gathering information and later testifying before a naval court of inquiry and at several civilian trials. Twenty sailors and sixteen civilians were arrested as a result of the "investigation."

The decoys reported that the YMCA (as well as beaches and wharves) was a haven of homosexual activity. Some gay sailors lived there, while others just rented rooms for the night. "Fagott" parties, the investigators found, were frequent at the Y in the evenings. The gay men who frequented the Y also engaged in homosexual activities in other cities and maintained contact with gay men in New York, Providence, and Fall River, Massachusetts. But, Chauncey found, in addition to the men who identified as "queer," there were trade who regularly enjoyed homosexual sex but thought of themselves as "normal" men.

Newport's YMCA reached its peak in 1951 during the Korean War, when approximately one and a half million servicemen used its facilities. When the Navy began downsizing during the Nixon administration, attendance at the Y fell off, and it was closed in 1971. It is now an apartment building for low-income residents.

> The Army and Navy Y.M.C.A. was the headquarters of all cocksuckers [in] the early part of the evening. . . . Everybody who sat around there in the evening . . . knew it.
>
> —Navy investigator, 1920

VERMONT

HINESBURG

Redbird Commune
Turkey Lane

From 1976 to 1979, a collective of eight lesbians and three children lived in the Vermont countryside in a commune they called Redbird. In 1974, the group began living together in nearby Burlington, and two years later they purchased twenty-two acres of land at this location. They were part of a growing lesbian separatist movement, withdrawing from patriarchal society and creating a self-sufficient retreat for themselves and their children. The women of Redbird built the main house themselves—a round, two-story post-and-beam structure—from materials they scavenged from old barns and sheds. While they were constructing their home, they camped outdoors in tipis and cooked meals in a fire pit. Joyce Cheney, one of the collective members, later recounted in her book *Lesbian Land* that the original plan was to make Redbird an alternative healing center for women. But as they completed the house, the idea of a healing center faded and a more personal motivation took root. "We all worked from waking to sleeping," Cheney related. "We were building a home, raising children, and saving the world."

Like other communes, Redbird had its share of problems and pitfalls. There was little privacy or money. "We each had two to five dollars a week 'allowance,'" Cheney wrote. "We all shared one car and one truck." Set up as a closed collective, no new members were sought or desired. Lovers were confined to members of the group, and sexual pairings were decided by drawing names out of a hat. This suffocating "inbreeding" eventually tore the collective apart. Member isolated themselves more and more from society and from the lesbian community in Burlington, scapegoating each other when something at the commune went wrong. In 1977, the first collective member ran away, charging that Redbird was emotionally abusive. Two years later, the commune dissolved, and the Redbird house is now a private residence—a tangible reminder of both the good and the bad aspects of "Lesbian Nation."

PLAINFIELD

Daughters, Inc.

Working out of an old farmhouse in a Vermont town so small it isn't on some maps, June Arnold and her lover, Parke Bowman, and others founded the lesbian-feminist publishing company Daughters, Inc., in 1973. That year, Daughters published its most famous contribution to lesbian literature—the first edition of Rita Mae Brown's *Rubyfruit Jungle*, which sold seventy thousand copies. Brown's second novel, *In Her Day* (1976), also bore a Daughters imprint. But in 1977, Brown urged Daughters to sell the reprint rights to *Rubyfruit*, which they controlled, to Bantam Books, launching her mass-market career and causing an ideological dilemma in the lesbian publishing world: Should lesbian writers "compromise" themselves by "selling out" to mainstream presses? The women of Daughters thought definitely not, but Brown, who was trying to make a living at writing, saw things differently. The success of Brown's novel allowed Daughters more financial freedom than other women's presses. In 1976, they were advertising that they could offer one thousand dollar advances and 15 percent royalties.

By early 1977, Daughters had moved camp to a loft at *22 Charles Street, Greenwich Village, New York City*. There, they continued to publish lesbian literati June Arnold, Blanche Boyd, Bertha Harris (who also worked part-time as an editor for the press), Elana Nachmann, Verena Stefan, and Monique Wittig. (They stated that their only requirements for publication were "quality and the verifiable sex of the author.") Daughters' novels were famous for experimentation with language and form. For example, Arnold's *The Cook and the Carpenter*, the story of a collective effort to make a women's space out of a public building, was written using the gender-neutral pronoun "na," which Arnold invented. The publishers and writers of Daughters transformed the politics of the women's movement into literary themes, and their works imagined the creation of Lesbian Nation—a separate women's community, "one untouchable safe sea of women," as June Arnold phrased it. Today Daughters publications such as *Sister Gin*, *Lover*, and *Riverfinger Women* are considered lesbian classics of that era.

ASIDE-STEP

Writer Helen Maria Winslow (1851–1938)—who was born in Westfield, Vermont—penned a novel called *Spinster Farm* in 1908, in which two women created a productive, healthy, independent life together, renovating and living on an abandoned farm. Winslow herself never married.

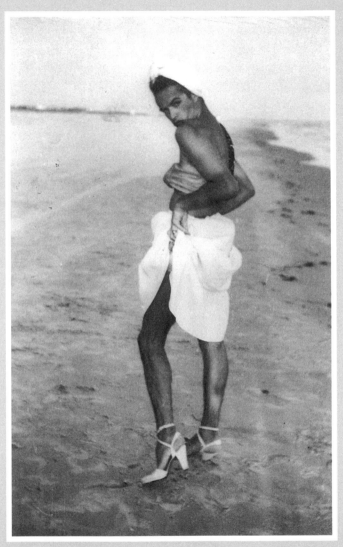

*Courtesy of the National Museum and Archive
of Lesbian and Gay History*

II

Mid-
Atlantic

Delaware

Wilmington

Alice Dunbar-Nelson home
1008 French Street

Born in New Orleans in 1875 to a seamstress and a merchant marine, Alice Moore began writing at an early age and published her first book of stories and poems, *Violets and Other Tales*, at the tender age of twenty. After graduating from Straight University (now Dillard University in New Orleans), Moore began teaching and writing to earn her living. One of her stories, which was accompanied by her photograph, appeared in the *Monthly Review* and attracted the attention of the young Paul Laurence Dunbar, who was himself a struggling writer. Dunbar wrote her a fan letter, beginning a passionate correspondence that resulted in their marriage in 1898 and a move to Washington, D.C.

The couple's relationship was stormy, ending after only four years, and Alice moved to Wilmington, where she taught at a local high school. Today Alice Moore Dunbar-Nelson (she remarried twice after she and Dunbar separated, but never adopted the name of the second husband) is unfortunately still remembered mainly as Dunbar's widow. Yet she was an accomplished poet, a historian, a syndicated newspaper columnist, and a lecturer in her own right.

Furthermore, research by Gloria Hull has revealed Dunbar-Nelson's romantic involvements with women and uncovered lesbian-themed poems in her diaries. After her move to Delaware, Dunbar-Nelson's intimate companion was Edwina B. Kruse, the principal of the Wilmington school where she taught. Kruse later remembered Dunbar-

Nelson's home on French Street as being "all alive with people all of the time." During the summers, Kruse studied school administration at New York University, and the two women wrote to each other daily. Dunbar-Nelson's unpublished novel *This Lofty Oak* was based on Kruse's life.

DISTRICT OF COLUMBIA

Benjamin Banneker Memorial
L'Enfant Plaza (east side of 10th Street, NW)
The self-taught Benjamin Banneker (1731–1806) is perhaps best remembered today as one of those chosen in 1791 to survey the boundaries of the nation's new capital district. But Banneker, a free black who lived all his life in Baltimore County, Maryland, was also an accomplished tobacco planter, mathematician, clock-maker, astrologist, and meteorologist who published numerous almanacs accurately forecasting the weather in an age when farmers relied on such predictions for their planting dates.

Speculations about Banneker's sexuality focus primarily on his lifelong bachelorhood, noted lack of interest in women, and apparent wrestling with "inner demons" in his almanac writings. In 1792, he warned readers in his first almanac, "Assemble all the evils which poverty, disease, or violence can inflict, and their stings will be found, by far, less pungent than those which guilty passions dart into the heart." (*See also* Oella, Maryland.)

Natalie Barney home
1626 Rhode Island Avenue
Born in Ohio, poet Natalie Barney (1876–1972) grew up in New York City and at this address in Washington, an Italianate palazzo in a neighborhood filled with elegant mansions. Her father was a successful but staid businessman and her mother the free-spirited artist Alice Pike Barney, from whom Natalie inherited her creativity and spunk. Alice made frequent so-

journs to Paris to study painting, taking along her two young daughters, who both moved to the French capital as adults.

Determined to introduce more art and culture to Washington society, Alice set up a salon and studio in a Mediterranean-style town house she called *Studio House*, facing Sheridan Circle. There she entertained luminaries such as Theodore Roosevelt, Oliver Wendell Holmes, Sarah Bernhardt, Anna Pavlova, and Ruth St. Denis. Natalie obviously absorbed Studio House's artistic ambience and learned well from her mother's example— she maintained her own celebrated salon in Paris at 20 rue Jacob for over fifty years.

Stephen Decatur House
748 Jackson Place, NW

At the corner of H Street and Jackson Place stands the elegant, Federal-style Decatur House, which serves as the headquarters of the National Trust for Historic Preservation. The building was designed by architect Benjamin Latrobe in 1819 as the home of Stephen Decatur, one of the U.S. Navy's most honored early heroes, who attained the rank of commodore following commendable service in the War of 1812.

But here's the dishy side of Decatur's story. Decatur and his beloved boyhood friend, Richard Somers, enlisted together as Navy midshipmen in 1798 and distinguished themselves in battles against the Barbary pirates. Several year later, on a night when Somers was to embark separately on a dangerous mission against the pirates, he gave Decatur a gold ring inscribed "R. S., to S. D. 1804," in case he didn't come back. Somers died in the course of duty that night, while his dear Decatur waited anxiously for news of his return. Hearing of Somers's death, Decatur fell into a deep, inconsolable depression, and he wore Somers's ring for the rest of his life.

A few years after Somers's death, Decatur entered into a marriage of convenience. The commodore reportedly had a "flair" for interior decorating and turned the Washington home he shared with his wife, Susan, into a showplace.

The Furies
219 Eleventh Street, SE

The Furies collective was founded in 1971 by lesbian-feminist separatists who wanted to live and work together, putting feminist theory into action. "We said goodbye to the New Left and to gay liberation because they were male-dominated," explained collective member Joan E. Biren (JEB), "and to the women's movement because they were unwilling to make room for visible lesbians and lesbian issues." Other members of the all-white collective included Rita Mae Brown, Charlotte Bunch, Helaine Harris, and Nancy Myron.

The following year at this address the collective launched a lesbian-feminist newspaper, also called *The Furies*, which they announced as "coming out monthly." Filled with news, opinion, and poetry (including in one issue Judy Grahn's now classic "Edward the Dyke") and operating under consensus ("all the politics and articles were agreed upon by the staff before anything was printed"), the newspaper, like so many other lesbian-feminist organs, died after only seven months when the original Furies collective disbanded, mainly over class differences, and the remaining editors burnt out. "It was clear," wrote two of the editors in *The Furies'* final issue, "that the paper was not the staff's major priority. . . . Everyone seemed to be spreading themselves thin. Perhaps the major portion of everyone's time was being spent at [full-time] jobs." Individual Furies members went on to help found Olivia Records, Diana Press, and *Quest/A Feminist Quarterly.*

Edith Hamilton home
2448 Massachusetts Avenue, NW

In the last twenty years of her life, classical scholar Edith Hamilton (1867–1963) lived in this house, which is adjacent to Rock Creek Park and is still a private residence. A Latin and Greek major at Bryn Mawr College, Hamilton was the popular headmistress of a girls' academy in Baltimore for twenty-five years. After retiring she embarked on a second successful career as a writer, almost single-handedly popularizing the study of ancient civilizations with such books as *The Greek Way* (1930), *The Roman Way* (1932), and *Mythology* (1942).

Hamilton cohabited with her life partner, Doris Reed, a stockbroker and former student of Hamilton's, from the 1920s until her death. The two women together raised Reed's four nieces and nephews, referring to them as "our children." Her relationship with Reed caused a split with Alice Hamilton, her younger sister, who was a professor of industrial medicine at Harvard University. Alice wrote to their other sister, Margaret, about the reason for the estrangement from Edith: "Until I can assure her [Edith] that I do not and never did consider her in any way abnormal mentally, there can be no coming together again."

Lafayette Park
Boundaries: Pennsylvania Avenue and H Street, NW; Jackson and Madison Places, NW

Across the street from the White House this public park has long been a cruising place for gay men. As early as 1892, Dr. Irving Rosse, a professor of nervous diseases at Georgetown University, addressed the topic of "the spread of sexual crime" in the park and elsewhere around the capital. "Only of late," he wrote, "the chief of police tells me that his men have made, under the very shadow of the White House, eighteen arrests in Lafayette Square . . . in which the culprits were taken away *in flagrante delicto*. Both black and white were represented among these moral hermaphrodites, but the majority of them were negros."

Lafayette Park also features statues of several prominent figures of the American Revolution, whom we now claim as gay. On the southeast corner of the park is a statue of Alexander Hamilton and John Laurens, who were inseparable in life and whose hands in the statue appear to be lightly touching. The two were colonels in the Continental Army and together served as interpreters for Baron von Steuben, the Revolutionary War hero and lover of men. John Laurens was killed during a battle with the British, and Hamilton later went on to become the first U.S. Secretary of the Treasury.

In 1777 Baron Frederick Wilhelm von Steuben, then a captain in the Prussian Army, faced charges of taking "familiarities with young boys," and to avoid a public scandal, he accepted a commission with the Continental Army, arriving in the American colonies with a seventeen-year-old French nobleman whom he called his "secretary." Von Steuben, who was well acquainted with the rigorous drills of the Prussian Army, is credited with introducing much-needed discipline into the revolutionary forces and thus aiding immeasurably in the eventual American victory over the British. The baron is honored by a statue at the northwest corner of Lafayette Park.

> I went into Lafayette Square and near the Von Steuben statue watched two fellows furtively engaged in mutual masturbation under cover of the dimness. . . . Both were handsome, clean-looking chaps, refined and cultured.
> —"Jeb Alexander" (a pseudonym), August 1920

Alain Locke African Collection
Howard University Gallery of Art
2400 Sixth Street, NW

African-American scholar and intellectual Alain LeRoy Locke (1886–1954) defined his role in the Harlem Renaissance as that of "philosophical midwife to a generation of young Negro poets, writers, and artists." The Harvard- and Oxford-educated Locke was a professor of philosophy at Howard University for many years, and one of the university's important research collections now bears his name. At Howard, Locke encouraged the study of black culture and history along with the classics and European literature, and founded *The Stylus*, the university literary journal in which Zora Neale Hurston published her first story. His attention tended to focus on the brightest and most attractive male students, however, and he routinely warned female students that they could expect no better than C's in his classes.

Locke shuttled back and forth between Washington and Harlem, where he mentored several young poets of the Harlem Renaissance. His protégé Countee Cullen introduced him to Langston Hughes. "You will like him," Cullen told Locke of the elusive and ambivalent Hughes; "I love him." A romantic triangle formed and may have been the root of the mysterious rift between Cullen and Hughes from 1924 on. (*See also* Philadelphia, Pennsylvania.)

off our backs
2318 Ashmead Place, NW

Founded in February 1970, *off our backs* was one of the first feminist news monthlies in the country, and from this address, its premiere issue was launched. According to its debut editorial, women's news organs were necessary because "existing institutions and channels for communication have ceased to meet the growing needs of the women's struggle." The editorial also pointed out that women journalists and feminist issues had gotten short shrift in both mainstream and radical left newspapers. "Women need to be free of men's domination," the *off our backs* collective asserted, "to find their real identities, redefine their lives, and fight for the creation of a society in which they can lead decent lives as human beings."

Throughout its history, *off our backs* served as inspiration and template for countless other feminist newspapers. Today, when many women's bookstores, journals, and newspapers have disappeared, *off our backs* continues to provide news, reviews, features, and commentary on feminist and lesbian issues around the globe.

Lucy Diggs Slowe home
1256 Kearney Street, NE

Lucy Diggs Slowe (1883–1937) was the first dean of women at Howard University, a position she held from 1922 until her death. A window in the Howard chapel honors her memory. As dean, Slowe worked for the empowerment of women, urging female students into the social sciences and other "nontraditional" fields. Concerned for the safety of young women in the "big city," Slowe expanded the university's dorm facilities so women could live on campus. Outspoken and headstrong, Slowe often locked horns with the university's president over the welfare of the female students.

Slowe shared this home with her life partner, writer and teacher Mary Powell Burrill, who had earlier been involved with Angelina Weld Grimké. Their residence was an informal gathering place for young Howard women, many of whom idolized their intrepid dean. In a bid to curb her power, Howard's president once suggested that Slowe live in a dorm instead—a seemingly homophobic attempt to break up the household that had become a source of strength for her.

Mathilda Coxe Stevenson home
1913 N Street, NW (near DuPont Circle)

The famous two-spirited Zuni We'wha (1849–1896) made an unprecedented visit to Washington in 1886 at the invitation of Mathilda Coxe Stevenson, an anthropologist who had done fieldwork on the Zuni Indians and had befriended We'wha. We'wha lived at the Stevenson home on N Street for six months and became the toast of Washington society, which mistakenly believed "him" to be a woman even while commenting on his "masculine carriage." At the Smithsonian Institution, We'wha demonstrated Zuni weaving, one of his several artistic talents, and participated in an amateur theatrical performance at the National Theater, where he was cheered by an audience of prominent politicians. During We'wha's stay in the capital, even President Grover Cleveland deigned to receive him at the White House.

Upon We'wha's death from heart disease in 1896, Mathilda Stevenson wrote movingly that her friend was "undoubtedly the most remarkable member of the tribe," with a "bright mind" and "an insatiable thirst for knowledge." Outing We'wha as "a man wearing woman's dress," Stevenson admitted that she herself had learned of We'wha's birth gender only after years of acquaintance, but would always think of and refer to her friend as "she," in deference to the custom of the Zunis. (*See also* Zuni, New Mexico.)

Union Hotel
30th and M Streets, NW (northeast corner)

Was Louisa May Alcott "one of us"? As a strong, independent, and feminist woman who disdained marriage, Alcott (1832–1888) is now often claimed by the lesbian community. Certainly, her self-modeled character Jo March in *Little Women* (1868) has served as a role model for generations of budding dykes. A later and also autobiographical novel, *Work: A Story of Experience* (1873), portrayed a classic romantic friendship between women, one of whom woos the other "as gently as a lover might."

In 1862 Alcott interrupted her promising literary career to travel south from her home in Concord, Massachusetts, and serve as a nurse in Washington, D.C. Alcott reported to what was at that time the Union Hotel, one of numerous area hotels that were converted into hospitals for Union troops. Her intense and agonizing work with soldiers suffering from infectious diseases precipitated a nervous breakdown and a return home to Massachusetts, where, in 1864, she collected her letters describing medical conditions during the Civil War into a volume titled *Hospital Sketches*. (*See* Boston and Concord, Massachusetts.)

Sumner Welles home
2121 Massachusetts Avenue, NW

This mansion is currently the location of the Cosmos Club, a private social club for individuals in the arts, literature, and science, which barred women from membership until as late as 1988. Before it became an exclusive club, however, this huge, imposing manor was first a railroad baron's estate and later the Washington residence of Sumner Welles, who served as undersecretary of state to President Franklin D. Roosevelt. Welles and his wife Mathilde were close personal friends of the Roosevelts and were famous for the elegant parties they gave at their home. Though married for many years, Welles was reportedly an active homosexual who frequented bars that catered to rough trade and whose conduct fell under the close scrutiny of J. Edgar Hoover's FBI. In 1941 Welles's "immoral activities" were brought to FDR's attention, but the undersecretary did not resign from the State Department until two years later, when enemies of the administration threatened to expose the scandal to reporters. (*See also* Cleveland, Ohio.)

The White House
1600 Pennsylvania Avenue, NW

Come on, you're saying—*the White House?* She's grasping at straws now! Not really. If you haven't read the listings for Abraham Lincoln in Springfield, Illinois, or for James Buchanan in Lancaster, Pennsylvania, maybe you should do that right now.

But the person I was really thinking of when I included this listing wasn't a president at all, but a president's sister. When Grover Cleveland took office as president for the first time in 1885, he was a bachelor in need of a First Lady and White House hostess. His "spinster" sister, Rose Cleveland, a teacher and editor of a literary magazine, stepped in to help her brother during his first term.

Cleveland was defeated for reelection, and Rose was once again her own woman. In 1890, she met and fell in love with a young widow named Evangeline Marrs Simpson. Gay historian Jonathan Ned Katz has written in detail about the two women's passionate relationship, including their intimate correspondence: "Oh, Eve," Rose wrote, "I tremble at the thought of you. . . . Sweet, Sweet, I dare not think of your arms." The two lived together until 1892, when Eve backed away from the relationship to seek a safer, more traditional male-female one. In 1893, Rose (once again ensconced at 1600 Pennsylvania Avenue, following her brother's successful campaign in 1892) wrote to Eve on White House stationery, wishing her dear companion "my best blessing—whatever you do." Eve went on to marry an elderly Episcopal bishop, Henry Whipple.

Following the bishop's death in 1901, Eve and Rose renewed their correspondence and finally reunited in Italy, where they lived together until Rose's death in 1918. Eve died in 1930 and requested that she be buried beside Rose and another woman friend.

Walt Whitman's haunts

In 1862, after his brother George was wounded at Frederick, Maryland, Walt Whitman (1819–1892) journeyed from his home in Brooklyn to the battlefield to be at his brother's side. The pain and suffering that Whitman witnessed at the front had a profound effect on his life and writing. Traveling with the Union Army, the poet ended up in the nation's capital, where for the next year he made the rounds of provisional army hospitals, offering comfort to the wounded soldiers. "I saw him, time and again," one New York reporter wrote, "wending his way . . . with a basket or haversack on his arm, and the strength of beneficence suffusing his face." In *Calamus Lovers*, Charley Shively has discussed how Whitman also used the hospital wards for "cruising" and would freely dispense kisses and other physical affection to the wounded.

During his stay in Washington, Whitman found part-time work writing dispatches on the war for the *New York Times*, but his meager salary and long hospital visits brought on a physical and mental breakdown that made army doctors send him back to Brooklyn in 1864.

When he first arrived in Washington, Whitman rented a small room at a boardinghouse (no longer standing) at *1407 L Street, NW*, for seven dollars a month. Later, he moved to another boardinghouse at *1205 M Street, NW*, which is now the site of Claridge Towers Apartments. Two of the makeshift army hospitals he frequented were the *Armory Square Hospital* at *Sixth Street and Independence Avenue, NW*, and the *"Patent Office,"* which now houses the National Portrait Gallery.

After the war was over, Whitman returned to Washington to live. It was there that Whitman became acquainted with Peter Doyle, one of the best known of his lover/companions. A former Confederate soldier, Doyle later spoke of their romantic first meeting aboard a streetcar on which Doyle was a conductor: "He was the only passenger [in the car], it was a lonely night, so I thought I would go in and talk to him. Something in me made me do it and something in him drew me that way. . . . We were familiar at once—I put my hand on his knee—we understood. He did not get out at the end of the trip—in fact went all the way back with me."

Whitman worked at the Bureau of Indian Affairs but lost his job when his boss found *Leaves of Grass*, which he was revising, in his desk and charged him with immorality. Friends who were outraged at the injustice of the firing found work for him at the Attorney General's office. During the next seven years in Washington, Whitman published *Drum-taps*, *Democratic Vistas*, and two revisions of *Leaves of Grass*, among other works. In 1873 Whitman suffered a stroke and moved back to Camden, New Jersey, where he lived until his death. (*See also* Camden, New Jersey; Brooklyn, New York; and Huntington, New York.)

Frances Willard statue
Statuary Hall
U.S. Capitol Building

In 1905, pioneering feminist and Women's Christian Temperance Union leader Frances Willard (1839–1898) became the first woman to have her white marble statue included in this traditionally all-male bastion. But even more amazing, she remained the only woman to be so honored for the next fifty-plus years! (*See also* Evanston, Illinois, and Janesville, Wisconsin.)

YMCA
1736 G Street, NW

Though never intended as such, since the early 1900s YMCAs provided gay men with places to meet, live, and have sexual encounters. For that reason, though, they could also become targets of police entrapment, as in the following incident.

In a crackdown on "tearoom" sex in October 1964, members of the Washington, D.C., vice squad began a stakeout of the men's room in the basement of this YMCA, just a few blocks from the White House. Concealing themselves behind the locked door of a shower room that was no longer in use, they spied through peepholes that afforded them a clear view of activities in the men's room, which the *New York Times* later described as "a 9-foot by 11-foot spot reeking of disinfectant and stale cigars." Did they expect to catch such big game? Arrested were Walter Jenkins, President Lyndon Johnson's Chief of Staff, and another man, who were charged with "disorderly conduct." Amazingly, Jenkins had been arrested on the same charge in the same bathroom five years earlier, but his prior offense had somehow escaped the notice of both the FBI and the White House. A married man described as "retiring and camera-shy," Jenkins was forced to resign from office a week later when the incident leaked to the Republican National Committee.

Maryland

Baltimore

Sylvia Beach home
1029 Edmondson Avenue

Born in Baltimore and raised in a Presbyterian parsonage in Bridgeton, New Jersey, Nancy Woodridge Beach as a teenager changed her name to Sylvia. While her minister father was associate pastor of the American Church in Paris from 1902 to 1905, young Sylvia determined that she would someday live in the French capital. During World War I, she and her sister took off for Europe to volunteer for the Red Cross, and Sylvia lived the rest of her life abroad.

Beach (1887–1962) is one of the best known of the American expatriates of the early twentieth century, and the founder of the bookshop Shakespeare and Company. The store was the first English-language shop on the Left Bank in Paris, serving as a literary center, lending library, and publishing company for the years between the two world wars. The bookshop was frequented by such notables as Gertrude Stein, Natalie Barney, André Gide, Ezra Pound, and Bryher. Beach is remembered in the literary canon as publisher of numerous editions of James Joyce's *Ulysses*, which mainstream publishers considered too radical a text to publish. Beach immortalized the store and the expatriate literary circle in a memoir called *Shakespeare and Company* (1959).

A confirmed liberal and a woman with a strongly anti-Fascist reputation, Beach's shop was closed by the Nazis in 1941, and she was interned for six months in a concentration camp as an "enemy alien." After the war, Beach did not reopen the shop but continued to lend books from her apartment.

The love of Beach's life was Adrienne Monnier, a Frenchwoman who owned a bookshop called La Maison des Amis des Livres, directly across the street from Shakespeare and Company. Beach and Monnier lived together from 1920 to 1936, when Monnier's affair with another woman caused them to separate. Still (in true lesbian fashion!), they remained friends until Monnier's death in 1955, having dinner together every evening. Though Beach lived all of her adult life abroad, she is buried in Princeton, New Jersey, with her family.

Diana Press
12 West 25th Street

First housed at this Baltimore address, Diana Press was one of the earliest lesbian-feminist publishing companies. Established in the mid-1970s, it was committed to making openly lesbian material available. Before she became a mass-market star, Rita Mae Brown published her collections of lesbian poems, *Songs to a Handsome Woman* and *The Hand That Cradles the Rock,* and a volume of essays, *A Plain Brown Wrapper,* with Diana Press. Other titles from Diana included Elsa Gidlow's *Sapphic Songs* and Judy Grahn's *True to Life Adventure Stories,* as well as poetry by Pat Parker. In the late 1970s, Diana had relocated to *4400 Market Street, San Francisco.*

Mary Elizabeth Garrett home
101 Monument Street

Mary Elizabeth Garrett was the heir to her father's B&O railroading fortune. She was also a lesbian philanthropist who used her father's money in the cause of feminism. In 1894, she promised the trustees of Bryn Mawr College a substantial sum if they would name her beloved, M. Carey Thomas, the first female president, which they promptly did. Garrett also subsidized Thomas's salary so that she could run a household and entertain in a manner befitting a college president. Though Garrett and Thomas were both involved with other women at the time, they maintained an intimate relationship, eventually living together at Bryn Mawr from 1904 until Garrett's death (*see also* Bryn Mawr, Pennsylvania). Even while cohabiting with Thomas, Garrett maintained this home in

Baltimore, which Thomas (Garrett's heir) eventually sold to the Art Institute of Baltimore.

Apart from her support of Thomas, Garrett was an ardent feminist who also helped raise money for the National American Woman Suffrage Association and was actively involved in NAWSA committee work. In addition, a Mary Garrett endowment helped found the Johns Hopkins Medical School, with the stipulation that women be admitted on equal terms with men.

Billie Holiday home
219 South Durham Street

Billie Holiday (1915–1959) had a rough childhood. As a young girl named Eleanora Fagan, she cut school so often she was sent to live at the House of the Good Shepherd, a home for "colored girls" run by the Little Sisters of the Poor (*Claverton Road and Franklin Street*). There she probably had her first lesbian experiences. Returned to her mother after a year, the two took up residence at this address, one of dozens over the years. At age ten, while living here, Eleanora was raped by her neighbor and sent back to Good Shepherd. But she was a handful, and the sisters refused to keep her for long, remanding her to her mother's care.

Only eleven years old, Eleanora earned money cleaning for a whorehouse madam. The madam let her listen to the records of Louis Armstrong and Bessie Smith, whose combined influence on her singing style was great. Eleanora began singing at various storefront churches, but her first professional gig was at Buddy Love's, a club located at *Orleans Street and Wayside*.

As a young teenager, Eleanora moved to New York with her mother, where she pursued her singing career and transformed herself into Billie Holiday. After years of touring with Count Basie and Artie Shaw, she was offered her first steady job in 1938 at Cafe Society for seventy-five dollars a week. From that, she went on to be a featured soloist at clubs all over the country, acquiring the nickname "Lady Day." Her distinctive voice—which she used like a musical instrument—transformed jazz singing. "I don't think I'm singing," she once said of her style. "I feel like I'm playing a horn."

Holiday had many affairs with men and women but was known as a "les" among many of her peers in the music industry. One of her female lovers reported that "Billie even got the name Mister Holiday, because she was seldom seen with fellas." Holiday once told a colleague, "Sure I've been to bed with women, . . . but I was always the *man*."

Sadly, by the 1940s Holiday was addicted to heroin and alcohol, and she was arrested on drug charges several times. Many club owners would no longer take the risk of hiring her because she was often high during performances. Her career went progressively downhill, and she finally died in 1959 of liver cirrhosis and numerous other complications of substance abuse.

A commemorative statue of Billie Holiday stands on *Pennsylvania Avenue, between Lanvale and Lafayette Streets.*

Pre-Stonewall bars
Leon's, located at *870 Park Avenue,* has been a gay men's bar for at least fifty years. The downstairs of *1101 Cathedral Street* has also been a queer hangout since the 1940s, when it was a lesbian club reputedly frequented by actress Tallulah Bankhead. Now it is a primarily gay men's bar called Allegro's, though there is a women's night on Thursday.

Gertrude Stein home
215 East Biddle Street
Gertrude Stein's (1874–1946) first ambition was not to be a writer, but a psychologist. After studying psychology with William James at Harvard, Stein was accepted at the Johns Hopkins Medical School, where her brother, Leo (with whom she was very close), was also enrolled, and the two lived together at this address on East Biddle Street.

Stein was unhappy and unfulfilled in medical school. She was also on the brink of discovering her lesbianism. While living in Baltimore, Stein ran with a lesbian crowd, a group of Bryn Mawr College graduates led by a young woman named Mabel Haynes. Sadly for her, Stein fell unrequitedly in love with Haynes's "romantic friend," May Bookstaver. The experience made a deep impression on Stein, whose first novel, *Q.E.D.*, completed in Baltimore in 1903, is an autobiographical account of this lesbian love triangle.

Unlike Stein's later novels, *Q.E.D.* is openly lesbian in content and language. Always internally homophobic, Stein put the finished manuscript away for thirty years. In 1932, she unearthed it and showed it to her agent, who advised against trying to publish it because of its "controversial" theme. *Q.E.D.* was finally published in 1950, four years after Stein's death.

Stein left Baltimore in 1903 to visit Leo, who had moved to Paris, and to try to forget May Bookstaver. Paris agreed with her, and she lived the rest of her life there, meeting Alice B. Toklas, her life partner, there in 1907. And what happened to May Bookstaver and Mabel Haynes? They both pursued much more traditional lives, ending their affair and marrying men.

OELLA

Mt. Gilboa Chapel
Oella and Westchester Avenues

Benjamin Banneker (1731–1806)—surveyor, clock-maker, astrologist, almanac compiler, and probable queer—lived all his life in this area of Maryland. Born a free black on a farm near Oella, Banneker worshiped with the Mt. Gilboa congregation (though the original structure is gone and the present one dates only from 1869) and attended school here. The self-taught Banneker is best remembered today as one of those chosen in 1791 to survey the boundaries of the nation's new capital district. (*See* Washington, D.C.)

White Oak

Rachel Carson home
11701 Berwick Road

Now a private residence, "Quaint Acres" was once home to Rachel Carson (1907–1964), scientist and environmental activist. The phenomenal success of her book *The Sea Around Us* (1951) allowed Carson to purchase this home and a summer cottage off the coast of Maine. It was at Quaint Acres that she feverishly wrote most of *Silent Spring* (1962), an attack on pesticides, while suffering from what she called "a catalogue of illnesses," including breast cancer and heart disease. There has been speculation that Carson suspected environmental causes for her own cancer and that of a beloved college professor, who fired her so that she would continue working tirelessly to expose the chemical industry. Between her hospital confinements, Carson worked late into the night on what was to be her final book. "No time for anything," she wrote to her intimate friend Dorothy Freeman, "unless it is somehow related to the great projects that are uncompleted."

Carson lived to see both the serialization of *Silent Spring* in the *New Yorker* and its publication as a book late in 1962. She was heartened by the public's strong response and hoped it would bring about a ban on the use

Aside-step

At his Maryland estate called Oxon Hill Manor *(6411 Oxon Hill Road, Oxon Hill),* Sumner Welles, the undersecretary of state to FDR, enjoyed a private study with wall murals of seminude young men in classical garb *(see also* District of Columbia). Oxon Hill Farm is now a public space maintained by the National Park Service, which can be rented for wedding receptions and other events. In 1994, the Democratic National Committee hosted President Bill Clinton's fundraiser birthday party there.

of DDT. But Carson quickly became too sick to enjoy the great acclaim that *Silent Spring* brought with it. "Now all the 'honors' have to be received for me by someone else," she wrote to Freeman. "And all the opportunities to travel to foreign lands—all expenses paid—have to be passed up." Carson died at her Maryland home in the spring of 1964. Two years later, the Environmental Protection Agency was born after a presidential commission corroborated Carson's findings about the hazards of pesticides. (*See also* Wells, Maine; Pittsburgh, Pennsylvania; and Springdale, Pennsylvania.)

New Jersey

Camden

Walt Whitman home
328 Mickle Street

In 1873, after suffering a stroke in Washington, D.C., poet Walt Whitman (1819–1892) moved to Camden to live with his brother, George, who nursed him back to health. George's house was located at 322 *Seventh Street*, and it was there that Oscar Wilde visited Whitman on his 1882 lecture tour. Wilde remembered later that the poet's room was filled with stacks of dusty newspapers.

In 1884, Whitman purchased his own gray clapboard row house on Mickle Street, which he called his "little old shanty." This was the only house he ever owned and the place where he lived out his final years. Whitman was considered an eccentric old lecher in the neighborhood. From his knapsack he peddled copies of his book, *Leaves of Grass*, on the street. For five years, Whitman's "special friend" was a teenager named William Duckett, an orphan who lived with him and was presumably his lover (Whitman was then in his late sixties). When Duckett moved out, Whitman had a second stroke that left him virtually bedridden for the remainder of his life. The companion of his last years was Horace Traubel, a man in his early thirties, who served as his scribe, confidante, and errand boy.

Whitman's house is now a museum and looks much as it did when he resided there. His bedroom, which he described as a "low-ceilinged room something like a big old ship's cabin," still holds his carved oak bed and assorted piles of books, newspapers, and manuscripts. Also on display are the knapsack in which Whitman carried his books for sale, and a rare first edition of *Leaves of Grass*, with its tooled green leather cover and embossed gold leaves. The museum is easily accessible by public transportation from Philadelphia (call 609-964-5383 for information).

Whitman is buried at the *Harleigh Cemetery* in Camden.

HACKENSACK

Gay Activists Alliance–New Jersey Building
176 Kansas Street
In the late 1970s, this site was a hub of gay and lesbian organizing in northern New Jersey. Besides GAA-NJ meetings (the local chapter of the gay rights group founded in New York City directly after the Stonewall Rebellion), the building hosted the Lesbian Feminist Collective, publisher of *Lavender Express*, the state lesbian newsletter that started in 1978 and was still being published seventeen years later. LFC also sponsored speakers, dances, and a weekend coffeehouse. Sports-minded members could meet every Sunday afternoon at two o'clock at the *corner of Union* and *Passaic Streets* to play touch football or softball. In the early 1980s, LFC had moved its operations to Kearny, and its weekly meetings were held at William Paterson College.

HOBOKEN

Stephen Foster home
601 Bloomfield Street
While living at this address, composer Stephen Foster (1826–1864) wrote his classic "Jeannie with the Light Brown Hair." Foster was born near Pittsburgh (*see* Pittsburgh, Pennsylvania) and lived much of his adult life in or near New York City. Though many of his most famous songs had southern themes—"Oh! Susannah," "Camptown Races," "Old Folks at Home (Swanee River)," and "My Old Kentucky Home," to name just a few—Foster visited the South only once on a brief trip to New Orleans in 1852. He drew his knowledge of the South primarily from camp meetings and minstrel shows.

The major relationship of Foster's life was not his wife but his collaborator, the poet George Cooper, who was fifteen years his junior. Cooper cared for Foster in his last days, when an alcoholic fall in his New York boardinghouse room proved fatal.

MT. LAUREL

Alice Paul home
"Paulsdale"
128 Hooton Road
Feminist and suffragist Alice Paul (1885–1977) was born at this location to a prosperous Quaker family that stressed education, tolerance, and nonviolence. The three-story farmhouse, which is reached from a dirt road, is two hundred years old and was a wedding gift from Alice's father to her mother. Currently in disrepair, Paulsdale is open only by special arrangement, and the Alice Paul Centennial Foundation is raising funds to restore it and open it to the public as a center of leadership for women and girls. Nothing in the house today is original to it, except for a bookcase that belonged to Paul. The lush yard, with a variety of trees and a vegetable garden, has been carefully maintained by the Foundation.

Paul was a tomboy who took on difficult tasks around the family farm. Shy and bookish, she graduated first in her class from Moorestown Friends High School (in her graduation picture, she was the only girl wearing a tie). She attended Swarthmore College, where she also was first in her class, majoring in social work. Paul went on to earn three law degrees and a doctorate in economics.

During her studies at the London School of Economics beginning in 1908, Paul became active with the women's suffrage movement in England. At a speech given by Christabel Pankhurst, Paul witnessed men in the audience harassing Pankhurst and throwing things at her, and she stood up in Pankhurst's defense, overcoming the shyness that had characterized her in childhood. Over the next few years, she worked closely with the Pankhursts, organizing parades, demonstrations, and hunger strikes, and was at times jailed along with the British women.

In England, she met Lucy Burns, another American who was also active in the British suffrage movement. Back in the United States in 1912, the two women were intimate friends, working side by side on the American suffrage campaign for eight years. They organized a 1913 suffrage march in Washington, D.C., mobilizing eight thousand people, and staged a demonstration the day of President Woodrow Wilson's inauguration to protest his lack of support for suffrage. Though the demonstration was peaceful on the part of the women, they were attacked by violent men who injured a hundred demonstrators. The incident turned suffrage into a national issue, but Paul's in-your-face activism against Wilson riled the National American Woman Suffrage Association, who asked her to leave the organization because she was too "radical."

In 1915, Paul formed the National Women's Party, which staged numerous actions on behalf of suffrage. During this time, Paul lived in a room upstairs at the party's headquarters at the Sewall-Belmont House in Washington, D.C., which is today a national historic monument. Paul was a workaholic who could work days at a stretch without even taking her hat off.

After suffrage was attained, Paul's activist work continued because she never saw the vote as an end in itself. In the 1920s she authored the Equal Rights Amendment and worked fifty-four years for its passage. During the 1930s and 1940s, Paul became actively involved with the peace movement in Europe and initiated the inclusion of sex equality in the United Nations

Charter. She was also responsible for organizing the coalition that success-fully got gender added to the Civil Rights Act of 1964. After moving to Connecticut, Paul suffered a stroke in 1972 and spent her final years in a nursing home in Moorestown near her hometown.

Paul never married, and there is no mention of men in her life. She was considered a "radical" by her family, and the silences around her personal life are suggestive of lesbianism. Her intense relationship with Lucy Burns appears to have been the most significant one of her life. Perhaps the up-coming biography by Amelia Fry will reveal more about her personal life.

NEWARK

Allen Ginsberg home
163 Quitman Street

This was the first home of poet Allen Ginsberg (1926–1997). When he was little, Ginsberg remembered that his father, who also wrote poems, used to wander around the apartment reciting Poe, Shelley, Keats, and Milton as he did household chores. His father called Allen "the little kiss-ing bug," because the boy was so openly affectionate. When Allen was six, the family moved to *155 Haledon Avenue*. During Allen's youth, his mother was often institutionalized for being suicidal.

The family moved around a lot, finally settling in Paterson at *288 Gra-ham Avenue*, where they stayed until Allen went away to Columbia Uni-versity. There, he would meet the men who would change his life—William Burroughs and Jack Kerouac—and who with him would form the nucleus of the Beat poetry movement in the 1950s and 1960s. (*See* Lowell, Mass-achusetts, and St. Louis, Missouri.) In 1945, Allen began writing poetry and eventually became one of the best-known poets of his generation. His "Howl," with its frank language about homosexuality and its condemnation of middle-class values, was a sort of credo of the counterculture. (*See also* New York City, New York.)

PRINCETON

Thomas Mann home
65 Stockton Street

Born in Germany, the Nobel Prize–winning writer Thomas Mann (1875–1955), an ardent anti-Fascist, went into exile in 1933 when the Nazis came to power. From 1938 to 1941, he lived at this address, after accepting an offer to lecture at Princeton University. The early Victorian house had a large library, several large reception rooms, and a study for Mann's use alone. After several years, though, Mann decided to leave the rigors of teaching and university life to "get on with my writing."

Though he married in 1905 and fathered six children, Mann's primary erotic leanings were toward his own sex. (He and his wife, Katia, had separate bedrooms.) Two of Mann's children, Erika and Klaus, were also gay, and Erika had a marriage of convenience with queer poet W. H. Auden. In Mann's fiction, a veiled, unnamed homosexual desire is often at the core, as in the classic novella *Death in Venice* (1912), in which an older man pines for a beautiful blond Polish youth he never meets. The story was based on Mann's own obsession with a boy in Venice. Mann's diaries and letters spoke more directly of his attraction to handsome young men and boys, though most critics over the years have tried to paint him as straight.

ASIDE-STEP

Dr. Sara Josephine Baker (1873–1945) and her lover, screenwriter Ida (I. A. R.) Wylie (1885–1959), who wrote *Keeper of the Flame*, shared a "pleasant house" in Princeton in the 1930s. With them lived Dr. Louise Pearce, who formed the third side of their triangle. After "Jo" Baker died, Wylie and Pearce became a couple. But Pearce continued to wear a bracelet given to her by Baker, which had a charm in the shape of the state with a jewel marking the site of the trio's home.

Princeton Graduate College
College Road

After his graduation from Yale University, playwright Thornton Wilder (1897–1975) taught secondary school at the Lawrenceville School near Princeton from 1921 to 1928. (His novel, *The Eighth Day* [1967], ridiculed the headmaster of the elite boys' school.) Wilder later remembered that the idea for his Pulitzer Prize–winning play, *The Bridge of San Luis Rey* (1927), occurred to him on one of his many walks into the center of town. In a quiet corner on the top floor of the Princeton Graduate College, Wilder began writing the famous play.

Wilder is buried in nearby Lyndhurst, at the *Mt. Carmel Cemetery*.

New York

Austerlitz

Edna St. Vincent Millay home
"Steepletop"
East Hill Road

At the top of a winding dirt road shaded by a thick bower of trees is the home that poet Edna St. Vincent Millay (1892–1950) shared with her husband, Eugen Boissevain, from 1925 until his death in 1949. Steepletop, a large, white clapboard house, took its name not from its mountaintop location, but from a wildflower that the couple found growing in the meadows surrounding their farmhouse.

At college, Millay was primarily lesbian-identified. Her early play "The Lamp and the Bell" and poem "Memorial to D. C." are her most lesbian works. When she moved to New York City, however, her first male lover, Floyd Dell, set out to "cure" her of "Sapphism." Throughout her bohemian Greenwich Village years, she continued to have relationships primarily with men, though she also had an affair with Thelma Wood, who later became the lover of Djuna Barnes. After Millay married Boissevain and moved with him to rural upstate New York, there is no further evidence of her "candle burning at both ends." Still, at Steepletop, Millay always kept a bronze bust of Sappho on a marble pedestal.

Steepletop was a quiet retreat where Millay spent many hours birdwatching in a favorite living-room chair by the front window. Boissevain was a house-husband, taking care of all the household chores and attending to his wife's personal and career needs, which left Millay free to compose the numerous collections of poetry that won her fame. Posted on the door of Millay's second-floor "poetry room" was a sign that read simply "Silence." On the walls hung a portrait of Robinson Jeffers, her favorite poet, and a pencil sketch of Percy Shelley. Millay's actual writing studio was a small cabin in the woods just beyond the house, furnished only with a simple desk and a couple of chairs.

The year after her husband's death, Millay herself died of a heart attack on the staircase of her home, holding a page of poetry in one hand and a glass of wine in the other. Her grave—shared with Boissevain—is in an overgrown area of the woods near the house, marked by a plaque.

Today, Steepletop is home to the Millay Colony, a residence for artists that is closed to the visiting public. The barns across from the main house serve as dorms for residents. At the entrance to East Hill Road stands a plaque noting the years that Millay lived in the sleepy hamlet of Austerlitz. But the actual house is so well hidden that if you drive by when trees and shrubs are in bloom, you will catch only a passing glimpse of the famous poet's home, tucked almost out of sight on the left side of the road.

BRONXVILLE

Dorothy Thompson home
17 Wood End Lane

Born near Buffalo to a family "so poor you wouldn't believe it," Dorothy Thompson (1894–1961) was one of the preeminent journalists and foreign correspondents of her day. An "unfeminine" girl bored with boys, Dorothy's first job after college was stumping for women's suffrage in western New York for eight dollars a week. Her early published articles in the New York papers chronicled her suffrage work. In 1920, with a friend from the suffrage movement, she went abroad and began her career as a foreign correspondent in Vienna. "Since you are obliged to earn your own living, it will not always be possible for you to remain a lady," her father warned her. "But I pray you, Dorothy—please promise me, that you will always remain a gentleman."

Thompson's intimate relationships included men and women. In 1921, she met Edna St. Vincent Millay, whom she alternately called "an angel" and "a little bitch." "We went swimming in the Danube, stark naked, late at night. . . . And drank champagne, afterward," Thompson remembered. "And drove out to the castle, and danced, and in the morning we ate an immense breakfast."

In 1928, Thompson married writer Sinclair Lewis, whose friends called him "Red." Lewis bought them a three-hundred-acre farm near Woodstock, Vermont, but Thompson continued pursuing her career. She interviewed Hitler in 1931 and spoke louder than any other journalist against Nazism. About that same time in Berlin she fell in love with Christa Winsloe, a writer whose most famous work was *The Child Manuela* (upon which the early lesbian-themed movie *Madchen in Uniform* was based). Winsloe had a "mannish" haircut and wore tailored suits with ties. Of meeting Winsloe, Thompson later reminisced, "Her name suddenly had a magic quality. . . . I wanted to say it. To use it. I talked about her to others, to hear her name." When they were apart, Winsloe signed her letters to Thompson "Christian" and used the German masculine pronoun for both of them.

At this home in Bronxville (bought for her by "Red"), Thompson spent much of 1933 living with Winsloe. When Winsloe returned to Europe in 1934, she presented Thompson with an ultimatum: "You've got to separate from Red somehow, that's for sure—otherwise you're *kaput* with me." Though by then her relationship with Lewis was no longer sexual, Thompson remained married to him until 1942. Her internalized homophobia appears to have been great, since she once described lesbian sex as a "perversion" and a "futility." Not surprisingly, the passion with Winsloe fizzled. For the rest of her life, though, Thompson preserved all of Winsloe's love letters.

When her Bronxville house burned in 1941, Thompson moved to a brownstone in New York (*see* New York City, New York). There is no evidence of another great love in her life after Winsloe; instead, she devoted herself to travel and adventure. In 1944, Winsloe was shot and killed in Paris in a street disturbance that followed the liberation of the city from the Nazis.

BUFFALO

In their ground-breaking local history, *Boots of Leather, Slippers of Gold*, Liz Kennedy and Madeline Davis document the growth of Buffalo's lesbian community from the 1930s to the 1960s. Their study is noteworthy for its concentration on the lives of the working-class butches and fems, who created a community and a culture for themselves. Some of the popular hangouts that Kennedy and Davis discuss are:

Galante's, Wilkeson Street (behind City Hall): Located in a rough neighborhood, this was a speakeasy that catered to gay men and women and a few straight people. The target of numerous police raids, it closed shortly after Prohibition ended.

Winter's, William Street (near Michigan): After Galante's closed, a group of women who had been friends there began frequenting Winter's. One patron described it as having two rooms and a kitchen infested with rats. Winter's also had rooms upstairs where "gay girls" could spend the night.

Ralph Martin's, Seneca and Ellicott Streets: Kennedy and Davis call this "the most open gay bar of the 1940s." Here, women were allowed to slow dance together, though only in the back room—something that was not regularly permitted in lesbian bars at that time for fear of police raids. Ralph's was "girl-cotted" by lesbians in 1945 when a fem had a run-in with the owner and was banned from the club.

Five Five Seven, Cherry Street, and Two Seventeen, Cherry Street: In the early 1950s, these two lesbian bars opened in the city's black neighborhood and had a large black clientele. Both places served a straight crowd during the day and lesbians at night.

CHERRY GROVE (FIRE ISLAND)

As far as I'm concerned, the entire resort of Cherry Grove is itself a historic site. Founded in 1869, it is the oldest community on the barrier island known as Fire Island, and the oldest gay resort in the United States. Gay men and lesbians—primarily theater people—first started migrating to Cherry Grove in the 1920s, mingling with the straight families who enjoyed summer homes there. When a hurricane destroyed most of the resort and its cottages in 1938, making real estate inexpensive, gay visitors began buying up land that others found too precarious. Many gay people are familiar with life on the edge, and an isolated island provided much-desired privacy. Later, Provincetown (at the tip of Cape Cod) and Key West, Florida, would become other gay vacation spots set on solitary points of land.

The Belvedere
Bay View Walk

In the late 1950s, gay developers John Eberhardt and Joe Guren built this imposing three-story Rococco guest house on the bay in the heart of the country's oldest gay resort, Cherry Grove. With its gleaming cupolas, Roman statues and columns, mirrors, fountains, and formal wisteria-draped arbors, the antiques-furnished Belvedere sits in sharp contrast to the simple shingled beach cottages of the Grove, rising above them like a white elephant. Eberhardt and Guren were famous for the elaborate parties they threw at the Belvedere every few days. The couple went on to become the Grove's largest landowners, buying up most of the eastern end of the resort and building numerous gingerbread cottages until the late 1960s.

GREENVILLE

Greene County in upstate New York was the site of the log home of "Miss Willson and Miss Brundage," two early-nineteenth-century "maids" whose real-life story inspired the classic lesbian novel *Patience and Sarah*.

According to one contemporary observer, Willson and Brundage had "a romantic attachment for each other" in the 1820s. Brundage was the farmer, who plowed and planted their few acres of land, while Willson painted watercolors. The intimate companions lived in Greenville on the northern border of the county for "many years" until Brundage's death, when the grief-stricken Willson "removed to parts unknown."

Over a hundred years later, Mary Ann Willson's folk painting of a mermaid, which was being exhibited in a Cooperstown art museum, attracted the attention of writer Alma Routsong, who noticed that the label on the painting mentioned Willson's "farmerette" companion. Routsong was inspired to try to research the women's herstory, but even in the New York Public Library's extensive genealogical division, she was unable to trace them. Finally, she fictionalized her subjects in a novel called *A Place for Us*. Self-published in 1967 under the pseudonym Isabel Miller, the novel proved so popular that it was later picked up by a mainstream press—under the revised title *Patience and Sarah*—and remains in print over twenty years later.

HUNTINGTON

Walt Whitman birthplace
246 Old Walt Whitman Road (off Route 110)
In the midst of a sprawl of suburban development (across from the "Walt Whitman Mall") is the carefully preserved family home of "the Good Gay Poet" (oops, I mean, "the Good *Gray* Poet"), Walt Whitman. Built somewhere between 1810 and 1816 by Whitman's father, the small shingled house, originally located on sixty acres of farmland, was the site of the poet's birth and very early childhood. The Whitmans had been farming in the vicinity known as West Hills since the mid-1600s, and the region is still sprinkled with historic structures associated with the extended family.

Whitman's birthplace is now a museum and state historic site that is open to the public. Downstairs are period rooms, while upstairs is a modern exhibit with photos and documents from Whitman's life, including a first edition of *Leaves of Grass*. Not surprisingly, the museum's interpretation of Whitman is missing any overt reference to his homosexuality. His lover, Peter Doyle, for example, is referred to as his "Confederate veteran pal"—but to their credit, the curators do display the well-known photo of Walt and Pete sitting close together, looking very much like a queer couple.

Whitman's father moved his family to Brooklyn in 1823 to pursue a career in carpentry and construction, but when an economic depression hit in the late 1830s, the family returned to Long Island. Over the next few years, young Walt—who himself left his formal schooling behind at age eleven—taught school in a number of Long Island towns, including briefly at the *Smithtown Schoolhouse, 9 Singer Lane,* earning $72.70 for five months of work. The desk he used as a schoolmaster at the *Woodbury School, Woodbury Road and Jericho Turnpike,* is on display at the birthplace.

During his teaching years, Whitman used his early training in printing to found *The Long Islander,* a weekly newspaper out of Huntington that is still in circulation (its masthead includes, "Founded by Walt Whitman"). On his own, he wrote, edited, typeset, and delivered the paper. Restless to try something else, he sold the paper the following year, but over the next twenty years, he continued to hold editorial positions at various newspapers on Long Island, in Brooklyn, and in New York. In his editorials he was outspoken in his advocacy of social, economic, and political reform.

The years he spent on Long Island proved an influential part of Walt Whitman's upbringing. A frequent swimmer at Montauk Point, Whitman's poetry abounds with sensual references to the power and beauty of the ocean. Many of his early sketches and short stories from the 1830s contain typical Long Island scenes. And his 1882 *Specimen Days and Collect* in-

> You sea! I resign myself to you also—I guess what you mean,
> I behold from the beach your crooked inviting fingers,
> I believe you refuse to go back without feeling of me,
> We must have a turn together, I undress, hurry me out of sight of
>   the land,
> Cushion me soft, rock me in billowy drowse,
> Dash me with amorous wet, I can repay you.
> —Walt Whitman, "Song of Myself"

cludes many recollections of the people among whom he had lived—the most "hospitable, upright, common-sensible people anywhere about."

HYDE PARK

Eleanor Roosevelt home
"Val-kill"
Route 9G

Intrepid First Lady, women's rights activist, and humanitarian Eleanor Roosevelt (1884–1962) was most at home here at her private retreat, Val-kill, named after the stream that runs beside it. Orphaned as a child, Eleanor was raised by a grandmother and educated in England at a girls' academy. At age twenty, she married her fifth cousin, Franklin Roosevelt, and for the next dozen years was a "proper" wife to an aspiring politician, living mostly in homes owned by her controlling mother-in-law, Sara Delano Roosevelt. But after Eleanor discovered Franklin's affair with her social secretary, Lucy Mercer, she offered him a divorce, and they reached the turning point of their marriage. The ambitious Franklin opted for his wife and children—and his political ambitions. Not long after, he contracted polio, which Eleanor nursed him through and which threatened to cut short his career. While he was recovering, Eleanor kept the Roosevelt name alive by making public appearances and speeches and becoming involved in Democratic politics herself. Within the party, she made many good friends, among them the lesbian couple Nancy Cook and Marion Dickerman.

In 1924, Franklin offered Eleanor, Nancy, and Marion ("the girls," as he called them) some wooded land on the Roosevelt estate in Hyde Park, on a rocky stream called Val-kill, where they could build a house and enjoy the serenity of the place without being at the large, imposing Roosevelt mansion, Springwood, two miles away. By 1925, a stone cottage in the Dutch colonial style (now called "Stone Cottage") was built on the site, and Nancy laid out the grounds and gardens. Nancy and Marion began living at the cottage full-time that year, with Eleanor visiting them on weekends and during the summers. According to historian Blanche Wiesen Cook, Franklin teasingly dubbed the place "The Honeymoon Cottage," and Eleanor embroidered the linens "E. M. N.," the women's three initials.

After a year, the trio (with another Democratic Party friend, Caroline O'Day, a former companion of Lillian Wald) had a second cottage constructed on the grounds for Val-kill Industries, an experimental business designed to provide work for local residents. Artisans were trained to create high-quality early American furniture reproductions, but it folded ten years later under the financial pressures of the Depression. Nancy and Marion continued to occupy the Stone Cottage until 1947, and Eleanor had the factory remodeled into her own home (now "Val-kill Cottage"), the first and only house that belonged to her. After Franklin's death in 1945, Val-kill became Eleanor's permanent residence. Now operated by the National Park Service and open to the public, Val-kill Cottage is a cozy, unpretentious house filled with comfortable furnishings (most made by Val-kill Industries) and decorated with photographs of Eleanor's friends and family. You can almost see her in the warm pine-paneled rooms, relishing her independence and freedom from the Roosevelt family.

Eleanor has largely been constructed by history as an unattractive, asexual woman whose main function was to further her husband's career. But Blanche Cook's recent biography shows Eleanor in a different light, revealing her activity within the women's committee of the Democratic Party, her feminist activism, her circle of lesbian friends, and most importantly, her decade-long intimate relationship with reporter Lorena ("Hick") Hickock. At Val-kill, however, you won't hear even a hint about Eleanor's lesbianism in the official Park Service interpretation and film, in which Nancy and Marion are painted as "good friends" and Hick—one of the major relationships of her life—isn't mentioned at all. (*See also* New York City, New York.)

NEW ROCHELLE

Carrie Chapman Catt house
120 Paine Avenue

Suffrage activist and founder of the League of Women Voters, Carrie Chapman Catt (1859–1947) purchased this home in 1928 with money inherited from her second husband, George Catt, who had wholeheartedly supported her work. Here she resided with her life partner, suffragist Mary Garrett (Molly) Hay (1857–1928), who had been cohabiting with Catt since 1905, when George died. Sadly, after living here only a few months and decorating and landscaping their home, Hay suddenly passed away on her seventy-first birthday. Hay's death, one friend reported, "shook Mrs. Catt to the soul." After a period of deep despondency in which she had to resort to drugs in order to sleep, Catt resumed her activism, becoming increasingly involved in the peace movement. At her death, she was buried next to Hay and shares one tombstone with her, the inscription of which Catt herself had written. (*See also* The Bronx, New York.)

NEW YORK CITY
The Bronx

Woodlawn Cemetery
East 233rd Street and Webster Avenue

At least two prominent queer people are buried in New York's northernmost borough. Though she married twice, suffrage leader Carrie Chapman Catt (1858–1947) chose to rest for all eternity beside Mary Garrett (Molly) Hay, her partner in the fight for women's votes. The two companions had lived together since 1905 (*see* New Rochelle, New York), supported in their suffrage work by money Catt's second husband had left her. At Woodlawn, they share one gravestone, which is inscribed: "Here lie two, united in friendship for thirty-eight years through constant service to a great cause." (*See also* Charles City, Iowa, and Ripon, Wisconsin.)

Also buried at Woodlawn is author Herman Melville (1819–1891), who had faded into obscurity by the time of his death in New York City. Melville's marble headstone, simply adorned with a scroll, quill pen, and vine, lists only his name and birth and death dates. (*See also* Pittsfield, Massachusetts, and New York City, New York.)

Brooklyn

W. H. Auden, Carson McCullers, et al., residence
7 Middagh Street

In the fall of 1940, George Davis, then the fiction editor of *Harper's Bazaar,* signed a lease on a three-story house at this address in Brooklyn Heights. His intention was to invite friends working in the arts to live there in community, renting rooms at moderate cost. The artists' commune that Davis created flourished until 1945, and the names of Davis's "friends" have passed into the canon of the creative arts—W. H. Auden, Carson Mc-Cullers, Richard Wright, Benjamin Britten, Peter Pears, Marc Blitzstein, Louis MacNeice, and Jane and Paul Bowles. Many more—like Janet Flanner, Leonard Bernstein, Lincoln Kirstein, and Anaïs Nin—visited the house on Middagh Street to experience firsthand what poet and critic Louis Untermeyer called "that queer aggregate of artists."

The Middagh Street residence was so well known at the time that there was a waiting list of artists who wanted to become tenants. Jane Bowles once snottily told a prospective tenant that he wasn't "important enough" to live there! While stories abound about the party atmosphere of the house and the many "queer dramas" that took place there, much serious work went on, too. One compelling story is about Carson McCullers, who was struggling with a draft of a novel she at the time called *The Bride and Her Brother.* Thanksgiving afternoon of 1940 proved crucial for her. After the meal, while the tenants and their guests enjoyed brandy before the fire in the drawing room, McCullers heard the whine of a fire engine siren drawing closer and closer, as though headed for Middagh Street. She and exotic dancer Gypsy Rose Lee, another tenant, rushed outside and ran sev-

OTHER NEW YORK CITY RESIDENCES OF THE MIDDAGH STREET ARTISTS

W. H. Auden: 77 St. Marks Place, Manhattan (in 1997, the brick facade was destroyed through "renovation," and a plaque indicating Auden's residence here was removed)
Jane and Paul Bowles: 28 West Tenth Street, Manhattan; 207 DeGrauw Avenue, Jamaica, Queens; and 1116 Woodrow Road, Staten Island
Carson McCullers: 321 West Eleventh Street, Manhattan
Oliver Smith: 28 West Tenth Street, Manhattan (with the Bowleses); 70 Willow Street, Brooklyn

eral blocks down Middagh toward the firehouse at the end of the street. Suddenly, McCullers caught Lee's arm, shouted breathlessly for her to stop, and cried out, "Frankie is in love with her brother and the bride, and wants to become a member of the wedding!" Lee had no idea what McCullers was talking about, but the latter's novel took on shape and focus—and its famous name—that day in the middle of Middagh Street.

Unfortunately, the block on which the celebrated house stood was razed in 1945 to make way for an entrance ramp to the Brooklyn-Queens Expressway. But other buildings on Middagh Street have not changed much since Auden's and McCullers's time there, and if you stand approximately where No. 7 was and look east, you can almost imagine that other time.

Montgomery Clift grave
Brooklyn Quaker Cemetery
Prospect Park
Born in Omaha, Montgomery Clift (1920–1966) began his career as a stage actor, before becoming a leading film star of the late 1940s and 1950s. He starred in such now-classic movies as *A Place in the Sun, Suddenly, Last Summer* (both with Elizabeth Taylor, who was unrequitedly in love with him), *Red River, Judgment at Nuremberg,* and *From Here to Eternity.*

But an automobile accident in 1956 nearly ended his career, and Clift underwent massive reconstructive surgery on his handsome face. In the middle of filming *Raintree County*, again with Taylor, Clift had to take months off before he was able to resume work on the film. Mentally and physically affected by his ordeal, Clift continued to make movies but more and more mourned his "disfigurement" through alcohol and drug abuse and died at the early age of forty-five of a heart attack.

Clift's homosexuality was well known in Hollywood, though he tried to keep it from becoming public knowledge for fear it would hurt his career. He had the reputation of being a loner, and most of his sexual encounters were one-night stands with male hustlers. In 1949, he was arrested for trying to pick up a hustler on Forty-second Street, but the incident was hushed up by his handlers. In the early 1950s, he had a quiet romance with the playwright Thornton Wilder, another gay man who prized "discretion" and suffered from internalized homophobia.

Clift's primary residence was in Manhattan from 1951 until his death, first at *209 East Sixty-first Street* (destroyed by fire in 1960), and then at the elegant three-story brownstone at *No. 217*, a house with four bedrooms and six baths. After a funeral service at the *Friends Meeting House, East Fifteenth Street*, he was buried at this site in Brooklyn, and his grave was planted with crocuses by his friend, actress Nancy Walker. (*See also* Omaha, Nebraska.)

Hart Crane apartment
110 Columbia Heights

Poet Hart Crane (1899–1933) was born in a small town in Ohio and came to New York City on his own while still a teenager. That year, 1916, his parents finally divorced after a stormy marriage, in which his father was abusive and his mother spent time in a sanatorium. Crane shuttled between Ohio and New York for several years, finally settling in the East in 1923. Crane supported himself and his writing by taking odd jobs writing advertising copy and borrowing money from friends and family. At first, he lived in a series of cheap furnished rooms in Greenwich Village, where he actively pursued sexual relationships with men.

In 1924, a young ship's steward, Emil Opffer, with whom Crane was having an affair, got him this apartment in Brooklyn Heights, in a building owned by the sailor's family. An art school was located on the first floor, while upstairs were numerous rooms and apartments for rent. Crane's room was on the fourth floor and looked out onto the Brooklyn Bridge. In fact, 110 Columbia Heights was the same house Washington Roebling, the son of the bridge's designer, occupied while carrying out his father's bridge design.

Crane enjoyed a rare period of peace and contentment while living in Brooklyn Heights. It was at this address—inspired by his view—that he began writing his most famous long poem, *The Bridge* (1930). But Crane was a tortured, self-destructive soul who battled alcoholism and his own homosexual desires. In 1933, on a ship from Mexico (where he had spent his last year compliments of a Guggenheim Fellowship) back to New York, he was beaten up by sailors he solicited for sex. Distraught, he flung himself from the deck of the ship into the sea and drowned.

Gay brothel
329 Pacific Street

In a three-story brick home at this location there was a male brothel in the early years of World War II. The establishment was operated by a Swede, George (Gustav) Beekman, who had run two earlier male brothels, one on West Forty-third Street in Manhattan and one near Court Street in Brooklyn. Conveniently located near the Brooklyn Navy Yard, Beekman's Pacific Street brothel catered to servicemen, who found the setting "warm and cozy . . . relaxed and friendly," to quote one guest. "We felt as if we had entered a happy family circle, George being Dad and Mom combined."

Visitors to the brothel could "order" a man to suit their tastes—"All details," one guest noted, "were jotted down in George's notebook." The waiting list for rooms was usually a long one, and occupancy of a bedroom on busy nights was limited to thirty minutes. While waiting, visitors relaxed on easy chairs or, on warm evenings, mingled in the outdoor garden.

In early 1942, the presence of so many strangers in the neighborhood began to alarm residents of Pacific Street, and they reported the suspicious activity at No. 329 to the police. Thus began six weeks of surveillance, ending in a raid and arrests on March 14, 1942. The tabloid newspapers had a field day with the raid, and rumors spread about the brothel—that it was being used for Nazi espionage, and that Senator David Walsh of Massachusetts, the chair of the Naval Affairs Committee, was a habitué. The *New York Post* called the scandal "a stinking mess." No evidence was found for the espionage claims, however, and the senator was exonerated. But poor George Beekman was sentenced to Sing Sing prison for twenty years on sodomy charges and served his full term there. For an entertaining fictional account of the brothel based on the actual events, pick up Christopher Bram's historical novel *Hold Tight*.

Walt Whitman homes and haunts

Born near Huntington, Long Island, Walt Whitman (1819–1892) moved with his family to Brooklyn when he was a young boy so that his father could find carpentry work during the housing boom there. (*See* Huntington, New York.) Whitman lived and worked at various Brooklyn addresses for the next forty years. Some of the most significant sites in Brooklyn associated with the great poet include the following:

149 Fulton Street: This was the office of the *Long Island Patriot*, where in 1831 Whitman got his first job. It was here that he learned to set type and where his future newspaper career was launched.

Cranberry and Fulton Streets (Cadman Plaza West): Until 1961, the building that housed the Rome Brothers print shop, which published the first edition of *Leaves of Grass*, was at this address, which is now an ugly concrete plaza. Whitman would come in every day from his home at *99 Ryerson Street* to help set the type. The finished volume was an oversized book of under ninety pages containing a mere twelve poems, bound within a green leather cover elegantly embossed with sprigs of gold leaves.

99 Ryerson Street: The Whitmans' Ryerson residence is still standing, though it has had a third floor added to it since the 1850s. It was in the Ryerson house that Whitman finished his masterpiece, *Leaves of Grass* (1855), and it was there that he brought the newly printed book for his family to admire. "I saw the book—didn't read it at all," his brother George later wrote unkindly, "—didn't think it worth reading—fingered it a little." The neighborhood around Ryerson is still full of pre–Civil War frame houses, which carpenters like Walter Whitman, Sr., constructed during the Brooklyn housing boom.

91-1/2 Classon Avenue: Walt frequently helped his family financially and lived with them in various rented houses. After Walt, Sr., died, the remaining Whitman family lived on Classon Avenue from 1856 to 1859, and it was there that Walt took in Fred Vaughan, a young "apprentice," to share his room and his bed. According to Charley Shively in *Calamus Lovers*, Walt and Fred's room was decorated with erotic drawings of Hercules, Bacchus, and a satyr. The teenaged Fred has been cited as the inspiration for the Calamus sequence of poems, which was written during this time. Shively speculates that Fred's marriage in 1862 may have prompted Walt's eagerness to depart for Washington. (*See* District of Columbia.)

Harlem

It's not a separate borough, but Harlem merits its own section by virtue of all the queer history that has been made there. Many significant sites are identified with the Harlem Renaissance of the 1920s and early 1930s, but queer culture thrived there through the following decades. A few Harlem sites include:

James Baldwin home
131st Street and Fifth Avenue
A housing project has been on this site for over forty years, but the first home of writer James Baldwin (1924–1987) was once located here. Baldwin wrote vividly and movingly of the deteriorating neighborhood in his

essay, "Fifth Avenue Uptown: A Letter from Harlem," calling the avenue "wide, filthy, hostile." "Walk through the streets of Harlem," he admonished his readers, "and see what we, this nation, have become."

Baldwin remembered a bleak, poverty-stricken childhood, where his playgrounds were the roof of his building and a nearby garbage dump. He escaped a brutal stepfather and a troubled home life through books and writing. One of his junior-high teachers, Countee Cullen, spent much time working with him on his fiction and poetry. Baldwin also found solace in the church, becoming an evangelical minister at age fourteen. *Go Tell It On the Mountain* (1953), his first novel, is an autobiographical work focused on his early life in Harlem.

Baldwin worked a number of after-school jobs to help his family, and at one such job in downtown Manhattan in 1940, he met the painter Beauford Delaney, who became his mentor and possibly his lover. Delaney introduced Baldwin to jazz, art, and to a circle of African-American artists. "The reality of his seeing," Baldwin later wrote, "caused me to begin to see." As a young man Baldwin left his family and Harlem for Greenwich Village, where he worked odd jobs to support his writing. In 1948, he took off for Paris, where he lived on and off for the rest of his life. Though he returned to live in New York for periods of time, he didn't like to stay long, saying that the racism of the city made him too "sad."

Baldwin treated homosexuality and bisexuality in many of his works, most notably *Giovanni's Room* (1956), *Another Country* (1962), and *Tell Me How Long the Train's Been Gone* (1968). His own life included affairs with both men and women, but the love of his life seems to have been a Frenchman named Lucien Happersberger, whom he met in 1949. "I starved in Paris for a while, but I learned something," Baldwin later wrote. "For one thing I fell in love." Happersberger became Baldwin's lover for a while but didn't share the dream of two men building a life together. He eventually married a woman and named his son after Baldwin.

In addition to fiction writing, Baldwin authored numerous important works exploring race and racism, particularly *Nobody Knows My Name* (1961) and *The Fire Next Time* (1963). He was himself active in the civil rights movement of the 1960s and continued to speak out about racism until his death from cancer in 1987.

Countee Cullen home
2190 Seventh Avenue

Facts about poet Countee Cullen's (1903–1946) early life are few. He was born Countee Leroy Porter and raised by his grandmother in Kentucky and New York. After her death around 1918, the boy was adopted by Frederick Cullen, pastor of Salem Methodist Episcopal Church, and his wife Carolyn. Countee came to live with the Cullens at the parsonage, located at this address.

The Cullens provided Countee with a privileged education. He graduated from DeWitt Clinton High School and New York University and obtained an M.A. degree from Harvard. A prominent figure in the Harlem Renaissance, he won numerous literary awards and was a prolific writer who frequently published in *The Crisis* and *Opportunity*. He was part of the black writers' community at the Harlem public library, where he met and fell in love with Langston Hughes in 1922.

In 1928, Cullen married Yolande Du Bois, the daughter of W. E. B., in an elaborate ceremony at Salem Methodist, ensuring his place among the "Talented Tenth." But he couldn't escape his homosexual desires. After a few tense months, the marriage fell apart, and Cullen took off for Europe with his lover and DeWitt Clinton classmate, Harold Jackman—who had also been his best man.

In the 1930s, Cullen was a teacher at Frederick Douglass Junior High School, where one of his most promising students was a young writer named James Baldwin.

Drag balls

During the Jazz Age, Harlem hosted a variety of well-attended and highly publicized costume balls, which Langston Hughes dubbed "spectacles in color." These balls—sanctioned by police permits—naturally attracted gay people, since they were occasions when men and women could legally dress in drag and dance with whomever they pleased. A "Queen of the Ball" was crowned at the end of the evening. The two most famous locations for the drag balls were:

Hamilton Lodge, 111th Street and Seventh Avenue: This was the largest of the Harlem balls, held in a space that accommodated up to six thousand people, mostly black. Though officially called the Masquerade and Civic Ball, historian George Chauncey states that by the late 1920s it was commonly referred to as the Faggots Ball.

Savoy Ballroom, Lenox Avenue between 132nd and 133rd Streets: This space boasted a crystal chandelier and a marble staircase. It was located right down the street from the famous Cotton Club.

Gumby's Bookstore
Fifth Avenue between 131st and 132nd Streets

Gay men and lesbians of the Harlem Renaissance enjoyed literary gatherings at the salon of Alexander Gumby, called "Gumby's Bookstore" because of the bookshelves lining the walls. Gumby came to Harlem around the turn of the century and worked as a postal clerk. He was enamored of artists and theater types and found a white patron to help him rent a studio/salon to attract them. But intellectual conversation reportedly wasn't all you got at Gumby's—there was also bathtub gin, marijuana, and sexual liaisons.

Harlem YMCA
181 West 135th Street

With over two hundred small rooms, communal bathrooms, and hall phones, the Harlem YMCA served as home to many young men when they first arrived in the city. This was the first address of poet Langston Hughes when he came to New York in September 1921. For seven dollars a week, Hughes rented a room on the fourth floor. When he arrived in Harlem, Hughes later wrote, "I stood there, dropped my bags, took a deep breath and felt happy again." New York, he felt, was "truly the dream city—city of the towers near God, city of hopes and visions, of spires seeking in the windy air loveliness and perfection." Shortly after, Hughes enrolled at Columbia University with money given to him by his father.

The YMCA's rent had increased fivefold by 1939, when musician Billy Strayhorn (1915–1967) stayed here. Strayhorn arrived from his hometown of Pittsburgh to join the Duke Ellington band. Ellington paid the young man's rent of five dollars a night. But Strayhorn's stay at the Y was short—he soon moved into the Ellington's seven-room apartment at *409 Edgecombe Avenue* and became like a member of the family. (*See also* Pittsburgh, Pennsylvania.)

The Harlem YMCA was also a temporary home to queer poet Claude McKay when he returned to New York after a long stay abroad (*see below*).

Langston Hughes homes
634 St. Nicholas Avenue and 20 East 127 Street

Raised in Kansas and Ohio, poet Langston Hughes (1902–1967) came to New York after high school to study at Columbia University. Hughes lived first at Hartley Hall, one of the Columbia dorms (much later Allen Ginsberg would room there, too), where he was assigned the worst room on account of his race. Unhappy at Columbia, Hughes left after less than a year.

A major figure of the Harlem Renaissance (ca. 1920–1935), Hughes in fact spent many of those years traveling abroad, always on a shoestring, and then studying at Lincoln University, an African-American college in Pennsylvania from which he graduated in 1929. He had occasional extended sojourns in New York, such as in the summer of 1926 when he lived at "Niggerati Manor" (*see below*). His essays "Harlem Literati" and "Parties" have captured the spirit and flavor of the Jazz Age. Some of his best-remembered works, such as *The Weary Blues* (1926), were written during the 1920s, but he published prolifically in many different genres until his death.

After years on the move, Hughes finally settled on St. Nicholas Avenue in Harlem during the 1940s, writing to his friend Arna Bontemps, "I never in my life intend to leave New York permanently. I never again will move another book or trunk of manuscripts." The top floor of this row house on

West 127th Street was where he lived from 1947 until his death twenty years later.

Hughes's sexuality has been much debated over the years. Some scholars were horrified when Isaac Julien titled his 1989 gay-themed film "Looking for Langston." One of Langston's biographers, Arnold Rampersad, has staunchly maintained that there is no hard "evidence" that Hughes was gay. But neither is there "evidence" that he was straight! In fact, his friends, acquaintances, and social circle all point toward his homosexuality. Gay scholars have also discussed the coded homoeroticism within Hughes's poems. (*See also* Lawrence, Kansas, and Cleveland, Ohio.)

Claude McKay home
147 West 142nd Street

Claude McKay (1890–1948) was born on a farm in Jamaica, the youngest of eleven children. At age seventeen, he met Walter Jekyll, a gay British expatriate, who mentored his writing, encouraging him to use the Jamaican patois in his poetry. In 1912, McKay immigrated to the United States, studying at Tuskegee Institute, working odd jobs, and making his way to Harlem two years later.

Though he spent much of the Harlem Renaissance in Europe, McKay wrote of Harlem often, about his love for "the warm accent of its composite voice, the fruitiness of its laughter, the trailing rhythm of its 'blues' and the improvised surprises of its jazz." His first volume of poetry, *Harlem Shadows* (1922), is usually considered the first major work of the Harlem Renaissance.

McKay's *Home to Harlem* (1928) was the first novel by an African American to hit the best-seller list—and it did so within two weeks of its publication. In it, he included a significant black gay male character and a discussion of lesbianism in Harlem. Langston Hughes called it "the finest thing 'we've' ever done."

McKay lived at this address after one of his many extended sojourns to Paris, Marseilles, and Tangiers.

Nella Larsen home
236 West 135th Street

Writer Nella Larsen (1891–1964) was born in Chicago to a white Danish mother and a "colored" West Indian father. It is unclear what happened to her father, Peter Walker. When Nella was three years old, her mother married Peter Larsen, a white man (or a light-skinned black man passing for white—possibly the same man as Peter Walker), who looked with displeasure on Nella's brown skin and determinedly positioned the family within the city's white society. The birth of a white half-sister made Nella even more of an outcast in her own family, and she spent many years traveling, searching for an undefined "something."

Trained as a nurse, Larsen worked at various nursing jobs, first at Tuskegee Institute and later in New York City. In 1919, she married physicist Elmer Imes, and the two enjoyed an active social life in the Harlem of the 1920s. She left nursing to pursue a career as a librarian and to write fiction, living at this Harlem address while working at the 135th Street branch of the New York Public Library (see below). (A reviewer of Quicksand in The Amsterdam News described Larsen's apartment as having "the air of a Greenwich Village Studio.") Her two novels, Quicksand (1928)—based in part on the career of performer Josephine Baker—and Passing (1929), were critically acclaimed, and she was the first African-American woman to win a Guggenheim Fellowship.

But an accusation of plagiarism (her final short story, "Sanctuary," was believed to resemble another author's work too closely), sensationalized in the press, and a bitter, public divorce brought about a reversal of fortune. Larsen returned to nursing to support herself and by the time of her death had largely been forgotten as a writer. Recent critics have pointed to the lesbian overtones of Larsen's work, particularly Passing, which, in addition to its overt story of "passing" for white, can be read as a story of "passing" for heterosexual. Larsen was such a private woman and the details of her life are so sketchy that we can only guess that Passing reflected her own hidden desires.

New York Public Library
135th Street and Lenox Avenue (Malcolm X Boulevard)

Now the Schomburg Center for Research in Black Culture, a premier research facility, this 1905 neoclassic building designed by the firm of McKim, Mead and White was once the Harlem branch of the public library. Novelist Nella Larsen (see above) was a librarian here before her literary career took off, and a community of black writers met here regularly during the Harlem Renaissance to discuss their work. It was at this site that Countee Cullen first met Langston Hughes, with whom he was in love. The Harlem branch of the NYPL is now named after Cullen and is located at the site of A'Lelia Walker's home (see below).

"Niggerati Manor"
267 West 137th Street

Zora Neale Hurston once wryly dubbed the premier Harlem artists of the 1920s, who were always winning literary contests and being feted at awards dinners, "the Niggerati." The nickname "Niggerati Manor" was quickly attached to this small rooming house, which queer poets Wallace Thurman, Bruce Nugent, and Langston Hughes all called home. The building was owned by Iolanthe Sydney, a black philanthropist who offered rooms here rent-free to artists in order to support their work. Nugent—a painter as well as a writer—reportedly painted brightly colored phalluses on the interior walls.

It was at this address that Thurman, Nugent, Hurston, Hughes, and others started the experimental literary journal *Fire!!* in the summer of 1926. Each of its seven founders pledged fifty dollars to the effort, but, according to Hughes's memoirs, only three ever paid up. Since Thurman was the only one with a steady job, his checks paid for the printing bill for the first and only issue.

The journal had a high price tag for the day—one dollar. Hughes later remembered *Fire!!* never seemed to make money because Bruce Nugent—who was unemployed at the time—distributed it to booksellers on foot, using the little bit of cash he got from its sale to buy food. (Nugent's

> . . . they walked in silence . . . Alex turned in his doorway . . . no need
> for words . . . they had always known each other . . .
>   —from Richard Bruce Nugent, "Smoke, Lilies and Jade," 1926

"Smoke, Lilies and Jade," the first published piece with a homosexual theme by an African American, was one of the notable pieces included in *Fire!!*) Ironically, several hundred copies of the journal, which were being stored in the printer's basement, were burned in an actual fire. It took Thurman four years to pay off the printing bills.

Pre-Stonewall gay hangouts and venues

Admiral Bar, Seventh Avenue and 132nd Street: Now a supermarket, this was a popular women's bar during the 1960s.

Apollo Theatre, 253 West 125th Street: Built as a burlesque theater in 1913, the Apollo has been a premier venue for African-American entertainers since the 1930s. Queer entertainers Alberta Hunter, Billie Holiday, Bessie Smith, Ethel Waters, and Jackie "Moms" Mabley all performed here regularly. In the 1960s, the Apollo hosted the famous drag show, the Jewel Box Revue.

The Clam House, 146 West 133rd Street: During the 1920s, the Clam House was described by one observer as "a narrow room in Jungle Alley [West 133rd Street between Seventh and Lenox Avenues] . . . not for the innocent young." Big, sassy lesbian Gladys Bentley (1907–1960) sang and played piano here, performing in full male drag—a white tuxedo and top hat—with her feet pounding the floor and her fingers flying over the keyboard. Bentley was one of the most popular performers in Harlem, belting out raunchy parodies of Broadway tunes and encouraging the club's patrons to sing along. Her success brought her an expensive apartment, servants, and a car. "The club where I worked," she remembered, "overflowed with celebrities and big star names nightly. . . . I had made my mark in show business."

Club Hot-Cha, Seventh Avenue and 132nd Street: Billie Holiday used to sing here before she became famous, and queer celebrities such as architect Philip Johnson and composer Virgil Thomson used to frequent it. An early nightclub map of Harlem stated that "nothing happens before 2 A.M." at Club Hot-Cha. There were two floors, with drinking on the first floor and "action" on the second.

Clinton Moore's, Seventh Avenue and 135th Street: This town house (painted white) was home to Clinton Moore's interracial after-hours club of the 1920s and 1930s. Moore's club was exclusive, catering to celebrities such as Noël Coward, Lorenz Hart, Cary Grant, and Cole Porter. The "entertainment" included a piano player who would extinguish a lighted candle by sitting on it until it disappeared—yikes!

Old Lady Cunard's, Lenox Avenue between 141st and 142nd Streets: This location housed a women's buffet flat during the late 1950s and early 1960s. Buffet flats, which originated in Harlem in the 1920s, were private parties infamous for sexual experimentation of every variety (a virtual "buffet" or "smorgasbord" of sexual tastes). Though not exclusively gay, the open sexual atmosphere of buffet flats appealed to gay men and lesbians.

Purple Manor, 125th Street between Fifth and Madison Avenues: During the 1950s and early 1960s, this was a men's bar. The front room was for straights, the back for gay men (and some lesbians).

Ubangi Club, 133rd Street: A Mafia-run nightclub in the 1930s, the Ubangi boasted queer performers Gladys Bentley (*see above*) and comedian Jackie "Moms" Mabley, both of whom had large gay followings, and a chorus of female impersonators.

> It seems I was born different. . . . From the time I can remember anything, even when I was toddling, I never wanted a man to touch me. . . . Soon I began to feel more comfortable in boys' clothes than in dresses.
>
> —Gladys Bentley

A'Lelia Walker home
"The Dark Tower"
108–110 West 136th Street

This was the site of A'Lelia Walker's (1885–1931) famous haven for writers and artists during the 1920s, nicknamed "The Dark Tower" after a poem by queer poet Countee Cullen. Walker's fortune came from her mother, Madame C. J. Walker, an enterprising woman who created a multi-million-dollar empire from beauty salons and hair-straightening products for black women. With her inheritance, A'Lelia purchased two Stanford White–designed town houses on West 136th Street in "Sugar Hill," combined them into one residence with a new facade, and furnished them lavishly. Here she hosted soirees for the Harlem and Greenwich Village "glitterati," serving caviar and bootleg champagne and providing entertainment by queer performers Alberta Hunter and Jimmy Daniels. Intellectual discussions took place on the third floor. Langston Hughes later wrote that A'Lelia's parties "were as crowded as the New York subway at the rush hour." She herself was a striking figure, whom Hughes called "a gorgeous dark Amazon."

Sadly, Walker's historic brownstone was demolished in the 1940s, but appropriately, the Countee Cullen branch of the New York Public Library now stands on the site.

Manhattan

Lesbian and gay Manhattan could take up a hefty volume of its own. Two very good walking tours are available for visiting queer sites in the Big Apple: Daniel Hurewitz's *In Their Footsteps* (Footsteps Publishing, 1994), and "A Guide to Lesbian and Gay New York Historical Landmarks," published by the Organization of Lesbian and Gay Architects + Designers (OLGAD). Below is a very subjective sampling of the city's queerest places.

Berenice Abbott studio
50 Commerce Street

Photographer Berenice Abbott (1898–1991) is probably best known for her portraits of artists and writers in the 1920s expatriate community in Paris. Born in Ohio, Abbott left the Midwest at age twenty-two to study in New York, Berlin, and Paris. In Paris, she was the assistant to the celebrated Man Ray from 1923 to 1925. She then set out to do her own photographic portraits of such subjects as Jean Cocteau, André Gide, and James Joyce.

In 1929, Abbott retuned to the United States and began a visual documentary of the city of New York. Much of the old architecture of the city was scheduled for demolition, and Abbott wanted to capture it on film before it disappeared. She kept a studio here on one of the tiniest, most charming streets in Greenwich Village. Abbott's important volume, *Changing New York* (1937), recorded the shifting cityscape before the advent of World War II.

In the years after the war, she became fascinated with new technological advances and particularly with using photographs to illustrate the laws of physics. Much of her later work was done at the Massachusetts Institute of Technology.

Though never openly identifying as gay, Abbott had several intimate relationships with women during her life. During the early 1920s, she was lovers with Thelma Wood, who Abbott then introduced to Djuna Barnes (*see below*). Barnes, who met Abbott in 1918, once commented: "I gave Berenice the extra 'e' in her name and she gave me Thelma. I don't know who made out better."

"Angel of the Waters"
Bethesda Fountain
Central Park (just north of 72nd Street)

The fountain made famous by Tony Kushner's epic *Angels in America* was sculpted by a lesbian, Emma Stebbins, in 1873. Stebbins (1815–1882) was one of several intimate companions of actress and lesbian bon vivant

Charlotte Cushman, whom she accompanied to Italy in the late 1850s and lived with for twenty years. They called themselves the "jolly female bachelors." After Cushman died in 1876, a devoted Stebbins wrote her biography.

Remarkably, Stebbins didn't begin studying sculpture until age forty-two, proving it's never too late to explore your dreams and talents. "Angel of the Waters," her most well-known piece, was made in her studio in Rome and cast in Munich. Unveiled in 1873, it was justly hailed as a masterpiece. Stebbins is also remembered for the Columbus statue in the Brooklyn Civic Center.

James Baldwin home
81 Horatio Street

Writer James Baldwin (1924–1987), who was born in Harlem (*see above*) and as a young writer lived in Greenwich Village, preferred Paris, where he found, as other black expatriates had, that his race was not an issue. Though Paris was his primary residence after 1948, he occasionally came back to the United States for several months or years at a time. From late 1957 to 1959, he lived at this address in the Village, paying one hundred dollars a month for a small, three-room apartment. He had to borrow the fifty-dollar security deposit from his brother, David, to whom he reported that there were "a couple of Negroes in the building already." Here he began work on his novel of interracial and bisexual love, *Another Country*, and wrote a number of essays that would eventually appear as the nonfiction collection *Nobody Knows My Name* (1961).

Djuna Barnes apartment
5 Patchin Place, No. 2F

Djuna Barnes (1892–1982) was a novelist, playwright, poet, and newspaper reporter who enjoyed a prolific forty-year writing career leading up to the publication of *Nightwood* (1936), the novel for which she is best remembered. *Nightwood* is today considered a masterpiece of modernist writing, though in the mid-1930s it was rejected for publication in this country and was first published in England. Adding an introduction by her friend T. S. Eliot helped sell the book in the United States, though it was neither a popular nor critical success at that time.

The book's lesbian content made the public assume that Barnes was a lesbian. But in her cranky old age, Barnes told a friend that if she'd known that would happen, she never would have written the novel at all and claimed that the "accusations" that she was a lesbian were "nonsense." Though Barnes also had sexual relationships with men and never identified as lesbian, the person she called her "great love" was a woman. Thelma Wood, with whom she lived in Paris in the 1920s and who had earlier been the lover of photographer Berenice Abbott and poet Edna St. Vincent Millay. *Ladies Almanack* (1928), Barnes's roman à clef about the lesbian community in Paris, was written to entertain Wood during a stay in the hospital.

Wood was an alcoholic who had numerous affairs while involved with Barnes. The two finally separated in 1929 after a stormy, alcohol-driven relationship. But Wood remained a prominent figure in the writer's life, inspiring the character Robin in *Nightwood*. Until her death, Barnes kept a scrapbook from the 1920s, more than three-quarters full of photos of the

A BEVY OF EARLY NYC BATHHOUSES

> *Everard Baths, 38 West 28th Street:* opened in 1888, but destroyed by fire in 1977
> *Lafayette Baths, 403–405 Lafayette Street:* the heart of gay New York in the first decades of the century. In the teens, Charles Demuth painted a series of interiors (complete with naked men) of the Lafayette Baths.
> *St. Marks Baths, 6 St. Marks Place:* opened in 1915, it was closed by the city at the height of the AIDS epidemic
> *Mt. Morris Baths, 1944 Madison Avenue:* opened in 1891 and still in operation

androgynously lovely Thelma Wood, often dressed in trousers and men's shirts. As a very old woman, Barnes spoke bitterly about the love of her life: "I gave Berenice [Abbott] the extra 'e' in her name and she gave me Thelma. I don't know who made out better."

During the second half of her life, Barnes published very little. Following her own treatment for alcoholism in the late 1930s, Barnes's last forty plus years were spent in self-imposed seclusion in a twelve-by-fourteen- foot studio on the second floor of this apartment building. Instead of her name on the buzzer, there was a typewritten notice, "Do Not Disturb!" Hank O'Neal, a companion to Barnes in her old age, described the apartment in his memoir, *"Life Is Painful, Nasty and Short . . . In My Case It Has Only Been Painful and Nasty": Djuna Barnes, 1978–1981*, as badly lit, crowded, unadorned, and drab. The writer's desk, he noted, was littered with incomplete poems, drafts of manuscripts, and stubs of pencils. "Everything in the room," O'Neal recorded, "seems to be in a state of decay, a room full of despair, disarray, and confusion. It appears to be a place shut away from time, but the ravages of time are there."

"I wonder why I wrote so little," Barnes pondered on one of O'Neal's visits, seemingly oblivious to the combined effects that depression, alcoholism, and an abusive relationship might have had. "But as Tom [T. S. Eliot] said, some of it was marvelous."

Caffe Cino
31 Cornelia Street

From 1958 to 1967, Joe Cino ran a coffeehouse at this address that has gone down in performance history as the place where both gay theater and Off-Off-Broadway were born. At the beginning the Beat generation café was not intended as a theater or a gay hangout, though Cino himself was gay. "My idea," he said in a *Village Voice* interview in 1965, "was . . . to start with a beautiful, intimate, warm, non-commercial, friendly atmosphere where people could come and not feel pressured or harassed. I also thought anything could happen. The one thing I never thought of was fully staged productions of plays." But that's exactly what happened. On a dark, narrow street, in a room described by one reporter as a "shoebox," gay playwrights such as William M. Hoffman, Doric Wilson, Robert Patrick, and Lanford Wilson got their start, as did gay-friendly writers Sam Shepard and John Guare.

Sadly, the accidental death of his lover, lighting designer John Torrey, sent Cino into despair and drugs. Cino committed suicide in 1967, and the "magic time," as William Hoffman called it, came to a close.

Willa Cather homes
82 Washington Place and 5 Bank Street

Though we associate Willa Cather (1873–1947) mainly with Nebraska, where she was raised and about which she often wrote, she spent most of her adult life in New York City. Offered a job she couldn't refuse at *McClure's* magazine, Cather moved to the city in 1907 and lived in a studio apartment at *60 Washington Square South* (now the NYU Loeb Student Center), where Edith Lewis, who would soon become her life partner, also resided. By 1908, the two had moved into their first shared apartment on Washington Place and lived there for the next five years.

Following the advice of her friend and mentor Sarah Orne Jewett, Cather left her demanding job at *McClure's* to dedicate herself to writing fiction, her first love. It was at the apartment on Washington Place that she did much of the work on her early novels *Alexander's Bridge* (1912) and *O Pioneers!* (1913). In 1995, New York's Historic Landmarks Preservation Center added a medallion to the front of the building to note its significance to American literary history.

Cather and Lewis spent the years 1913 to 1927 living at 5 Bank Street, a brick town house on one of the loveliest blocks in Greenwich Village. In their spacious, seven-room apartment Cather worked on such now-classic novels as *My Ántonia* (1915), the Pulitzer Prize–winning *One of Ours* (1922), *A Lost Lady* (1923), and *The Professor's House* (1925). The period on Bank Street was unquestionably her most productive as a writer. The building was torn down in 1927, and Cather and Lewis moved uptown to *570 Park Avenue (at East 62nd Street)*, where they lived until Cather's death. During this time, personal losses and stinging professional criticism converged on Cather, making writing difficult. She also became obsessed with protecting her private life as a lesbian and destroyed most of her correspondence. Her will forbade scholars to quote from any of her surviving letters. (*See also* Red Cloud, Nebraska; Jaffrey, New Hampshire; Santa Fe, New Mexico; Pittsburgh, Pennsylvania; and Gore, Virginia.)

Katharine Cornell/Guthrie McClintic home
23 Beekman Place

Actor Katharine Cornell and director Guthrie McClintic bought this brownstone in 1923 for twenty thousand dollars, after the success of Cornell's first starring role in the Broadway hit *A Bill of Divorcement*. They placed both of their names on the doorplate, scandalizing their proper Beekman Place neighbors, who believed it to be an admission of an illicit relationship.

In fact, Cornell and McClintic were married, but they were simply "beards" for each other, occupying separate bedrooms from early on. Cornell referred to their lavender marriage as "forty years of companionship." Over the years, she enjoyed intimate relationships first with Gertrude Macy, her secretary and "general representative," and later with playwright Nancy Hamilton, both of whom lived with her. And the joke around town about McClintic was that he was so adept at directing his wife because he secretly wanted to play all her roles—the most famous of which were Joan of Arc, Juliet, and Elizabeth Barrett Browning.

Elsie de Wolfe/Elisabeth Marbury home
"Irving House"
122 East 17th Street

Elsie de Wolfe (1865–1950) had two careers, first as an actress and then as the first professional interior decorator. In 1892, she and her lover, Elisabeth (Bessie) Marbury, a theatrical agent and producer, made a home together at this address, a residence that had been built in 1830 for writer Washington Irving—hence called "Irving House." (Today, a plaque on the building mentions Irving but not de Wolfe.) Though East 17th Street was not fashionable at that time, their block was situated firmly in the elegant Gramercy Park district, which held a certain cachet for the two women.

De Wolfe tired of touring in theatrical productions in the late 1890s and spent more time at home. Marbury suggested that she begin to focus her attention on the remodeling of Irving House, her first interior decoration project. De Wolfe removed the dark woodwork and wallpaper, velvet curtains, and heavy furniture that had marked the tastes of the mid-Victorian era. She had the walls painted ivory and light gray and the house completely refurnished in eighteenth-century French style.

When the remodeling was finished, "the Bachelors"—as de Wolfe and Marbury called themselves—established a Parisian-type salon at their residence. Each Sunday afternoon from 1897 to 1907, an eclectic assortment of guests met at Irving House for literary talk, gossip, tea and snacks, and an exchange of wit. Guests included such famous personalities as Sarah Bernhardt, Ellen Terry, Oscar Wilde, Nellie Melba, Henry Adams, and Isabella Stewart Gardner. "You never know who you are going to meet at Bessie's and Elsie's," one salon-goer remarked, "but you can always be sure that whoever they are they will be interesting and you will have a good time."

De Wolfe's first public decorating commission came through Marbury's contacts. Marbury was the first successful theatrical agent, who represented most of the big playwrights of her era, including Oscar Wilde and George Bernard Shaw. Marbury pulled some strings to land her lover the job of redecorating the Colony Club in New York, the first private club for women. After that, more and more projects opened up for de Wolfe—a commission to decorate the mansion of Henry Clay Frick made her a millionaire.

Marion Dickerman/Nancy Cook home
171 West 12th Street

Marion Dickerman and Nancy Cook were life partners who met as graduate students at Syracuse University in 1909. Suffragists and pacifists, they first became acquainted with Eleanor Roosevelt in the early 1920s. When her politically ambitious husband Franklin became ill with polio, Eleanor kept the Roosevelt name alive by taking an active part in the women's committee of the Democratic Party, where she made fast friends with Dickerman and Cook. At the time, Dickerman and Cook were living at this address, in a twenty-four-unit cooperative apartment building filled with other politically active lesbians—including Polly Porter and Mary "Molly" Dewson, and Grace Hutchins and Anna Rochester.

In the early 1920s, Eleanor, Nancy, and Marion embarked on several joint projects, including the Val-kill furniture factory (*see* Hyde Park, New York) and the Todhunter School for girls on Manhattan's Upper East Side. From 1925 until the 1940s, Nancy and Marion lived on Eleanor's Val-kill property in the building called "Stone Cottage," where Eleanor was a frequent visitor. According to historian Blanche Cook, Franklin Roosevelt dubbed the place "The Honeymoon Cottage," and Eleanor embroidered the linens for the house "E. M. N.," the women's three initials. Blanche Cook also suggests that there was a particular intensity in the relationship between Nancy and Eleanor, though it is unclear whether it was ever anything more than just friendship.

> [Nancy Cook was] an attractive woman who had distinct artistic ability and could do almost anything with her hands.
>
> —Eleanor Roosevelt

Murray Hall home
457 Sixth Avenue (formerly no. 145)

Murray Hall (c. 1830–1901) came to New York in the 1870s and opened an employment office on Sixth Avenue near Twenty-third Street. Within a short time, Hall became an important political organizer with the Tammany Hall Democratic machine. According to a contemporary account in the *New York Times*, Hall was regarded as "a 'man about town,' a bon vivant, and all-around 'good-fellow.'" A heavy drinker, a poker player, and a

> Why, I saw him play poker with a party of the Jefferson Market clique one night, and he played the game like a veteran. And for nerve, well, I can't believe that he was a woman, that's all. . . . He had a cigar in his mouth that night, but I don't believe he lit it.
>
> —Joseph Bremer, hotel owner, on the revelation in 1902 that Murray Hall was born female

ladies' man who was "sweet on women," Hall had two wives (in succession) and an adopted daughter, to whom he left his modest estate of five thousand dollars. He and his second wife lived at this address from about 1894 until his death.

What was not discovered until Hall's death was that he had been born a female named Mary Anderson, an orphan who had donned men's clothes to make her way in the world. Hall had been suffering for six years from breast cancer but decided to forgo medical help until it was too late, because he wanted to keep his birth gender hidden. When the news about Hall's secret hit the local papers, headlines such as "Murray Hall Fooled Many Shrewd Men" filled the *Times* and the *Tribune*. One of the greatest

ASIDE-STEP

In 1958, Allen Ginsberg (1926–1997) wrote the poem "Kaddish" for his mother, Naomi, at whose funeral the Kaddish was not read. Naomi had suffered from suicidal tendencies and had been institutionalized many times when Ginsberg was young. At the time he wrote "Kaddish," Ginsberg was living with his lover, Peter Orlovsky, at *170 East 2nd Street* on the Lower East Side. Ginsberg completed the entire poem in one marathon session, starting at six o'clock on a Saturday morning and continuing straight through until the following evening. When he finished, many of the fifty-eight pages of manuscript were marked with tears. (*See also* Newark, New Jersey.)

causes for concern was that Hall had regularly voted in elections—which at that time was not legal for women to do.

Henry Street Settlement
265 Henry Street

Lillian D. Wald (1867–1940) was one of many women from her generation who felt the need to make a contribution to society rather than settle into a comfortable middle-class life. After training as a nurse, an experience that brought her into contact with the dire health-care needs of the immigrant poor of New York's Lower East Side, Wald and classmate Mary Brewster decided to start a settlement house in the neighborhood in 1895. International banker Jacob Schiff provided the red-brick building that became the Henry Street Settlement and Visiting Nurse Service, which is still standing and in operation today.

Like Jane Addams in Chicago, Wald attracted a group of dedicated women to live and work with her on Henry Street, providing low- or no-cost health care to the poor in their homes. Within the next dozen years, the Visiting Nurse Service included one hundred nurses, who made almost a quarter of a million house calls a year. One nurse recalled later that Wald was always "the first to hear a knock at the front door to respond to an incoherent stumbling appeal for a nurse." But Henry Street became more than just a health-care facility; it acted as a community center, providing classes and cultural experiences.

Wald shared her life with a community of women and enjoyed intimate relationships with several women. Among them were Mabel Kittredge, a wealthy donor, and Helen Arthur, a lawyer and theater producer, who once wrote to Wald of longing "to get back to your comfortable lap . . . instead of being solicitously hustled from your room at ten o'clock." Wald's intimate companions quickly discovered that her relationship with Henry Street Settlement would always be primary.

During World War I, Wald became actively involved in the peace movement, which made her work and travel schedule more hectic. She purchased a country house in Connecticut in 1917 (*see* Westport,

Connecticut) and periodically took time off there to retreat and recover. She finally retired from her settlement work in 1933 and spent her remaining years in Westport, Connecticut.

Helen Hull / Mabel Louise Robinson home
322 West 106th Street

Helen R. Hull (1888–1971) shared this home with her partner of fifty years, Mabel Louise Robinson. They met in 1912 while both were English instructors at Wellesley College and moved to New York together to teach at Columbia University. (One of Hull's students was the young Carson McCullers.) In addition to their apartment not far from Columbia, the couple shared a farm on the Maine coast, where they spent the summers from 1914 on (*see* North Brooklin, Maine).

Hull was also a successful novelist and short-story writer. Her short story "The Fire," published in *Century* magazine in 1919, and her novels *Quest* (1922) and *Labyrinth* (1923) are notable for their early depictions of positive relationships between women-loving women. By the mid-1920s, however, psychological theories about "inversion" had become deeply entrenched in society, and Hull began to change the focus of her writing to unhappily married heterosexual couples. She became increasingly guarded about her private life, refusing to do interviews or public promotions for her books.

Hull continued to write and publish until the early 1960s, when her beloved Mabel died. Though her early novels were likened in the press to those of Willa Cather, Hull's later works were dismissed by reviewers as "women's books." She fell into obscurity until the late 1980s, when some of her works were reprinted by The Feminist Press and Naiad Press.

Elisabeth Irwin / Katharine Anthony home
23 Bank Street

Elisabeth Irwin (1880–1942) and her lover of thirty years, Katharine Anthony (1877–1965), were two dynamos of the Progressive era. Irwin was an educator and psychologist who founded the city's experimental *Little*

Red Schoolhouse (*196 Bleecker Street at Sixth Avenue*), which is still in operation today. Anthony was a prolific writer who authored "brilliant biographies" (in the words of feminist colleague Inez Haynes Irwin) of important feminists such as Susan B. Anthony and Margaret Fuller. Both women were members of Heterodoxy, a radical feminist club that met in Greenwich Village from 1912 to 1940.

Among their friends and associates, Irwin and Anthony were an acknowledged couple. Together they raised several adopted children. Besides their pretty home on Bank Street, they enjoyed a summerhouse in Gaylordsville, Connecticut, where they jokingly referred to themselves as "the gay ladies of Gaylordsville."

Esther Lape / Elizabeth Read home
20 East 11th Street

Political activists and life partners Esther Lape and Elizabeth Read lived together for over two decades in this brick building, which Lape owned, on a quiet Greenwich Village block. Lape was a journalist and publicist, while Read was an attorney. They met Eleanor Roosevelt in 1921 through the League of Women Voters, which Lape and Read had helped to found. The three spent many happy evenings together on East 11th Street, following elegant candlelit dinners with poetry readings and discussions of Democratic political strategy.

Lape and Read also owned a home in Connecticut, a 147-acre estate they called Saltmeadow. Painted in large green letters on the doormat of the country house was the maxim "Toujours Gai." Eleanor occasionally spent weekends with them, and according to her biographer, Blanche Wiesen Cook, it was at Saltmeadow that she spent the last vacation weekend of her life.

From 1933 to 1942, Eleanor rented an apartment in Lape's building, which she used as a hideaway when she was in New York. Like Val-kill (*see* Hyde Park, New York), her apartment there was a haven from the pressures of being a public figure. Since these were also the years of her passionate relationship with Associated Press reporter Lorena Hickock, the address seems to have provided the First Lady with the privacy to pursue that affair. A plaque on the front of the building notes Eleanor's years of residence here.

Lesbian and Gay Community Services Center
208 West 13th Street

Founded in 1983, the second-largest gay community center in the country (only L.A.'s is bigger) is located in this one-hundred-fifty-year-old former public high school. The Center not only provides meeting space to local gay, lesbian, bisexual, and transgender groups, but also sponsors its own award-winning social service programs, a variety of cultural events, a groundbreaking gay parents' and families' organization, and an active voter registration drive. On any given night, you can attend a gay AA meeting, a poetry reading, an exhibit, or a dance, or borrow books from the city's first gay lending library. ACT UP, GLAAD, and Queen Nation all had their beginnings at public meetings at the Center. The Center is now in the midst of a multimillion-dollar renovation of its venerable old building. Future plans include constructing an additional building next door to accommodate the enormous demand for queer meeting space and programs.

Lesbian-feminist Manhattan

When I first moved to New York City over fifteen years ago, the metropolitan area—besides being home to a handful of lesbian bars—boasted two women's bookstores, a three-story women's center, a feminist art institute and gallery, a women's vegetarian restaurant and coffeehouse, a lesbian storefront theater, a lesbian archives, and numerous lesbian-feminist organizations, including a couple of newspapers with their own private offices. Away from my nine-to-five mainstream publishing job, I traveled through "women's space." Within that world, I rarely had to come out to anyone—just showing up in a predominantly lesbian space was enough to signify sexual orientation. Most of those spaces—which catered primarily to white women—are now gone from the cityscape. Some of the sites associated with "lesbian-feminist Manhattan" include:

Djuna Books, 154 West 10th Street: This bookstore was named for the writer Djuna Barnes, who highly disapproved of it. "How dare they," she once said. "It is probably a terrible little lesbian bookshop." Well, Djuna had some problems with internalized homophobia, but her namesake was a cozy little nook carrying feminist books and periodicals.

Medusa's Revenge, 10 Bleecker Street: Founded in 1976 by a women-of-color collective, Medusa's Revenge billed itself as "an experimental theater of women dedicated to the creation of original plays . . . exploring a homo-esthetic sensibility." The theater group lasted only a few years, but its direct descendant was the *W.O.W. Cafe* (*Women's One World*), founded in 1980 and first located in a storefront at 330 *East 11th Street. W.O.W.* is still in operation in the East Village at 59 *East 4th Street.*

Womanbooks, 201 West 92nd Street (at Amsterdam Avenue): Right down the block from the Lesbian Herstory Archives (*West 92nd Street at Broadway*) and my first therapist, Womanbooks was a big, homey place that encouraged browsing and reading and had a children's section with toys and games.

Women's Liberation Center, 243 West 20th Street: Located in an old firehouse, the three-story Women's Center housed such organizations as Lesbian Feminist Liberation (LFL) and the Lesbian Switchboard. There were also dances and meetings held in the downstairs hall.

A SIDE - STEP

Gay Manhattan's first social and community center was at the *Gay Activists Alliance Firehouse, 99 Wooster Street*, which opened in 1970. GAA was one of the leading groups of the early gay liberation movement, and it sponsored meetings and dances at this site. Arson curtailed activities at the firehouse in 1974, though GAA continued as an organization until the early 1980s.

OTHER EARLY GAY COMMUNITY CENTERS STILL IN OPERATION IN THE MID-ATLANTIC REGION

Capital District Gay and Lesbian Community Council (founded 1970)
332 Hudson Avenue
Albany, New York

Gay Alliance of the Genesee Valley (founded 1973)
179 Atlantic Avenue
Rochester, New York

Penguin Place (founded 1974)
201 South Camac Street
Philadelphia, Pennsylvania

Gay and Lesbian Community Center of Baltimore (founded 1977)
241 West Chase Street
Baltimore, Maryland

Herman Melville plaque
104 East 26th Street

After giving up on farming in 1863 (*see* Pittsfield, Massachusetts), Herman Melville moved his family to New York City into an apartment building at this address. Though the building has been demolished, a plaque marks its location, and the intersection of Twenty-sixth Street and Park Avenue South, which is just west of here, is called "Herman Melville Square." From this address, Melville commuted daily to his job in lower Manhattan as deputy inspector of customs, earning about four dollars a day. In the evenings he worked on the novella *Billy Budd*, which remained in manuscript at his death and is the only known fiction he wrote during his last thirty years.

In 1891, Melville died at home in relative obscurity. Many of his contemporaries thought he had died years earlier! His brief obituaries labeled

> And farther afield in Brooklyn . . .
> *La Papaya Coffeehouse and Bookstore, 331 Flatbush Avenue:* Opened
> in 1980, La Papaya served vegetarian snacks and dinners, as well as
> hosted poetry readings, concerts, and art shows. They also sponsored a
> feminist seder at Passover.

his first book, *Typee* (1846), his most famous. At *Woodlawn Cemetery* in
the Bronx (see above), his small marble tombstone also has remarkably little to say about a man whose work has passed into the literary canon:
"Herman Melville—Born August 1, 1819—Died September 28, 1891."

Pre-Stonewall gay hangouts

The Bagatelle, 86 University Place: This was one of the few lesbian
bars open in the city in the 1950s. In her autobiographical *Zami: A New
Spelling of My Name*, Audre Lorde recalled nights at "the Bag"—"the most
popular gay-girl's bar in the Village"—when she would get carded though
her white friends would not.

Columbia Hall/Paresis Hall, 392 Bowery: This was one of the earliest
recorded hangouts for gay men in the city. Historian George Chauncey has
traced it back to the 1890s, when "fairies" frequented the club as well as

> When Claggart's unobserved glance happened to light on belted Billy
> rolling along the upper gun deck in the leisure of the second dogwatch,
> exchanging passing broadsides of fun with other young promenaders in
> the crowd, that glance would follow the cheerful sea Hyperion with a
> settled meditative and melancholy expression, his eyes strangely suf-
> fused with incipient feverish tears. . . . Sometimes the melancholy ex-
> pression would have in it a touch of soft yearning, as if Claggart could
> even have loved Billy but for fate and ban.
>
> —Herman Melville, *Billy Budd*

gawking tourists who wanted to explore the city's demimonde. Another early gay spot was the *Artistic Club, 36 West 30th Street*, which is also mentioned in police reports of the 1890s.

Julius', 159 West 10th Street: Julius' has been a bar since the Civil War and was a popular speakeasy during Prohibition (the side door still has a peephole). It has been attracting a primarily gay clientele since the 1950s, making it the oldest gay bar in the city. Reputedly, it was a favorite hangout of Tennessee Williams and Truman Capote. A sign on the wall used to state that "Patrons Must Face the Bar While Drinking."

Mona's, 135 West 3rd Street: Mona's was an early lesbian bar that dated back to World War II. In a later incarnation, it was called The Purple Onion.

San Remo, 93 MacDougal Street: Though never exclusively gay, the San Remo attracted a number of gay artists and writers during the 1940s and 1950s, including Allen Ginsberg, W. H. Auden, and Merce Cunningham.

Stewart's Cafeteria, 116 Seventh Avenue South: Stewart's Cafeteria opened in 1933 in Greenwich Village at Sheridan Square and quickly became a gathering spot for gay men and some lesbians, who were not discouraged from idling there, as they were in other public places. Stewart's and its successor in the late 1930s, the Life Cafeteria, were advertised in restaurant and tourist guides of the time as spots that provided a "show" of "eccentrics" and "Villons." Sightseers ventured down to the Village to soak up the "bohemian" atmosphere and gape at real-life "dykes" and "fairies" through the cafeteria's wide front window, as if they were animals in the zoo.

According to historian George Chauncey, the cafeteria's queer clients played along with the tourists, amusing themselves by camping it up for the "jam" (slang for straight people). Though gays and lesbians were on display, both Stewart's and the Life served as community centers, alternatives to seedy gay bars. As one gay man later remembered, "It [the Life] attracted young people, like me. They could go there because they didn't know anywhere else to go. . . . It was a place where they could meet people." A General Nutrition Center store now occupies the cafeteria's corner of Sheridan Square.

Edna St. Vincent Millay residence
75-1/2 Bedford Street

Following her 1923 marriage to businessman Eugen Boissevain, Edna St. Vincent Millay lived at this address in Greenwich Village in what she nicknamed "the dollhouse." The diminutive brick house on Bedford Street was only nine and a half feet wide, with one room and a fireplace on each of the three stories. Behind the house was a beautiful but tiny courtyard. In 1995, New York's Historic Landmarks Preservation Center installed an oval medallion at Millay's former residence with the inscription, "The irreverent poet, who wrote 'my candle burns at both ends,' lived here in 1923–1924 at the time she wrote the 'Ballad of the Harp-Weaver,' for which she won the Pulitzer Prize." Conveniently, Millay's house was only a few blocks from Chumley's, a speakeasy (still in operation as a bar and eatery) that was one of her favorite hangouts. From Bedford Street, Millay and Boissevain moved to a farmhouse in upstate New York, which they renovated and lived in until their deaths. (*See also* Austerlitz, New York.)

ASIDE-STEP

I received a poignant, anonymous message on-line about a TriBeCa loft building, which has been vacant since 1988. "I've been waiting to tell someone for years," the message read, "that 'How to Have Sex in an Epidemic: One Approach,' which marks the invention of safe(r) sex, was written at 129 Duane Street, between Church and West Broadway."

^   ^   ^

Stonewall Inn
51–53 Christopher Street

At last!—the point of reference for all those entries I've included for "Pre-Stonewall gay hangouts." The Stonewall Inn was a popular bar in the late 1960s, a time when police raids on gay bars were seemingly *de rigueur*. But on the night of June 28, 1969, the patrons of the Stonewall decided to just say no to police harassment. When the bar was raided early in the morning and those inside were forced out onto Christopher Street by the police, the patrons—many of whom were drag queens and people of color—and a crowd of supporters began pelting the cops with beer cans and rocks, forcing them to take cover inside the bar. The crowd then set the bar on fire, but the police managed to put out the flames. Though after several hours the police claimed to have "secured" the area, a weekend of riots ensued, during which gay people bravely stood off the city cops and claimed their right to live openly.

The term "Stonewall" has become the international symbol of gay resistance and liberation, and the anniversary of the riots is an annual celebration around the world. Gay history is now commonly marked as being before or after Stonewall. In 1989, the short strip of Christopher Street where the bar was located was officially designated "Stonewall Place" by the city in commemoration of the riots. The original site of the bar has gone through many metamorphoses since June 1969—in the early 1980s, when I first came to New York, it was a cafeteria-style eatery called "Bageland"—and is now once again called the Stonewall Inn.

Dorothy Thompson house
237 East 48th Street

Dorothy Thompson (1894–1961), the intrepid foreign correspondent and author of *I Saw Hitler*, was once married to writer Sinclair Lewis, but the great love of her life was Christa Winsloe, author of the novel upon which *Madchen in Uniform* was based (*see* Bronxville, New York). After the break with both of them, Thompson lived alone in this three-story brownstone in Turtle Bay from 1941 to 1957. She spent over twenty thousand dollars for renovations to make it, as she wrote, "the most perfect small house I have ever seen."

Thompson's home included a "small and lovely library" with over three thousand books, five fireplaces, and a third-floor study for writing. In the drawing room, a wine satin sofa could hold, Thompson bragged, five of "the most distinguished bottoms in New York." When the renovations were complete, Thompson invited a reporter from *Look* magazine to inspect the final product, and he remarked admiringly on the many telephones, intercoms, and labor-saving devices throughout the house.

In the front door were eight painted glass panels showing Dorothy in medieval attire performing various jobs—writing, lecturing, greeting guests. There was also displayed the house's motto: "Gallus in sterquilinio suo plurimum potest." ("The rooster on his own dunghill is very much in charge.") Thompson's brownstone is now marked by a medallion placed by New York's Historic Landmarks Preservation Center in 1995.

Carl Van Vechten home
150 West 55th Street

Carl Van Vechten (1880–1964), a critic, novelist, photographer, and bon vivant, moved to this address with his wife, Fania Marinoff, in 1924. Though married, both Van Vechten and Marinoff took a liberal part in the gay subculture of their time. It's to Van Vechten that the famous quote, "A thing of beauty is a boy forever," is attributed.

ASIDE-STEP

Near the West 40th Street entrance to Bryant Park (in front of the Bryant Park Grill), there is a small sculpture of writer Gertrude Stein (1874–1946) in a Buddha-like pose, deep in thought. In a Valentine's Day action in 1993, the New York Lesbian Avengers mounted a papier-mâché Alice B. Toklas (1877–1967) next to Gertrude, reaching out to lightly touch her lover's face.

"Carlo," as Van Vechten was known in his intimate circle, was a tall, blond, white man who began "slumming" in Harlem in the 1920s after reading Walter White's *The Fire in the Flint*. Outfitted with a hip flask, bracelets, and English cigarettes, Van Vechten became such a fixture at drag balls and cabarets that a popular song of the day, "Go Harlem," spoke of going "inspectin' like Van Vechten."

Van Vechten was so enamored of the New Negro Movement (now called the Harlem Renaissance) that he became a patron and supporter of many of the most significant writers and artists of the day, including Langston Hughes and Countee Cullen. His contacts at the publishing house Alfred A. Knopf were instrumental in getting the work of Hughes and Nella Larsen published. He turned his home on West 55th Street into an artists' salon. Guests remembered Van Vechten's flamboyantly colorful decorating style—the study was black and orange, and the drawing room was green, purple, and raspberry with a Venetian glass chandelier. (It was the drawing room that Van Vechten missed most when he and Fania moved in the 1950s to Central Park West.) At Van Vechten's parties, the "casual" entertainment might include Paul Robeson singing spirituals, George Gershwin playing the piano, and Countee Cullen giving Charleston lessons.

Van Vechten's controversial novel *Nigger Heaven* (1926) depicted life in Harlem through his eyes and was a best-seller that went through nine printings in four months. But both the title and the content made some enemies for Van Vechten—his friend Countee Cullen, for example, didn't speak to him for over a decade! Beginning in the 1930s, Van Vechten discovered photography and set out to document the major African-American artists of his day through stunning black-and-white portraits.

Oscar Wilde Memorial Bookshop
291 Mercer Street

This was the first location of the oldest gay bookstore in the country. Gutsy gay activist Craig Rodwell opened the store two years before the Stonewall riots, and it served as an informal community center as well as a place to buy books. In 1973, it moved to its present location at *15 Christopher Street*.

SOME FAMOUS QUEER-IDENTIFIED MANHATTAN APARTMENT BUILDINGS AND HOTELS

The Algonquin Hotel, 59–61 West 44th Street: The famous Algonquin Round Table—a gathering of New York glitterati—met here regularly beginning in 1919. Queer members included drama critic Alexander Woollcott and writer Edna Ferber (*see also* Appleton, Wisconsin). Frequent visitors included actresses Tallulah Bankhead and Eva LeGallienne. Founder Dorothy Parker's second husband, Alan Campbell, was also gay. Recent historians have questioned just how "witty" the Round Table actually was; contemporary sources suggest that it may have been duller than participants wanted the public to believe.

The Chelsea Hotel, 222 West 23rd Street: The Chelsea has long been a haven for artists, particularly queer ones; one former resident called it "a refuge from an unsympathetic world." Composer Virgil Thomson lived at this address for years, and William Burroughs (*see also* St. Louis, Missouri), Jane and Paul Bowles (*see also* Brooklyn, New York), and Janis Joplin all had rooms here. Andy Warhol's *Chelsea Girls* was filmed here in part.

The Dakota, 1 West 72nd Street: Besides going down in infamy as the site of John Lennon's murder, the venerable old Dakota Apartments, built in the 1870s, have been home over the years to many queer celebrities, including Leonard Bernstein, Judy Holliday, William Inge (*see also* Independence, Kansas), and Rudolf Nureyev.

∧　　∧　　∧

Staten Island

Alice Austen home
"Clear Comfort"
2 Hylan Boulevard

When photographer Alice Austen (1866–1952) lived there, Staten Island was a quiet, bucolic, upper middle-class suburb of picturesque "cottages." The Austen family home, Clear Comfort, was a seventeenth-century Dutch farmhouse purchased by Austen's grandfather in 1844 and renovated and added on to over the years. When Alice's father abandoned them, she and her mother came to live at Clear Comfort, where Alice was surrounded by a family of supportive relatives, including an uncle who presented her with her first camera when she was ten years old. One of this country's earliest female photographers, Austen was also the first woman to take her camera into the streets of New York City, leaving behind an invaluable record of life at the turn of the twentieth century. Her earliest documentary photographs predate those of Alfred Stieglitz and Edward Steichen, whose work is now renowned while that of the gifted Austen, who died in obscurity, is largely neglected.

Austen frequently focused her camera on the upper-class world she knew best, recording what she referred to as "the larky life"—tennis matches, bicycling, swimming, amateur theatrics, auto races. But her subjects also included the poor of lower Manhattan—street vendors, immigrants in Battery Park, shoeshine boys, ragpickers—who were far removed from her comfortable life on Staten Island. Austen took photographs almost every day, at a time when cameras and photographic equipment were heavy and bulky and glass plates cost about two dollars each. During her lifetime, she produced about nine thousand photographs, and the extant glass plates and negatives are today part of the collection of the Staten Island Historical Society (located at *Historic Richmondtown, 441 Clark Avenue*).

Austen shared more than half of her life with an intimate companion, Gertrude Tate, who came to live with her at Clear Comfort in 1917. But the curators of the historic house steer away from the "L" word. Today, visitors to Clear Comfort view an introductory videotape that labels Austen "a personality" who led an "unconventional lifestyle"—code words that attempt to explain why, as narrator Helen Hayes puts it, "Alice Austen was never to marry," though she had "no shortage of suitors."

Austen's home is now a National Historic Landmark. The first floor is open to the public, but only one room, the downstairs parlor, has been completely restored to look much as it would have in Alice's time. As her finances dwindled after the Crash of 1929, Austen began selling furniture and art objects to New York museums, and some of these items have been retrieved for exhibit at Clear Comfort. Fortunately, Austen, for posterity, left a complete photographic record of both the interior and the exterior of the house.

NYACK

Carson McCullers home
131 South Broadway
This rambling three-story clapboard house in the sleepy village of Nyack was the home of writer Carson McCullers (1917–1967) from 1945 until her death. The front of the grand Victorian house faces one of the main streets of Nyack, while the rear sun porch enjoys a stunning view of the Hudson River. It is still a private residence, divided into a number of apartments.

After the death of Carson's father in 1944, her mother, Marguerite Smith, didn't have the heart to remain in the Georgia house where she and her husband, Lamar, had raised their family (*see* Columbus, Georgia). At the time, Carson's husband had gone into the army, and she, too, was faced with living alone. Since Carson had always loved the scenic village of Nyack, just twenty-five miles up the Hudson from New York, she, her mother, and her sister Rita decided to take up residence there in the fall of 1944. Nyack reminded Marguerite of the small, friendly towns she had known in Georgia, so she felt immediately at home.

Carson's family first rented a spacious apartment at 129 South Broadway, and then in the spring of 1945 moved to the house next door, which Marguerite purchased with nine thousand dollars from the sale of her Georgia house. When her mother's funds became low in the early 1950s, Carson purchased the house from her with the money she received for selling the screen rights to *The Member of the Wedding.*

Carson used Nyack as her home base in between trips to the artists' colony at Yaddo, where she did much of her writing (*see* Saratoga Springs, New York), and speaking and teaching engagements all over the country. It was at this home that she gave a luncheon to honor her idol, Isak Dinesen, after the two met at a literary function in 1959. Other guests included Marilyn Monroe and husband Arthur Miller. The high point of the afternoon was a spellbinding tale Dinesen related—in true Scheherazade fashion—about killing her first lion in Africa.

Plagued by ill health, depression, and alcoholism throughout her life, Carson suffered her final stroke in this house in the summer of 1967. According to Carson's biographer, Virginia Spencer Carr, the last words she spoke were to the young actor who rented living space in the basement of the house. He stopped by her bedroom and told her he was appearing in a play called *Stop the World—I Want to Get Off.* "Oh, darling, isn't that a marvelous title," Carson said. "Ahh, to get off. Wouldn't that be something. Wouldn't that be marvelous." She suffered a massive brain hemorrhage only twenty minutes later and died at Nyack Hospital. (*See also* Brooklyn, New York; Charlotte, North Carolina; and Fayetteville, North Carolina.)

ROCHESTER

Lillian D. Wald home
3 East Avenue
Social reformer and settlement activist Lillian D. Wald (1867–1940) was born into a prosperous Jewish family, the daughter of a successful optical goods business owner. Her parents' families had fled the anti-Semitism of Central Europe twenty years earlier and settled in Cincinnati, which at

that time was the heart of Reform Judaism. When Lillian was still a young child, the family relocated for business reasons first to Dayton, Ohio, and then in 1878 to this address in Rochester, an optical supplies center. (The house was later destroyed by fire.) As an adult, Wald remembered a happy and uneventful childhood in Rochester, where she attended private schools and traveled in a wealthy social circle.

But Wald was bored by the social life of the upper middle class and was determined to have a fuller life. In her application to nursing school, Wald wrote, "My life hitherto has been . . . a type of modern young womanhood, days devoted to society, study and housekeeping duties, such as practical mothers consider essential to a daughter's education. This does not satisfy me now. I feel the need of serious, definite work." Her comfortable early life in Rochester did nothing to prepare her for the poverty and indigence she would witness during her nursing training in New York City, which would lead her to found the Henry Street Settlement and Visiting Nurse Service in 1894. (*See also* New York City, New York, and Westport, Connecticut.)

SARATOGA SPRINGS

Yaddo
Union Avenue (between racetrack and Interstate 87)
Originally the home of wealthy stockbroker Spencer Trask and his wife, Katrina, Yaddo was named by one of the Trask children—her pronunciation of "shadow." The Trasks had four offspring, all of whom died young, and Katrina's grief made her try to envision a brighter future for the estate as an artists' colony, after she and her husband had died. In 1926, following the Trasks' wishes, Yaddo welcomed its first colonists and continues to sponsor writers, who must apply for residence.

Yaddo is a gloomy, gothic estate, with ominous warning signs to visitors, crumbling statuary, and neglected gardens. Especially on an overcast day, it is easy to believe the rumors that it is haunted by the ghosts of the Trask children. It is also easy to imagine Patricia Highsmith creating her psychological thriller, *Strangers on a Train*, in this "shadowy" setting. Yaddo was also a favorite writing retreat for other queer writers, including John Cheever, James Baldwin, Langston Hughes, and Carson McCullers, who finished *The Member of the Wedding* while in residence. McCullers was a frequent visitor to the colony, who on her very first visit was placed in the coveted "tower room" that had belonged to Katrina Trask. A few years later, Truman Capote worked on his first novel, *Other Voices, Other Rooms*, in the very same room.

SENECA FALLS

National Women's Hall of Fame
76 Fall Street

This museum commemorates a significant number of lesbians and bisexual women, though it doesn't really address sexual orientation. Queer honorees include Jane Addams, Charlotte Bunch, Rachel Carson, Carrie Chapman Catt, Charlotte Cushman, Emily Dickinson, Babe Didrikson, Margaret Mead, Alice Paul, Eleanor Roosevelt, and Bessie Smith.

WOODSTOCK

Maverick Lunar Colony
Maverick Road

Poet Robert Duncan (1919–1988) lived in an informal artists' colony at this location in 1940. The "colony" consisted of a rustic cabin on Maverick Road (hence the name), where poet James Cooney lived with his wife and published a literary journal called *The Phoenix*. Near the Cooneys' cabin was a separate studio for the printing press, and in the loft above the pressroom Duncan's bedroom. Duncan learned typesetting by helping Cooney with the production of the journal.

Duncan, who fancied himself a poet-shaman, reportedly preached Sunday morning sermons in another cabin in the woods for anyone who wanted to listen. Barely twenty-one years old at the time, he was also apparently sowing his wild oats, and his Woodstock friends teasingly referred to him during this period as "Fanny the Fucker of the Village."

The Phoenix folded that same year, and the Cooneys left the area. But Duncan stayed on with his companion, Sanders Russell, and started his own journal, which he called *The Experimental Review*. The first issue in November 1940 contained a poem of Duncan's called "Toward the Shaman," which was openly gay. So controversial was the subject matter that one critic disparagingly labeled the publication "a handbook for homosexuals." The journal was short-lived, and Duncan moved to New York City to actively pursue his writing career. (*See also* Bakersfield, California, and Berkeley, California.)

> We are a community of people upon the Maverick—and we have times among us of buffoonery, we are silly, ridiculous—everything that human beings are, and then there are times when we are suddenly quite real, quite actual—when we are like tense points of electrical contact.
>
> —Robert Duncan, 1940

PENNSYLVANIA

BETHLEHEM

H. D. *birthplace*
110 Church Street

The modernist poet and novelist H. D. (1886–1961) was born Hilda Doolittle at this address, and a marker at the site notes: "H. D. sought the Hellenic spirit and a classic beauty of expression." Her family was of the Moravian faith and believed in a life of piety and grace. Hilda was the only girl child in a family that conceded total authority to the father, Charles Doolittle, a professor of mathematics and astronomy at Lehigh University. His hold over Hilda was particularly strong. H. D.'s partner, Bryher, later remembered that the poet spoke almost daily about "my father, the Astronomer."

In Bethlehem, Hilda, her parents, and her brothers lived in close proximity to her mother's family. H. D.'s biographer, Barbara Guest, has described the Bethlehem streets as close and claustrophobic—"each house," she writes, "seems to eye the other." Hilda attended private schools and eventually studied at Bryn Mawr College, living at home and commuting to classes. By that time, the family had moved to Upper Darby, following the professor's acceptance of a chair at the University of Pennsylvania. Hilda left college after only a year to pursue her own writing and to become engaged (against her family's wishes) to the young poet Ezra Pound, who introduced her to his literary circle. Around the same time, H. D. also became romantically and sexually involved with a woman, Frances Josepha Gregg, eventually forgoing Pound for Gregg.

Though she had several relationships with men and married once (the writer Richard Aldington), the great love of H. D.'s life was a British woman who called herself Bryher (Annie Winifred Ellerman). They met in

1919 when Bryher, an admirer of H. D.'s published poetry, sought out and introduced herself to the poet. Lovers for twenty-five years, they remained devoted to each other even after the sexual side of their relationship had waned. Bryher married twice, and H. D. enjoyed numerous passionate affairs. But it was Bryher who was at H. D.'s side when she died in Switzerland in 1961.

H. D.'s published work was closeted, though in the 1920s she wrote a trilogy of autobiographical novels—*Paint It Today* (1921), *Asphodel* (1921–1922), and *HERmione* (1926–1927)—that she chose not to publish, all of which honestly explored her erotic relationships with women. These novels have only recently been published with critical commentary by lesbian scholars.

BRYN MAWR

M. Carey Thomas home
"The Deanery"
Bryn Mawr College

M. Carey Thomas Library
Bryn Mawr College
Named for its illustrious president, M. Carey Thomas (1857–1935), Bryn Mawr's library honors the memory of the woman who turned the last of the Seven Sisters into a first-rate academic institution. Martha Carey Thomas was born and raised in Baltimore and educated at Cornell University. She was also one of the first female graduate students at Johns Hopkins University, of which her father was a trustee.

Thomas was a lifelong "woman-loving woman," carrying on passionate relationships with other girls and women from an early age. (Her recent biographer, Helen Lefkowitz Horowitz, has explored Thomas's lesbianism with refreshing honesty.) One of her greatest loves was Mamie Gwinn, another Baltimore girl, with whom Thomas lived in Europe while studying for her Ph.D. at the University of Zurich. On their return from abroad, the two women lived together at the newly founded Bryn Mawr College (Thomas as dean of faculty, then president, and Gwinn as a graduate student, then English professor) until 1904, when Mamie ran away with Alfred Hodder, who had been a professor at the school.

Thomas's second great love was Mary Elizabeth Garrett, whom she had also known as a young woman in Baltimore. (Garrett, Gwinn, Thomas, and two other young women had a study and writing group called the "Friday Evening.") Garrett was the heir of her father's B&O railroading fortune, and with it she bribed the trustees of Bryn Mawr to name Carey Thomas president of the college in 1894, in exchange for a hefty endowment.

For ten years, Thomas juggled passionate relationships with both Gwinn and Garrett, while Gwinn trysted with Hodder, her "boy on the side." After Gwinn and Hodder eloped, Garrett quickly moved into the deanery, Thomas's official residence, and the two were devoted companions until Garrett's death in 1915. Another famous scheme they cooked up with Garrett's inheritance was to endow Johns Hopkins with a medical school—if, and only if, women would be admitted to it on a par with men!

Thomas continually expanded the deanery over the thirty-plus years that she lived there. When she first moved into the house in 1885, it was a simple eight-room frame structure that required only one servant to maintain. As college president, Thomas enlarged the house to twelve rooms to accommodate important guests. In 1896, Mary Garrett financed an even larger expansion, which added a two-story wing and a third floor. By the 1920s, the deanery had become a luxurious residence with a staff of fifteen, nine of whom lived there. Thomas retired from Bryn Mawr in 1922 but was named as a trustee and continued to live at the deanery. In 1933, she finally transferred the deanery to the college to serve as the alumnae center and went to live in a villa on the French Riviera.

Today, the college library named for Thomas also contains a plaque dedicated to Mary Garrett, lesbian philanthropist extraordinaire (*see* Baltimore, Maryland). Another plaque honors Anna Howard Shaw, the prominent feminist orator of the same era, who lectured at Bryn Mawr (*see* Moylan, Pennsylvania).

LANCASTER

Charles Demuth home
109 North Lime Street

Born at this location, the artist Charles Demuth (1883–1935) belonged to a wealthy family that owned the oldest tobacco and snuff factory in the United States. Until he was six, Demuth lived on North Lime Street, when his family moved to *118 East King Street*, next to their tobacco shop. Fortunately for him, Demuth never had to work for a living, and his life was one of upper-class gentility. He did, however, grow up an outsider—a childhood disease left him lame, and he spent several years confined to his bed.

Demuth showed an early talent for painting and as a young man studied at the Pennsylvania Academy of Fine Arts. Later, he came under the aesthetic mentoring of another queer artist, Marsden Hartley. Inspired by Hartley's work, Demuth developed a precisionist style of painting, and his depictions of modern city architecture (including that of his hometown of Lancaster) are what critics consider his greatest contribution to modern art.

Today, gay critics are more interested in Demuth's renderings of the early homosexual community in New York City. In 1918, Demuth accomplished a series of paintings depicting gay men in the Lafayette Baths. Another group of paintings from 1930 bear the revealing names "Two Sailors Urinating," "Three Sailors on the Beach," and "Four Male Figures." Even Demuth's later still-life paintings of flowers and fruit are surprisingly phallic.

According to one biographer, Demuth was more a voyeur of gay life than an active participant, and he tried to camouflage his sexual orientation in order to pass. Traveling in bohemian circles, Demuth frequented Mabel Dodge's salon, was an ancillary member of the Provincetown Players, and spent several summers in Provincetown, where he roomed with Hartley. Eugene O'Neill patterned the sexually ambivalent (and cleverly named) Charles Marsden in the Pulitzer Prize–winning play *Strange Interlude* (1928) after the closeted Demuth.

Wheatlands
1120 Marietta Avenue

James Buchanan (1791–1868), the fifteenth president of the United States, was also this country's only "bachelor" chief executive. His sexual orientation has frequently been questioned, primarily because of his intimate friendship with William Rufus King, whom he met in 1834 when both were U.S. Senators and with whom he shared a flat in Washington. According to historian Jonathan Ned Katz, their relationship was the source of many biting comments in the nation's capital. King was perhaps more "queen" than "king" and was referred to by Washington insiders as "little Miss Nancy," "she," and "Aunt Fancy."

Buchanan bought this Pennsylvania estate in 1848, when he was James Polk's secretary of state. He had greater political ambitions, and Wheatlands, a seventeen-room federal style mansion, seemed to him more "presidential" than his flat in Washington. Running for president in 1852, Buchanan lost the Democratic nomination to Franklin Pierce, and party bosses selected Senator King as the vice-presidential candidate in a bid for Buchanan's support (and the votes he could deliver). Pierce and King won, but unfortunately, King died of tuberculosis after only one month in office.

Buchanan became his party's compromise candidate in the 1856 presidential election, and Wheatlands served as his campaign headquarters. Unlike today, when presidential candidates traverse the country in search of votes, Buchanan stayed at Wheatlands, receiving visitors who could help his bid for election. This proved a good P.R. move, since newspapers across the country carried descriptions of Buchanan's beautiful estate and of the many dignitaries who passed through Wheatlands during the campaign.

Buchanan served only one uneventful term as president. After his retirement from office, he returned to Wheatlands, where today many of his belongings are still on exhibit. Buchanan is buried at the nearby *Woodward Hill Cemetery*.

Q: Why does the Scripture say that there shall be no marriages in heaven?
A: Ah, my dear friends [drawing a long sigh], someone has answered that by saying, because there will be no men there.
—Anna Howard Shaw, during a Q & A after one of her speeches

MOYLAN

Anna Howard Shaw home
240 Ridley Creek Road

This picturesque stone house with blue trim, now a private residence, was built in 1908 by suffragist Anna Howard Shaw (1847–1919), who lived here with her intimate companion, Lucy Anthony, niece of Susan B. The house was "the realization of a desire. . . . No one could ask for a more ideal site for a cottage," Shaw wrote in her autobiography, *The Story of a Pioneer*, in which she noted the nearby stream, forest, and hilltop view. Shaw was a brilliant orator who traveled extensively on behalf of the suffrage movement. "From every country I have visited I have brought back a tiny tree," Shaw explained, and the pine grove she started planting at her home is now full-grown.

While she lived here, Shaw, a minister by profession (*see* Ashton, Michigan), was president of the National American Woman's Suffrage Association. Her early activism focused on temperance, but she was lured to the suffrage movement by Susan B. herself. It is estimated that Shaw gave about ten thousand speeches on suffrage during her career, mesmerizing her audiences with her powerful voice, dramatic delivery, and sharp wit.

PHILADELPHIA

Billie Holiday home
331 South Broad Street

The future Billie Holiday (1915–1959) was born Eleanora Fagan to a nineteen-year-old single mother who earned a living doing housework. Eleanora's mother, Sadie, scrubbed floors at Philadelphia General Hospital in exchange for receiving care during her pregnancy and delivery. The baby's father was Clarence Holiday, who at the time was also a young teenager but later became a well-known banjo and guitar player in Harlem.

At the time of her daughter's birth, Sadie gave 331 Broad Street as her address, but mother and daughter moved many times over the years. By 1920, Eleanora had been sent to Baltimore to live with Sadie's sister and brother-in-law, and it was there that she grew up, experiencing a rough childhood of abuse, neglect, and being shunted from place to place. (*See next entry*, and Baltimore, Maryland.)

Billie Holiday State Historical Marker
Douglass Hotel
1409 Lombard Street

Billie Holiday (1915–1959) endured a rough childhood and adolescence that included a stay in a home for delinquent girls. As a teenager, she moved to New York to pursue her singing career, transforming herself into Billie Holiday. For years, she toured with Count Basie and Artie Shaw, regularly performing in Philadelphia, where she always stayed at the Douglass Hotel. A marker outside the hotel lists the highlights of the short, stellar but troubled life of the great singer nicknamed "Lady Day." (*See also* Baltimore, Maryland.)

Alain Locke childhood home
2221 South 5th Street

A state historical marker notes the spot of the childhood home of the prominent intellectual and critic Alain Locke (1886–1954). Locke gradu-

ASIDE-STEP

Blues great Gladys Bentley (1907–1960) was born to a poor family in Philadelphia. In school, she suffered from ridicule because she was overweight and "unfeminine." From an early age, Bentley was aware she was different, especially when she developed a serious crush on a female teacher. "In class I sat for hours watching her and wondering why I was so attracted to her. At night, I dreamed of her. I didn't understand the meaning of those dreams until later." (*See also* New York City, New York.)

ated from Harvard University in 1907 and then went on to Oxford University as the first African-American Rhodes scholar (the next wasn't named for sixty years). As a philosophy professor at Howard University, Locke encouraged the study of black culture and history along with the classics. He founded Howard's literary magazine, *The Stylus*, in which one of his students, Zora Neale Hurston, published her first story. A misogynist, Locke had a particular fondness for attractive male students and reportedly warned female students that they could expect no more than C's from him.

The mentor of many young men associated with the Harlem Renaissance, Locke traveled back and forth from Washington to New York, where he actively promoted the careers of Countee Cullen, Richard Bruce Nugent, and Wallace Thurman, while neglecting women artists. Editor of the groundbreaking anthology *The New Negro*—which was, according to critic

ASIDE-STEP

Performer and actor Ethel Waters (1896–1977) got her start singing professionally in 1917 at the clubs along Kater Street in Philadelphia.

Cheryl Wall, the "manifesto" of the Harlem Renaissance—Locke saw his role as "a philosophical mid-wife" to the younger generation of artists. Another of his protégés and the object of his affection in the early 1920s was Langston Hughes. With Cullen, the three formed a romantic triangle, which led in 1924 to a mysterious and irreparable split between Hughes and Cullen. (*See also* District of Columbia.)

PITTSBURGH

Chatham College
Woodland Road
Founded in 1869 and formerly called the Pennsylvania College for Women (PCW), this women's college (my alma mater) claims as its most celebrated alumna ecologist Rachel Carson, class of 1929, for whom the school's science building and a scholarship are named. Born in rural Pennsylvania, Carson developed a love of writing early in childhood, which continued throughout high school and college. At PCW, Carson started as an English major but switched to science after an inspirational biology course with Professor Mary Skinker. "I have always wanted to write," she affirmed, "and biology has given me something to write about. I will try to make animals in the woods and waters, where they live, as alive to others as they are to me."

And she succeeded at that. Carson's brilliant exploration of sea life, *The Sea Around Us* (1951), won the National Book Award and was an instant best-seller that made her a celebrity and earned enough royalties to secure her living as a writer. *The Sea Around Us* remained on the best-seller lists for eighty-six weeks and prompted a reissuing of an earlier book, *Under the Sea-Wind* (1941), which also achieved success. *The Edge of the Sea* (1955) and her masterpiece, *Silent Spring* (1962), ensured their author a place in the annals of both science and literature. (*See also* Wells, Maine; White Oak, Maryland; and Springdale, Pennsylvania.)

ASIDE-STEP

Novelist Willa Cather (1873–1947) lived in Pittsburgh from 1896 to 1906, during which time she worked as managing editor of the women's magazine *Home Monthly*, and wrote articles for numerous other local publications. In 1899, she met and fell in love with Isabelle McClung, who invited Cather to live with her and her wealthy family in their mansion in Squirrel Hill at *1180 Murray Hill Avenue*. Isabelle and Willa shared a bedroom at the back of the house, where they would quickly retire together soon after dinner.

Stephen Foster Memorial
University of Pittsburgh
Forbes Avenue and Bigelow Boulevard

Stephen Collins Foster (1826–1864) was one of the most popular composers and songwriters of the pre–Civil War era. Born near Pittsburgh, Foster was educated mostly at home and received no formal training in music, composing his first song at age thirteen. His best-known works are simple folk songs that many children still learn in elementary school—"Oh! Susannah," "Old Folks at Home (Swanee River)," "Camptown Races," "Beautiful Dreamer," and "Jeannie with the Light Brown Hair" (*see also* Hoboken, New Jersey). Foster was well-paid for his songs during most of his life, but in his later years, suffering from alcoholism, he was reduced to poverty.

Though he married and fathered a daughter, the most significant relationship of Foster's life seems to have been with the young poet George Cooper, who collaborated on several dozen of Foster's songs. Cooper also cared for Foster when the latter, in an alcoholic haze, suffered a fall in his room in a boardinghouse in New York's Bowery and died at the young age of thirty-eight.

Gertrude Stein birthplace
850 Beech Avenue (formerly 71 Beach Street)
Gertrude Stein (1874–1946) was born in the town of Allegheny, later incorporated into the city of Pittsburgh, and a marker at this address indicates the site. (The street numbering and spelling have been changed since the 1870s; in the 1874 city directory, the Steins' home address is listed as *71 Beach*). Her father, Daniel, owned a prosperous clothing business, and young Gertrude never knew anything but a comfortable, middle-class life. She was the youngest child, a distinction she enjoyed. "One should always be the youngest member of the family," she later wrote. "It saves you a lot of bother, everybody takes care of you."

A year after Gertrude's birth, her family relocated to Vienna along with Daniel's business. The first six years of Gertrude's life were nomadic, with her family also living for brief periods of time in Paris and Baltimore. In 1879, they finally moved to California, where Gertrude stayed until she entered college. (*See also* Oakland, California, and Baltimore, Maryland.)

Billy Strayhorn home
7212 Tioga Street Rear
Composer Billy Strayhorn (1915–1967) lived at this address in the Homewood section of Pittsburgh from age nine until he left for New York as a young man. At that time, white families lived on the main streets of Homewood, while blacks lived in the alleys behind them (the "Rear" in the Strayhorn address). The Strayhorn home was "a four-room shack," according to one of Billy's childhood friends, with two rooms on each floor and a toilet in the basement. The kitchen was the biggest and most significant room in the house. Because of the crowded living conditions and Billy's father's alcoholic binges, Billy's mother often sent her eldest son for long stays with his grandparents in Hillsborough, North Carolina. Billy's grandmother owned and played a piano, and it was in Hillsborough that Billy first learned to play.

Though he was a musical prodigy, Strayhorn's family could not afford lessons to further his talent. As an adolescent, Billy found odd jobs selling papers and working as a soda jerk to purchase his first piano, a broken-down upright. "All the money he [Billy] could get hold of," a friend remembers, "he bought [sheet] music. . . . The house was swamped with music."

At Westinghouse High School, Strayhorn pursued music, becoming first pianist in the Senior Orchestra and playing at local social events and banquets with the school's Orchestra Club. Though he was often made fun of at school for being a "sissy," the shy, withdrawn Strayhorn concentrated on his work and his passion for music. After graduation, Strayhorn formed his own interracial jazz trio and played local nightspots. But he still had to work days at the drugstore soda fountain and pick up extra money by arranging music.

His big break came in 1938, when a friend of a friend got him an "audience" with Duke Ellington, who was playing with his band at the Stanley Theater in downtown Pittsburgh. Ellington was impressed by the talented young pianist, who could seemingly do everything—write music, lyrics, and arrangements. But he didn't have an opening in his band. Ellington made Strayhorn a promise of a job if the young musician ever got to New York and gave him exact directions to his home in Harlem. Eager to please Ellington, Strayhorn turned the directions into a song. "Take the A Train" turned out to be his most famous composition and eventually became Ellington's theme song.

Strayhorn did indeed make it to New York (see Harlem, New York), where he hooked up with Ellington and worked with him for the next thirty years. While Ellington was the public artist, Strayhorn worked behind the scenes as collaborator and arranger. Ellington supported Strayhorn's career, but he also sometimes took credit for the younger man's work. Strayhorn consoled himself with drink and died of cancer and alcohol abuse at age fifty-one. His song "Lush Life" (1936) sadly defines his own short life.

Strayhorn knew early on that he was gay and was open about his sexual orientation. According to his biographer, he never even danced with a girl. Ellington, who was straight, seems to have been supportive and tolerant of his collaborator's homosexuality. Strayhorn had a number of significant relationships in his life, most notably in his final years with a graphic designer, a white man named Bill Grove. Grove was the only man Strayhorn ever brought home to meet his family.

Andy Warhol grave
St. John the Baptist Byzantine Catholic Church Cemetery
Off Route 88 (Library Road)

Pop artist and avant-garde filmmaker Andy Warhol (1928–1987) was born Andrew Warhola in the Pittsburgh suburb of McKeesport and grew up in Castle Shannon. A devout Catholic, he is buried at his former parish cemetery. At his grave site, mourners have been known to leave flowers in Campbell's soup cans, to honor the memory of one of his most famous artworks.

Claimed as a gay artist, Warhol was in fact enigmatic about his personal life and seems to have been primarily asexual. After he graduated from Pittsburgh's Carnegie Institute of Technology (now Carnegie-Mellon University) in 1949, Warhol moved to New York and achieved fame first as a commercial artist. His silk screens of Campbell's soup cans and of Marilyn Monroe in the early 1960s launched his pop art career. Later, he directed such underground films as *My Hustler* (1965) and *Chelsea Girls* (1966). Others films, such as *Trash*, *Flesh*, and *Women in Revolt*, were made by director Paul Morrissey and produced by Warhol at his studio, a Manhattan loft called "The Factory," and gave prominence to such drag queens as Holly Woodlawn and Candy Darling.

In 1968, Warhol's life was almost cut short when Valerie Solanis, the violent founder of SCUM (Society for Cutting Up Men), shot him. Following his recovery, Warhol became more reclusive and abandoned directing, having already experienced significantly more than "fifteen minutes of fame." He died unexpectedly during a gallbladder operation in 1987. The *Andy Warhol Museum, 117 Sandusky Street*, opened in Pittsburgh in 1994.

SHARON HILL

Bessie Smith grave
Mt. Lawn Cemetery
84th Street and Hook Road

Blues great Bessie Smith (1894–1937) was born into poverty in Tennessee and was discovered singing on streetcorners at a tender age by Ma Rainey, who may have been the first of her many lesbian lovers (*see* Chattanooga, Tennessee). During the 1920s, Smith's popular "race records"—including "Down-Hearted Blues," "St. Louis Blues," "Nobody Knows You When You're Down and Out," and "Gimme a Pigfoot and a Bottle of Beer"—won her the title "Queen of the Blues." Tragically, she was killed in an automobile accident in Mississippi and was buried at this site by her husband, a Philadelphia policeman. The grave has been maintained through the financial support of Smith's former maid and the late rock singer, Janis Joplin.

SPRINGDALE

Rachel Carson birthplace
613 Marion Avenue
Once surrounded by woods, this small farmhouse in the Allegheny Valley was the site of scientist Rachel Carson's birth in 1907. Both her rural upbringing and her mother's teaching instilled in her a deep appreciation of nature's beauty and mystery. "I can remember no time," Carson wrote, "when I wasn't interested in the out-of-doors and the whole world of nature." Her childhood love of the natural world translated into a career of interpreting environmental science for laypeople and exposing the harm being done to the physical environment by humans. "The beauty of the world I was trying to save has always been uppermost in my mind—that and the anger of the senseless, brutish things that were being done," Carson wrote to a friend after the publication of *Silent Spring*, her attack on the use of pesticides. "I have felt bound by a solemn obligation to do what I could—if I didn't at least try I could never again be happy in nature." (*See also* Wells, Maine; White Oak, Maryland; Pittsburgh, Pennsylvania.)

From the collection of the author

III

SOUTH

Arkansas

Clover Bend

Alice French house
State 228 (6 miles west of Mentura)

Here on the banks of the Black River, a marker indicates where writer Alice French (1850–1934) spent winters with her life partner, Jane Crawford. French was a novelist and essayist who wrote mostly under the name Octave Thanet, which she used to avoid antifemale bias in the publishing world. Though one of the highest paid writers of her day, French has now fallen into obscurity.

The lavish house, which was called Thanford, was an old plantation that French purchased in 1884. A decade later, the mansion burned to the ground and was rebuilt in 1896. French and Crawford, who were together for over fifty years, spent most of the year in Davenport, Iowa, where they had both grown up. (*See also* Davenport, Iowa.)

FLORIDA

JASPER

This little village of two thousand people near the Georgia border was the hometown of writer Lillian Smith (1897–1966), who is best remembered for her first novel, *Strange Fruit* (1944). Though it sounds like pulp fiction with homosexuality as its theme, *Strange Fruit* was actually a tale of miscegenation, which was turned down by seven publishers before being accepted. It was banned in cities like Detroit and Boston for its realistic treatment of the controversial theme. Despite that (or more likely, because of it), the book was a runaway best-seller, which sold three million copies and was translated into sixteen languages.

Smith was a white woman with a lifelong interest in racial issues. Her comfortable childhood was spent in "a rambling house of many rooms, surrounded by a big lawn, back yard, gardens, fields, and barn." When Lillian was young, her parents took in a foster child they believed to be a white orphan, only to find that she was part black. The girl was immediately sent away, and the cruel incident left a lasting impression on Lillian. Besides *Strange Fruit* (in which Jasper is thinly disguised as Maxwell, Georgia), Smith published five nonfiction books on the topic of racial justice and numerous articles in *Redbook*, *Saturday Review*, and *The Nation*. Smith's life partner was Paula Snelling, whom she met when the two helped run the Smith family's exclusive summer camp for girls on top of Old Screamer Mountain in Clayton, Georgia. Beginning in the 1930s, the two women collaborated to publish a magazine called *Pseudopathia*, devoted to reviewing literary works by African Americans. The journal was later renamed *North American Review* and finally *South Today*, before it folded in 1944, the year *Strange Fruit* was published.

KEY WEST

Elizabeth Bishop home
624 White Street

Poet Elizabeth Bishop (1911–1979) was born into a wealthy family from Worcester, Massachusetts. After her graduation from Vassar, she used a family inheritance to live a nomadic life in New York City, Europe, Florida, and other places. In 1938, she and her lover at the time, Louise Crane, purchased a house in Key West. Bishop lived at this residence off and on for the next nine years, first with Crane, then with a subsequent lover, Marjorie Stevens.

In letters to friends, Bishop described her island home this way: "It is very well made, with slightly arched beams so that it looks either like a ship's cabin or a freight car." The house was located right on the beach and was to Bishop "perfectly beautiful . . . inside and out." Bishop's first volume of poems, *North and South* (1946), was published during the time she lived in Key West.

It may sound idyllic, but Bishop battled alcoholism throughout her adult life, and the relationship with Stevens did not last. After they broke up, Bishop sold the Key West house and resumed an itinerant life, eventually being hospitalized for both depression and alcohol-related problems. In 1951, with the help of her mentor, Marianne Moore, Bishop secured a fellowship from Bryn Mawr College that enabled her to travel around the world.

But Bishop never got farther than Brazil, where she met the wealthy

Lota de Macedo Soares, who became her lover and tried to nurture her away from alcoholism. Bishop kept postponing her return, until her stay in Brazil had lengthened to sixteen years. At her home, Lota built a studio for Bishop that was separate from the house and had a stream running beside it. In that peaceful setting, Bishop was very productive and composed some of her greatest poems. But Bishop eventually returned to the States after Lota committed suicide in 1967, and her own alcoholism worsened.

Tennessee Williams home
1431 Duncan Street

In 1949, with several successful Broadway plays behind him and movie adaptations of them on the way, Tennessee Williams and his lover Frank Merlo decided to "winter" in Key West, where they rented this three-bedroom cottage. With them came Williams's much-loved maternal grandfather, a retired minister. Merlo took good care of both men, keeping house, cooking, and acting as their chauffeur. Said one friend of the Key West residence, "There was a very homey atmosphere. . . . Tenn wrote each day at the end of the dining room table, Frank cooked and ran the house, the Reverend was a respectable addition to the household—it was all very much a family."

In the fall of 1950, Williams purchased the Duncan Street house for ten thousand dollars, because his grandfather was happy there and Frank managed it for him. Over the next few years, he added a pool ringed with palm trees and shrubs and a small guest house. A gazebo constructed in front of the main house was dubbed "The Jane Bowles Summer House," in honor of one of his many famous friends. Later, Williams affixed small brass plaques to the gazebo, engraved with the first names of other cherished friends. His additions to and improvements of the house raised its value to one hundred thousand dollars at the time of his death in the early 1980s.

TAMPA

An article in the November/December 1957 issue of *ONE* magazine reported police raids on two lesbian bars in the Tampa area. One raid was at
Jimmie White's Tavern, in which a dozen women were arrested for wearing
"mannish" clothing. The second raid was at a hangout called Fungie's Tavern, where one woman was arrested.

ASIDE-STEP

Sports legend Babe Didrikson Zaharias (1911–1956) lived in Tampa
for the last few years of her life, in a house of her own design located
at the edge of the Tampa golf course. She lived at "Rainbow Manor"
with both her husband George and her protégée and intimate companion Betty Dodd. According to George, Babe "planned every inch of it
[the house], . . . remembering the rooms she had seen and liked as
she traveled back and forth across the country." (*See also* Beaumont,
Texas.)

GEORGIA

COLUMBUS

Carson McCullers home
1519 Starke Avenue

This modest white frame house was the childhood home of writer Carson McCullers (1917–1967), who was born Lula Carson Smith. (Her actual birthplace was at 423 *Thirteenth Street* in downtown Columbus.) Carson's first fantasy was to be a concert pianist, but a childhood spent reading books and writing and performing skits eventually led to her true vocation. In a 1948 article, "How I Began to Write," she remembered writing and producing plays in the Starke Avenue house, using the front sitting room as an auditorium and the back sitting room for the stage. The two rooms were separated by sliding walnut doors that functioned as a stage curtain. Carson enlisted her brother and sister as performers, and their proud and supportive mother invited people from the neighborhood to the performances. Carson described their theatrical repertory as "eclectic, running from hashed-over movies to Shakespeare and shows I made up and sometimes wrote down in my nickel Big Chief notebooks."

Carson was not popular in school—she was withdrawn and cared little about her clothes or appearance—and she was taunted by other girls as being "freakish" or "queer." She didn't date boys until she met Reeves McCullers, a soldier stationed at Fort Benning, in the summer of 1935. Reeves courted Carson at the Starke Avenue house, bringing her mother flowers and candy—and beer and cigarettes for Carson—and they married here two years later. Carson and Reeves had a stormy relationship, rife with drama, that ended finally with Reeves's suicide. Both were bisexual and at one time were in love with the same man, composer David Diamond.

Carson's mother lived in this house until her husband's death in 1944. Plagued by illness throughout her life, Carson frequently returned to Columbus to recuperate under her mother's care. Eventually, mother and daughter lived together in Nyack, New York, in a house bought with the money from the sale of the Starke Avenue house. (*See also* Nyack, New York; Charlotte, North Carolina; and Fayetteville, North Carolina.) A self-guiding tour map of the town of Columbus—including the McCullers house—is available from the Georgia Welcome Center (phone: 404-322-3839).

Ma Rainey home
805 Fifth Avenue

Gertrude Pridgett / "Ma" Rainey (1886–1939) was born in Columbus to parents who were minstrel performers, and she began her own professional singing career at the tender age of fourteen at the local Springer Opera House. In 1904, she married Will Rainey, who led a touring company called the Rabbit Foot Minstrels, and joined him on the road. Rainey enjoyed a thirty-year career, and through her live performances and recordings, she became a nationally recognized blues and gospel singer, nicknamed "Mother of the Blues." In 1934, Rainey retired to this house in her hometown, which today is listed on the National Register of Historic Places, and she is buried in the town's *Porterdale Cemetery*.

Ma Rainey also gave the world Bessie Smith, whom she discovered as a

> *Went out last night with a crowd of my friends,*
> *They must have been women 'cause I don't like no men.*
> *They say I do it, ain't nobody caught me,*
> *They sure got to prove it on me.*
> *—from Ma Rainey's "Prove It on Me Blues"*

young girl singing on the streetcorners of Chattanooga (*see* Chattanooga, Tennessee) and with whom she may have been lovers. Throughout her career, Rainey pursued affairs with women, and in the 1920s, she was arrested for holding a lesbian orgy in her apartment. She is often extolled by gay and lesbian historians today for writing and performing gutsy queer blues numbers. In "Prove It on Me Blues," the most famous of these songs, she openly defended cross-dressing and "woman loving" (*see box above*). An advertisement for the recording showed a woman in full male drag escorting two very feminine flappers. Rainey also wrote about her husband's sexual relationship with a "queen" named "Miss Kate" in a song called "Sissy Blues."

JULIETTE

Whistle Stop Cafe
McCrackin Road
Ninety miles south of Atlanta, this site was used for the location filming of the 1991 movie *Fried Green Tomatoes*. Originally a general store, it was transformed for the movie into the 1920s Whistle Stop Cafe. In the novel by Fannie Flagg, Whistle Stop Cafe owners Idgie and Ruth were lesbians, but Hollywood decided to blur the lines of their relationship in its

ASIDE-STEP

Lesbian writer Barbara Deming (1917–1984), an ardent peace and civil rights activist, spent one month in the Albany, Georgia, jail in 1964 during the Quebec-Washington-Guantanamo Walk for Peace. She and other demonstrators were arrested for marching through Albany's downtown area and refusing to walk on Oglethorpe Avenue—which local officials had designated as the march route—because it was a street that divided the black and white communities of the town.

inimitably homophobic way. Still, there are some fine, coded lesbian moments, as when young Idgie dresses in boy-drag for her sister's wedding. After the movie was released, the location spot became a tourist attraction, and the owners decided to capitalize on its popularity by turning it into an actual café.

KENTUCKY

LEXINGTON

"Sweet Evening Breeze" home
186 Prall Street

Born James Herndon around 1892, "Sweet Evening Breeze" or "Sweets" was well known and respected in Lexington before and after World War II as the most conscientious nursing assistant in town. Sweets was an African-American gay man who worked for many years as an orderly at *Good Samaritan Hospital, 310 South Limestone*. According to one former resident, all the elite of Lexington (including the Vanderbilts and the Whitneys) insisted on being placed in Sweets's careful charge when they were in the hospital. Sweets was also famous for his theatrical and campy manner and for his elaborate drag costumes. At hospital basketball games, Sweets was always the most ebullient cheerleader. In a conservative southern city that did not condone homosexuality or transvestism, Sweets was accepted and tolerated because of his kindness and expert nursing abilities.

Henry Faulkner home
462 West Third Street

Henry Faulkner (1924–1981) was born in a log cabin in rural Kentucky. After his mother died when he was only two years old, his father sent him and his brothers and sisters to the Kentucky Children's Home, a Louisville orphanage. Placed unsuccessfully in several foster homes, he finally went to live with tobacco farmers in the mountain community of Falling Timber. His new home was a stark three-room cabin papered in illustrated pages from the Sears, Roebuck catalog.

Henry began making art at an early age, because, he later wrote,

"Mountain children have such colorless homes they have more reason for imagination and a creative mind." Fond of playing with dolls, he was frequently taunted by other children as a "sissy" or a "nut." Henry ran away several times and was remanded to the orphanage, where he lived off and on between sojourns at other foster homes. Finally, at age eighteen, he was on his own.

Wandering from city to city, Faulkner made his way as a young man through con games—often ending up in jail—and odd jobs, sometimes with female impersonation acts. In addition, he was painting and writing poems. After studying art in California, he settled in Lexington, which was close to Falling Timber and the area where he had grown up. With sheer determination and a portfolio of colorful, rustic paintings, he brokered his own work in New York galleries and eventually became a prosperous "primitive" artist.

Faulkner's success bought him this elegant Lexington mansion, which he shared with a menagerie of animals, including a bourbon-drinking goat named Alice. Parties and extravaganzas were routine at Faulkner's residence. Faulkner spent the winters in Key West. He counted among his intimate friends Tennessee Williams and James Herlihy, the author of *Midnight Cowboy*. Williams's last play, *The Lingering Hour*, was about Faulkner, whom he labeled "the ultimate artist."

LOUISVILLE*

Cherokee Park
Located in the Highlands neighborhood, this park was designed by the Victorian landscape architect Frederick Law Olmstead, whose most famous project was Central Park in Manhattan. For decades Cherokee Park has been a popular cruising area for gay men and, until the AIDS crisis, a center of Louisville's gay male subculture.

*My thanks to David Williams of the Williams-Nichols Institute for identifying the Louisville sites.

Comm-Ten Center
1321 South Preston Street
The descendant of Gay Lib House (*see below*), the Comm-Ten Center was Louisville's gay and lesbian community center from 1984 to 1988 and the focal point of the community in the mid-1980s. Originally an elementary school, the building housed the Gay and Lesbian Hotline and the Comm-Ten Library. In addition, meetings, performances, drag shows, and a popular Sunday brunch were held there. Financial difficulties always plagued the Center, and it was forced to close after only four years.

First Unitarian Universalist Church
Fourth and York Streets
This church housed the first two gay churches in the city, Church of the Open Door (founded 1974) and the local MCC, Metropolitan Community Church (c. 1975). In 1985, the one-hundred-year-old church burned to the ground, and MCC met at other locations until securing permanent space elsewhere. The Unitarian church was rebuilt in the late 1980s and is now one of the most gay-supportive churches in the area.

Gay Lib House
1919 Bonnycastle Avenue
Louisville's first gay community center was founded at this location in 1971 but lasted less than a year. The rented building served as a drop-in center for the city's small gay liberation movement and was run by the Gay Liberation Front of Louisville. Gay Lib House published Kentucky's first gay newspaper, *Trash*; operated a gay hotline; and sponsored organizational meetings.

On October 17, 1971, a party at Gay Lib House was raided by the police, and twenty-five people were arrested for either disorderly conduct or felony narcotics charges (some partygoers had been smoking pot). Though all charges were later dropped or amended, Gay Lib House was forced to close, and Louisville had to wait over a decade for a new community center. (*See* "Comm-Ten Center" *above.*)

National City Bank
2123 Bardstown Road
In 1981, when this was the First National Bank and Trust Company, Sam Dorr, the branch manager, advised his supervisors that he had been elected president of the local chapter of Dignity/Integrity, a support group for gay and lesbian Roman Catholics and Episcopalians, and that this required him to be out publicly as a gay man. Dorr's supervisors in turn asked him to either resign the post as president or resign his job at the bank. He resigned his job under pressure, but the following year Dorr sued the bank, claiming his constitutional right to freedom of religion had been violated. Dorr lost the suit, but he appealed to a higher court. Before the case could be tried, Dorr and the bank settled out of court.

Sam Dorr's case fired up the sluggish local gay and lesbian community. In 1981, there were only three small gay and lesbian groups citywide. By the next year, the community gave birth to a gay hotline, an archives, a coalition group, a student group, and several other groups. In the spring of 1982, Louisville also witnessed its first Gay Pride Week. Sam Dorr's resistance to homophobia paved the way for future community organizing and is sometimes considered Louisville's Stonewall.

Pre-Stonewall gay bars
The Downtowner, located on Chestnut Street west of Third Street, opened in the early 1950s, just down the street from another old gay bar, the *Beaux Arts*, located in the Henry Clay Hotel. For twenty years, the Downtowner flourished at that location, sponsoring numerous drag shows, until arson destroyed it in 1974. The New Downtowner reopened on Main Street five years later and remained there until 1989, when the owners moved it to a large building at the corner of Floyd and Market and renamed it once again, this time The Connection Complex.

^   ^   ^

West Main Street
(between Brook and Second Streets)
In the 1970s and 1980s, this area of town was hopping with both gay and straight bars, and it was a popular weekend hangout for gay men and lesbians. By most accounts, Bob Seger's song "Main Street" focused on this lively street, though he concentrated on the straight clientele. Today, West Main Street has only two gay and lesbian bars and one restaurant. One of the bars, Sparks, is in the same location as an earlier series of gay and lesbian bars.

LOUISIANA

NEW ORLEANS

Truman Capote homes
Monteleone Hotel
Royal Street, corner of Iberville

711 Royal Street

A suite in this elegant hotel at the edge of the French Quarter (advertised as "The Finest Hotel in New Orleans") was the first home of Truman Streckfus Persons (later Capote) in 1924. Truman's mother was a sixteen-year-old former beauty queen, his father a traveling salesman, and the boy's first years were spent in an assortment of hotel rooms. When his parents went out, Truman recalled later, they locked him in the hotel room alone. Truman's parents were ill-matched and divorced after only a few years, leaving young Truman to be raised by different eccentric maternal relatives in Monroeville, Alabama. His creative imagination was forged early on. "By the time I was ten," Capote remembered as an adult, "I was sitting up all night long to write." He was also already putting himself to sleep by taking a few swigs of whiskey.

Capote first achieved literary recognition in his early twenties with a number of critically acclaimed short stories in major publications. He wrote much of his first novel, *Other Voices, Other Rooms* (1948), the story of a young homosexual southerner, while living in a rented room, also on Royal Street. His subject matter was considered scandalous and offensive, and a reviewer in the *New York Times* complained, "The distasteful trappings of its homosexual theme overhang it like Spanish moss." Capote went on to an active literary career anyway—his most famous works included *Breakfast at Tiffany's* (1958) and *In Cold Blood* (1966)—though one that was marred by alcoholism and ill health.

Daily Crescent office
95 St. Charles Street

In early 1848, Walt Whitman was fired as editor of the *Brooklyn Eagle* for defying the publisher by supporting the Wilmot Proviso, which opposed the extension of slavery into the territories. Shortly after, Whitman made the acquaintance of the owner of the *New Orleans Daily Crescent*, who offered him a job as a rewrite and clippings man for the newspaper. With two hundred dollars in traveling expenses, Whitman took off from New York with his brother Jeff, crossing the Allegheny Mountains by train, and then heading south by steamer from Wheeling. The brothers arrived in New Orleans in February 1848. According to biographer David S. Reynolds, the trip inspired Whitman's poem "The Mississippi at Midnight."

In New Orleans, Whitman and his brother lodged at a series of boardinghouses, but Walt spent most of his time at the *Crescent* office, located at this address. Steering away from the controversial issue of slavery that had gotten him sacked, Whitman wrote mostly light sketches of local characters such as con men and streetwalkers. It was during his stint at the *Crescent* that Whitman first started mixing up slang and colloquialisms in

ASIDE-STEP

Gay sculptor Richmond Barthé (1901–1989) was born in New Orleans. Barthé showed artistic talent early, creating his first paintings at age six and having his first exhibition at age twelve. Drawn to the theater, Barthé sculpted many busts of queer stage actors during his long career, including Katharine Cornell (*see* New York City, New York), Maurice Evans, Sir John Gielgud, and Gypsy Rose Lee (*see* Brooklyn, New York).

> *Once I passed through a populous city, imprinting my brain, for*
>   *future use, with its shows, architecture, customs and traditions.*
> *But now of all that city I remember only the man who wandered*
>   *with me, there for love of me,*
> *Day by day and night by night, we were together—all else has been*
>   *long forgotten by me,*
> *I remember, I say, only one rude and ignorant man who, when I*
>   *departed, long and long held me by the hand, with silent lips,*
>   *sad and tremulous.*
>
> —Walt Whitman, 1860

his writing with standard English. His new job, however, lasted only until May of that year, when Whitman and the *Crescent* owner had an argument over money, and the Whitman brothers decided to head back to Brooklyn.

Some of Whitman's early biographers made much ado of a supposed love affair with a New Orleans woman—which ended in her bearing his child—and pointed to this as proof of his heterosexuality. But David S. Reynolds found no evidence of such a relationship. In fact, the romance, Reynolds notes, was probably with a man, as suggested by the poem "Once I Passed Through a Populous City" from the Calamus series (*see box*).

Tennessee Williams home
632-1/2 St. Peter Street

Suffering from a physical and emotional breakdown in 1935, Tennessee Williams had recuperated at the home of his grandparents in Memphis (*see* Memphis, Tennessee). After his recovery, the young writer attempted to find work with the Works Progress Administration, which had hired thousands of unemployed writers to pen guides to American cities and states. Williams traveled to New Orleans in search of work, but WPA opportunities by that fall had dried up. Still, Williams decided to stay on, taking menial jobs—distributing handbills, working in restaurants—because he was sure the city would fuel his writing. At boardinghouses, he proudly registered as "Tennessee Williams, Writer." For a time he lived at *431 Royal Street* in a room that cost three dollars a week, and then later rented a "bohemian" attic apartment at *722 Toulouse Street.* The rent was ten dollars a week, and he took his meals at nearby inexpensive cafeterias. Favorite hangouts included Victor's Bar and Alpine's La Boheme Restaurant. Early in the mornings, Williams worked on a series of scenes filled with French Quarter settings, which would later be used in such plays as *A Streetcar Named Desire*; *Suddenly, Last Summer*; and *Auto-Da-Fe*.

During a stay in New Orleans in the fall of 1941, Williams roomed at *538 Royal Street.* "I have a room on Royal right opposite *the* gay bar—The St. James," he wrote to a friend, ". . . so I can hover like a bright angel over the troubled waters of homosociety."

A later sojourn in New Orleans in 1946 proved even more significant. Williams had already achieved Broadway success with his play *The Glass Menagerie*. In the fall, he rented an apartment with his lover, Pancho Rodriguez y Gonzalez, on St. Peter Street in New Orleans for the considerably higher rent of one hundred and fifty dollars. It was there that he completed the play he originally called *The Poker Night*, discovering a better title on the New Orleans streets right outside his apartment. "I live near the main street of the Quarter," he wrote in an essay that fall. "Down this street, running on the same tracks, are two streetcars, one named 'Desire' and the other named 'Cemetery'" (*see next entry*). By the time he submitted his finished play to New York producers the following spring, its name had changed to *A Streetcar Named Desire*.

Desire streetcar
Old Mint
Barracks Street
Streetcars were common transportation in the city when Tennessee Williams lived there in the mid-1930s and again in the mid-1940s. The Desire streetcar, which the playwright immortalized, has long been retired, but you can see it on display in front of the Old Mint at the edge of the

French Quarter. The Desire and Cemetery streetcars actually ran parallel to each other, but Williams used poetic license to make their routes perpendicular (and metaphorical) in the play (*see box*).

> They told me to take a streetcar named Desire, then transfer to one called Cemeteries.
> —Blanche DuBois's first line a *A Streetcar Named Desire*

Mississippi

Columbus

Tennessee Williams's first home
St. Paul's Episcopal Church Rectory
South Second Street

Edwina Dakin, the mother of playwright Tennessee Williams (1911–1983), was originally from the town of Columbus, the daughter of an Episcopal minister. She met Cornelius Williams, who worked for the local telephone company, when she was appearing in an amateur production of *The Mikado*. The two married in 1909, but Cornelius's drinking and frequent traveling for his job kept them apart during the years immediately following their wedding. The first home of their children Rose and Thomas Lanier (who would later take the name Tennessee, the home state of his father's family) was at Edwina's father's rectory. Mother and children lived with the grandparents until 1918, when Cornelius got a managerial position and moved his family to St. Louis.

His early childhood memories made Tennessee Williams extremely fond of his maternal grandfather, the Reverend Dakin. After his Broadway successes enabled him to buy a home in the Florida Keys, Williams brought his elderly widowed grandfather to live with him there. Williams's lover, Frank Merlo, cared for both men. Said one friend, "There was a very homey atmosphere. . . . Tenn wrote each day at the end of the dining room table, Frank cooked and ran the house, the Reverend was a respectable addition to the household—it was all very much a family." (*See also* Key West, Florida; New Orleans, Louisiana; and St. Louis, Missouri.)

Black Mountain

This summer resort town of three thousand people was once the site of Black Mountain College, an experimental school in existence from 1933 to 1956. According to historian Martin Duberman, who chronicled its history in his exhaustive group biography *Black Mountain*, the college was "the forerunner and exemplar of much that is currently considered innovative in art, education and life style." At Black Mountain, there were no required courses, no system of exams, and no formal grades. Students were considered responsible for planning their own course of education, participating in classes that often had fewer than ten students each.

Black Mountain was also the refuge and "nurturing ground" of numerous queer writers and artists, including Paul Goodman, Merce Cunningham, and John Cage. Other queer lecturers during its history included Thornton Wilder, Ted Shawn, and Robert Duncan. Artist Robert Rauschenberg was a student there. *The Black Mountain Review*, the college's literary journal (which gave rise to the term "Black Mountain poets"), published the work of Allen Ginsberg and Jack Kerouac, among many others. Though gay men taught and studied there, however, homosexuality was not openly tolerated at Black Mountain. When Paul Goodman, a lecturer in "psychotherapy (his own), literature, history, community planning and sex," according to Duberman's account, applied for a full-time teaching position, the faculty (including some homosexuals!) voted against him, fearing that he would prove to be a child molester.

The original site of the school consisted of church buildings constructed by the Blue Ridge Assembly as a summer conference center for its members. For most of the year, the buildings were vacant, and Black Mountain founder John Andrew Rice saw it as the perfect location for his school. The main building, called Lee Hall, included both common rooms and individual living and study spaces for the students.

The rental agreement with the church stipulated that the buildings and grounds had to be cleared of all college equipment and furniture by the beginning of the summer. Because of this, Lee Hall had a "Shaker plainness" to it, and many students had to construct their own desks and furniture. After a few years, the college purchased a more stable site at *Lake Eden*, a former summer resort with lodges and cottages on a human-made lake.

The college suffered chronic financial problems, and lack of money and students forced it to close in 1956. The property was sold off piece by piece, and part was leased as a boys' summer camp. Martin Duberman's history of the school also marked his own coming out as a gay historian.

CHARLOTTE

Carson McCullers home
806 Central Avenue

The upstairs apartment of this large frame house was an early home of newlyweds Carson and Reeves McCullers. (Their first apartment, which they occupied for only a few weeks, was at *311 East Boulevard*.) Carson was just twenty years old in 1937 when she married Reeves, who was her first boyfriend (*see* Columbus, Georgia). Both later discovered their same-sex desires. In Charlotte, Reeves went to work for the Retail Credit Corporation, and Carson began work on the first chapters of what would become *The Heart Is a Lonely Hunter*, but at that time was called simply *The Mute*. The following year, Reeves's company gave him a promotion and transferred him to Fayetteville (*see next entry*).

FAYETTEVILLE

Carson McCullers home
119 North Cool Spring

Carson and Reeves McCullers moved to the southeastern part of the state in 1938, following Reeves's promotion at the Retail Credit Corporation. Just prior to their move, Carson finished the first six chapters of *The Heart Is a Lonely Hunter* and submitted them to the publisher Houghton Mifflin, which gave her a contract and a five-hundred-dollar advance.

Carson and Reeves were at first unhappy in their move to the flat, humid town of Fayetteville. But their spirits improved when they rented a spacious second-floor apartment at this address in a white-columned building (the oldest in town) that had been built in the late eighteenth century as the Cool Spring Tavern and was steeped in local history. The McCullers's apartment had a veranda to which Carson would bring her typewriter and work.

In 1939, Carson finished her first novel and in a brief two months wrote her second, *Reflections in a Golden Eye*, while living here. But at the same time, her marriage began to fall apart, and in an effort to revive it, she and Reeves moved to New York City in 1940, following the publication of *The Heart Is a Lonely Hunter*. Sadly, both Carson and Reeves were plagued by depression and alcoholism throughout their lives, and after a stormy, on-again-off-again marriage, Reeves committed suicide in 1953. (*See also* Brooklyn, New York, and Nyack, New York.)

ASIDE-STEP

Novelist Bertha Harris (author of *Lover*, an early title from Daughters, Inc.—*see* Plainfield, Vermont) was born in Fayetteville in 1937 and educated at the University of North Carolina at Greensboro.

SOUTH CAROLINA

PENDLETON

Jane Edna Hunter birthplace
Woodburn Plantation
Route 279
Social worker Jane Edna Hunter (1882–1950) was born on this plantation
in a small cabin, the daughter of former slaves. After training to be a nurse
and migrating north to Ohio, she went on to fame as the founder of
the Phillis Wheatley Home and Association for Working Black Girls (*see*
Cleveland, Ohio). Hunter, who had one "brief and loveless" marriage,
"seemed to rejoice in the opportunity to make a life as a single female," according
to her biographer Adrienne Lash Jones, which only leads us to
wonder about her sexual orientation.

ST. HELENA'S ISLAND

Penn Center
Martin Luther King, Jr. Drive
In 1862, white abolitionists Laura Towne and Ellen Murray (companions
who are usually described as "good friends") arrived on St. Helena's Island
from Philadelphia, as part of the Port Royal Experiment. The Union fleet
off Port Royal Sound had driven white planters from the island, leaving ten
thousand liberated slaves with no means of supporting themselves. Abolitionists
saw this as their opportunity to educate and train the former
slaves, as well as to spread Christianity. Towne and Murray set up the
Penn School, holding classes first at the *Oaks Plantation House*, and then
at the *Brick Church*, two structures that are still standing. In 1870, they
began training their students to become teachers. The earliest known

black teacher was Charlotte Forten (later Grimké), who migrated from Massachusetts to help the island people and taught at the school from 1862 to 1864.

Laura Towne was in charge of the school for almost forty years, living in one of the abandoned white estates, Frogmore, with Murray. Sadly, Towne saw the purpose of Penn School not as preserving the residents' African culture and Gullah language but making them more "American." Many island families consequently resisted Penn School, staunchly safeguarding their native culture. After Towne's death in 1901, Penn School became Penn Normal, part of the state's segregated school system, and later Penn Center. It remains an educational center for island residents to this day, but now its focus is on African-American arts and culture.

Tennessee

Chattanooga

Bessie Smith birthplace
West Sixth Street
The area of Chattanooga where Bessie Smith (1894–1937) was born in a dilapidated, one-room shack is known as Blue Goose Hollow. Smith used to sing on streetcorners until, while still a teenager, she was discovered by Ma Rainey as she toured with the Rabbit Foot Minstrels. During World War I, Smith became a headliner for the black-run Theater Owners Booking Association, crisscrossing the country on the vaudeville circuit. By the "Roaring Twenties," she was one of the most popular black performers in the country, recording over one hundred and fifty "race records" in a ten-year span. Her interpretations of "Down-Hearted Blues," "St. Louis Blues," and "Nobody Knows You When You're Down and Out" are legendary and earned her the title "Queen of the Blues." "Gimme a Pigfoot and a Bottle of Beer" celebrated the rent parties of 1920s Harlem, where lesbians and gay men often congregated.

Smith's birthplace is no longer standing, but her piano and assorted memorabilia are on display at the *Chattanooga African-American Museum, 730 Martin Luther King Boulevard*, which is nearby.

Though Smith was married to a man, her biographer, Chris Albertson, has revealed that she enjoyed numerous sexual relationships with lesbians and bisexual women on the touring circuit, one of whom, Boula Lee, was the wife of her musical director. It has been suggested that her mentor, Ma Rainey, was her first lover. Smith's lesbian affairs were a frequent source of tension with her husband, Jack Gee. In 1937, the blues singer died of massive wounds incurred in an automobile accident in Clarksdale, Mississippi, and is buried near Philadelphia. (*See also* Philadelphia, Pennsylvania.)

MEMPHIS

Beale Street Historic District
168 Beale Street
Before emancipation, Memphis was already home to many freedmen, and after the Civil War, the area around Beale Street became predominantly black. By the late nineteenth century, Beale Street was the acknowledged capital of African-American Memphis and of the mid-South, also achieving a reputation as a raw, exciting center of music and entertainment. Blues composer W. C. Handy lived on the street and immortalized it in 1912 in his "Beale Street Blues." His talent drew such great performers as Ma Rainey, Bessie Smith, and Alberta Hunter (bisexuals all), who during the 1920s regularly played in the clubs and performances spaces lining the street, such as the Daisy Theater. Beale Street is now a National Historic District with markers pointing out its significant historic sites.

Broome's Variety Theater
37 Jefferson Street
In her article "The Trials of Alice Mitchell: Sensationalism, Sexology, and the Lesbian Subject in Turn-of-the Century America," historian Lisa Duggan documents the story of Annie (a.k.a. Marie) Hindle, a professional male impersonator on the late-nineteenth-century stage. Hindle was the "bright particular star," according to a contemporary Memphis newspaper report, of Broome's Variety Theater, a vaudeville house, during the 1869–1870 season. Broome's also specialized in female impersonators and others of "unconventional gender identifications," to quote Duggan, and those who performed there created a queer community for themselves.

Annie Hindle's "inclination was altogether toward women," the reporter in the *Memphis Public Ledger* stated, "and she inspired in them a like feeling toward herself." Two women who were Hindle groupies were said to have fought over her with knives at the "ladies' entrance" to the Overton Hotel. Leaving Memphis for New York in 1870, Hindle went on to an even greater career up north, the first male impersonator to achieve fame on the

American stage. Hindle married another woman, Annie Ryan, and they lived together until the latter's death in 1891.

Tennessee Williams's grandparents' home
1917 Snowden Avenue

During the summer of 1935, an ailing Tennessee Williams (1911–1983) recuperated at the home of his grandparents in Memphis. Williams had been living in a small St. Louis apartment with his family, working days at the International Shoe Company and staying up nights writing, smoking, and drinking pots of coffee (*see* St. Louis, Missouri). Homosexual panic and physical and mental exhaustion brought on a breakdown. Since his sister Rose was also mentally unstable and living at home, Williams was sent to Memphis to recover.

During his four months at the home of his supportive grandparents, Williams's health and confidence grew. He collaborated on a play, *Cairo, Shanghai, Bombay*, which was performed by the Memphis Garden Players that June and became his first play produced outside of a school setting.

ASIDE-STEP

Blues great Alberta Hunter (1895–1984) was born in Memphis, where she learned songs from her grandmother and from listening to player piano rolls in music stores. At the tender age of twelve, she ran away to Chicago to pursue a singing career. There she lived with Helen Winston, a friend of her mother's who may have been Hunter's lover. Her family was unable to locate her for several years. Pretending to be eighteen, Hunter got her first professional singing gigs with Winston's help. Though her first job was at a hangout for prostitutes and pimps, Hunter was soon a popular cabaret act, performing all over Chicago. She began her recording career in 1922. The following year she got her big break, when she was chosen to replace Bessie Smith in *How Come?* at the Apollo Theatre in Harlem, becoming an overnight hit.

Williams developed a strong and positive bond with the people and the place that nurtured him during his illness, and from that summer on, he identified as "Tennessee" instead of as Tom.

"Perverted Passion"

In 1892, a lurid crime in Memphis engaged the attention of the country. A nineteen-year-old named Alice Mitchell was arrested for the murder of Freda Ward, age seventeen, with whom she had an intimate friendship. At a hearing at the Shelby County Courthouse, medical specialists gave "expert testimony" on Mitchell's behavior, and the girl was judged to be insane.

At the hearing, Freda was described as "girl-like," while Alice was "a regular tomboy." Both girls were "familiar figures in society." Alice had reportedly exhibited an obsession for Freda, becoming despondent and threatening suicide when her friend's family moved to another city. In three separate letters, Alice asked Freda to marry her, and Freda finally agreed, accepting an engagement ring from Alice in the summer of 1891. Alice's correspondence, one expert said, showed "all the warmth of lover for lover."

Alice schemed to pass as a man so that the two could be married and live together, but their plan to elope to St. Louis was foiled. Freda's older sister, with whom she was living, found Alice's letters and prevented Freda from leaving. Freda returned the engagement ring that Alice had given her, indicating that she could have no further contact with her. Rather than lose Freda, the troubled Alice became determined to kill her. While Freda was visiting Memphis in early 1892, Alice murdered her by cutting her throat with her father's straight razor. Of course, medical specialists rushed to study the case of "perverted passion," using it to back up their own theories and to conveniently link mental instability with lesbianism.

Texas

Beaumont

Babe Didrikson home
850 Doucette Avenue

This house in the south end of Beaumont was home to the young Mildred "Babe" Didrikson (1911–1956), one of the greatest athletes of all time. The Didriksons moved to Beaumont when Babe was a child, after a flood destroyed their Port Arthur home. As one biographer put it, Doucette Avenue was "full of rednecks and roughnecks, hard-knuckled families living in washboard poverty." The busy, noisy street had an oil refinery at one end and a trolley line running down the middle. Around the neighborhood, Babe wore boys' pants, overalls, and athletic undershirts. Her boyish manner made her a social outcast at school, but she later advised that "a girl that wants to become an athlete and do some winning should . . . start by being a tomboy."

And she was indeed an athlete who did "some winning." From 1930 to 1932, Babe held the American, Olympic, or world records in five different track and field events. After her stunning gold-medal victories at the Los Angeles Olympics in 1932, one newspaper headline declared, "Babe Breaks Records Easier Than Dishes." When she returned from her Olympic triumph, Babe's father built an apartment for her and her sister on the second floor of the Doucette Avenue house, consisting of two small rooms, a hallway, and a bathroom. Her sister called the bathroom "Babe's Hollywood bathroom . . . the most beautiful bathroom in Beaumont," complete with a bright green tub like one that she had seen and admired in Los Angeles.

Babe went on to excel in numerous sports, including softball, bowling, javelin throwing, boxing, billiards, tennis, and diving. But her greatest distinction by far was as a golfer. In 1935, she came under the protective wing of Bertha Bowen, a powerhouse in Texas golf, who not only helped her game but transformed her looks and physical demeanor as well. Babe—whose "masculine" appearance and competence in male sports had given rise to the suspicion that she was a lesbian—went from cross-dressing to cultivating a traditionally feminine look, including skirts, waved hair, rouge, and red nails; she even acquired a husband, the wrestler George Zaharias, in 1938. During her short career, the "ultimate Amazon" won eighty-two professional and amateur golf tournaments, was named Associated Press Woman of the Year six times, and was a founding member of the Ladies Professional Golf Association.

Also in town is the *Babe Didrikson Zaharias Memorial Museum, 1750 I-10 East*, a tiny octagonal building that documents her life and achievements, housing many of her athletic trophies. Don't be surprised when you can't find any reference to her lesbianism or to her intimate companion, the young golfer Betty Dodd, who is treated solely as a friend. Babe, Betty, and George all lived together in Florida from 1950 until Babe's death from colon cancer in 1956. Of Babe's husband, Betty later said, "We always had a lot more fun when he wasn't around" (*see* Tampa, Florida).

Babe is buried at the *Forest Lawn Memorial Park, 5220 Pine Street*, in Beaumont. The state of Texas maintains a historical marker at her gravesite.

BELTON

Sanctified Sisters commune
Central Hotel
Main Street
One hundred and forty miles south of Dallas is the small town of Belton. Here in 1866, Martha McWhirter and her followers, who called themselves the Sanctified Sisters, set up a successful feminist separatist commune for themselves that lasted for twenty-five years at this location. (They later moved north to Washington, D.C.) The women believed that

"God made man and woman equal, and to woman . . . he has revealed his will concerning his own elect few. We are to come out and be the 'peculiar people.'"

The Sisters built Belton's Central Hotel to support their community. The hotel had a simple interior, and the Sisters maintained a separate living area and entrance for themselves. When the hotel was crowded, they would double up and offer their own rooms to paying customers. Through their frugality and economic common sense, they amassed a fortune of more than two hundred thousand dollars during their stay in Belton. They branched out beyond the hotel, building houses, improving the land, and providing the major impetus for the development of the town. The Sanctified Sisters were a prototype of the separatist women's communities of the late twentieth century, though none of the 1970s experiments achieved the financial success or longevity of McWhirter's early commune.

DALLAS

Cathedral of Hope / MCC Dallas
3834 Ross Avenue

Founded in 1970 as MCC Dallas by a group of twelve friends, the Cathedral of Hope is today the largest gay congregation in the country. In 1972, the congregation moved into its first permanent home at this location on Ross Avenue. Growing by leaps and bounds, it was able to purchase its own building four years later at *2701 Reagan Street*, also home to Dallas's Gay and Lesbian Community Center (*see below*) and other gay organizations.

In 1990, MCC Dallas officially changed its name to the Cathedral of Hope. To accommodate its rapidly expanding membership, the Cathedral completed a new and dramatic church building in late 1992, located at *5910 Cedar Springs Road*. By its silver anniversary in 1995, the congregation was once again planning for its imminent growth, commissioning renowned architect Philip Johnson, a gay man, to design a new cathedral to be completed in the next millennium. From a dedicated group of a dozen gay people, the Cathedral of Hope has expanded to serve a congregation of three thousand.

Columbo's Restaurant
Mockingbird Lane and Greenville Avenue

The pizzeria is gone, but in 1970, this was the site of the historic meeting between lawyer Sarah Weddington and Norma McCorvey, in which McCorvey, who was pregnant, agreed to be the plaintiff "Jane Roe" of *Roe v. Wade*. McCorvey had already given birth to two children, wanted an abortion, but couldn't afford a safe illegal one. Weddington failed, however, to explain that the suit would take longer than McCorvey's pregnancy. Though McCorvey ultimately helped other women, the Supreme Court's legalization of abortion came several years after her own baby had been born.

In her 1994 autobiography, *I Am Roe*, McCorvey came out as a lesbian. The following year she reversed her pro-choice position, publicly declaring that she had been "born again" and was now working with the anti-choice Operation Rescue—"serving the Lord and helping women save babies."

Gay and Lesbian Community Center
2701 Reagan Street

One of the leading gay community centers in the country, the Dallas Center was started in 1984. The Center offers a community hot line and switchboard, a speakers' bureau, an adult education program, a welcome wagon, and an archives and research library. In addition, meeting space is available for local groups to rent.

EL PASO

John Rechy home
1225 Olive Street

Born in 1934, writer John Rechy's first home was at this address. Rechy's parents had fled Mexico during the purges of Pancho Villa and relocated in

Texas. Interested in journalism, Rechy studied at Texas Western and later at the New School for Social Research in New York. After a stint in the army and a few years of drifting and hustling, he wrote his most famous novel, the autobiographical *City of Night* (1963), while living once again in El Paso.

City of Night is now considered a classic of gay literature, though its focus is on sex rather than on identity. Rechy, in fact, does not like to be labeled a "gay writer."

> Nowhere else in the world . . . is there a sky as clear, as blue, as Deep as that.
>
> —John Rechy, *City of Night* (1963), writing about his home state of Texas

OTHER EARLY GAY COMMUNITY CENTERS STILL IN OPERATION IN THE SOUTH

Atlanta Gay Center (founded 1976)
71 Twelfth Street
Atlanta, Georgia

Gay and Lesbian Community Services of Central Florida (founded 1978)
714 East Colonial Drive
Orlando, Florida

The Oasis Gay, Lesbian and Bisexual Community Resource Center (founded 1982)
2135 NW 39th Street
Oklahoma City, Oklahoma

FORT WORTH

Patricia Highsmith home
508 Broadway

Born Patricia Plangman at this address, writer Patricia Highsmith (1921–1995) achieved fame with her first novel, *Strangers on a Train* (1949). Most of *Strangers* was written while she was in residence at Yaddo, the artists' colony, where Truman Capote had helped her gain admittance (*see* Saratoga Springs, New York). The sinister novel was translated into an equally sinister film by Alfred Hitchcock in 1951.

Her parents divorced early (her mother later remarried a man named Highsmith), and she never met her father until she was twelve years old. Her mother traveled extensively as an illustrator for *Women's Wear Daily*, and Highsmith was raised by her grandmother, who lived in Greenwich Village and who taught her to read at age two. By the time she was eight years old, Highsmith had read all of Sherlock Holmes. From age fifteen until her death, she religiously kept what she called "cahiers"—identical 7 x 8¼ notebooks—in which she wrote down dreams and story ideas. As a child, her two great ambitions were to live abroad and to write a book.

And she indeed did both. The sixty-eight hundred dollars Alfred Hitchcock paid her for the film rights to *Strangers* allowed her to move to Europe in the early 1950s, and, except for brief trips back to the States, she lived abroad the rest of her life. Her last years were spent in a small mountain village in Switzerland in a two-hundred-year-old farmhouse, living alone but with a coterie of friends nearby.

Highsmith is best remembered for her crime novels and psychological thrillers—including a series with the antihero Tom Ripley—in which she often explored the seemingly ordinary individual's potential to commit violent acts. "I write about somebody who is compelled to commit a crime," she said in 1988, "and the feelings of guilt or the absence of guilt."

But lesbians also know her as the author of *The Price of Salt* (1952)—originally titled *Carol*—a classic lesbian love story that she published under the pseudonym Claire Morgan. The novel detailed a passionate affair between a young department store salesclerk and a married woman and was a resounding best-seller, distinguished for being the first lesbian novel with a happy ending. Several years before her death, Highsmith finally permitted the novel to be published under her own name.

SAN ANTONIO

Hertzberg Circus Collection
210 West Market Street

Harry Hertzberg, who died in 1940, was a prominent local lawyer and state senator, whom recent research has revealed to be gay. Hertzberg and his longtime companion Tom Scaperlanda were circus fans who began collecting Big Top memorabilia in the 1920s and amassed one of the largest collections of that type in the country, totaling over twenty thousand individual items. The two left their collection to the city of San Antonio, where it is now on permanent exhibit at a museum called the Hertzberg Circus Collection, housed in a former public library. On exhibit are a miniature model of a three-ring circus, posters, costumes, literature, and specialty items, such as the 1843 carriage built for Tom Thumb. Hertzberg also had a passion for rare books and bequeathed his personal library of over ten thousand volumes to the San Antonio Public Library.

William Pahlmann home
2403 West Commerce Street

William Pahlmann (1900–1987) was a native San Antonian who went on to international fame as an interior designer. Growing up at this address, Pahlmann attended local schools before studying at the Parsons School of Design in New York. Head of the interior design department at the New York department store Lord & Taylor, he is considered the founder of the Eclectic School of interior design, for his integration of antiques into modern rooms.

In the service during World War II, as director of an army camouflage school in South Carolina, Pahlmann distinguished himself by redesigning the combat uniforms used in warfare. The camouflage design that we are familiar with today is attributed to Pahlmann. After the war, Pahlmann continued his interior design career, and his credits include the Ziegfeld Theater, the Overseas Press Club, the home of showman Billy Rose, and buildings at the University of South Carolina and Texas A&M. Today, the Pahlmann Research Library at the Texas A&M Architectural School contains his personal collection of books. Throughout his life, Pahlmann, a gay man, maintained homes in San Antonio and New York, where he lived with his life partner, Jack Conners.

San Antonio Country
1122 North St. Mary's

A parking lot and a small "wailing wall" are all that stand where there was once the biggest gay bar that the city—and perhaps the entire state—ever knew. Opened in 1973 by Gene Elder, San Antonio Country occupied a large stone house that had originally been the home of a local opera singer. The name of the bar commemorated an earlier, defunct gay bar located on Culebra Road outside of the city limits.

Harassment by city police and the state alcoholic beverage commission began almost immediately after the Country opened. With five major military bases in the city, military police, too, made frequent raids on the premises. When the bar was declared "off-limits" to military personnel, the gay community—inspired by the Stonewall Rebellion in New York a few years earlier—fought back, mounting a major legal defense against the military hierarchy that resulted in the withdrawal of the "off-limits" ban. After years of being victimized by military police, the gay community considered this its "Stonewall." Unfortunately, the Country was sold to another owner in 1980, who razed it to make way for a parking lot.

^   ^   ^

WEATHERFORD

Mary Martin home
414 West Lee Avenue

Stage and screen star Mary Martin (1913–1990) was born at this address—"a big rambling house," as Martin called it—to a father who was a lawyer and a mother who taught violin. Martin attended elementary school right up the hill from the house. The family later moved to *314 West Oak Street*. When Martin was an eighteen-year-old wife and mother, starving for meaningful work, her older sister encouraged her to open a dance school, and her supportive parents built her a studio at *No. 311*. There she ran the popular "Mary Hagman's School of Dance" for three years, serving several hundred students during that time.

While growing up in Weatherford, Martin was a tomboy who preferred "boxing gloves, punching bags, [and] bicycles" to the dolls her mother kept buying for her. An avid reader, she claimed to have read *The Well of Loneliness* at age eleven. (The novel, however, wasn't published in this country until 1928. She also claimed that she "didn't have the remotest idea what [it was] all about.") Married twice, the first time at age sixteen, Martin left her first husband and young son (the actor Larry Hagman) to pursue a career in Hollywood and on the stage. Her second husband, Richard Halliday, liked to shop for antiques with his mother and decorate their home and Martin's dressing rooms—you figure it out! Martin enjoyed a lifelong companionship with fellow actress Janet Gaynor, whom she called her "closest, most special friend" and who was in a lavender marriage with costume designer Adrian. Martin's intimate circle of friends included other queer theater couples, such as Katharine Cornell and Nancy Hamilton and Alfred Lunt and Lynn Fontanne.

One of the greatest Broadway musical stars of all time, Martin created the roles of Maria Von Trapp and Nellie Forbush on the stage but is probably best remembered for her portrayal of the boy who refused to grow up, Peter Pan. In the 1950s and 1960s, she flew into our living rooms in the televised version of the stage play, singing such classics as "Never-Neverland" and "I Won't Grow Up" and quickly becoming a lesbian icon. She epitomized the popular lesbian aesthetic of boyishness and resisted female cultural norms. In front of the Weatherford Public Library at *1214 Charles Street* is a statue of Peter Pan.

VIRGINIA

ARLINGTON

Benjamin Banneker Boundary Stone
Eighteenth and Van Buren Streets

Now a National Historic Landmark, this marker originally defined the southwest corner of the District of Columbia when astrologer and mathematician Benjamin Banneker (1731–1806) helped to site the capital's cornerstones in 1791 (*see also* Oella, Maryland, and District of Columbia). The district's southern boundary changed, however, in 1847, when part of the land Virginia had donated was returned to the state and the cornerstone was shifted slightly north.

Leonard Matlovich grave
Congressional Cemetery

Air Force Sergeant Leonard Matlovich's (1943–1988) tombstone reads "Never Again, Never Forget—A Gay Vietnam Veteran—When I was in the military they gave me a metal for killing two men and a discharge for loving one." Matlovich, who did three tours of duty in Vietnam and earned a Bronze Star, was discharged from the U.S. Air Force in 1975 when he publicly declared his homosexuality. After three years of fighting the decision, Matlovich won his case and was given the opportunity to be reinstated in the USAF or settle. He chose to settle and donated some of his money to lesbian and gay organizations, including the San Francisco Gay Men's Chorus. The rest he used to open a pizza parlor in Guerneville, the gay resort on the Russian River north of San Francisco, which he operated until illness made it impossible for him to work.

Matlovich succumbed to AIDS in 1988 and received a veteran's burial in Washington, D.C., complete with caisson, eight-member honor guard, a

USAF bugler playing taps, and an Arlington burial plot. But gay activists were his pallbearers, and his mourners carried lavender flags. "I've always been gay," Matlovich once said, "and for most of my life I prayed not to be that way. . . . However, the harder I prayed the queerer I got. That must have been God's response."

GORE

Willa Cather home
"Willowshade Farm"
Route 50W
Willa Cather (1873–1947) was born in Virginia, raised in Nebraska, and spent most of her adult life in New York City. The majority of her stories and novels are set in the Great Plains, and only one, *Sapphira and the Slave Girl* (1940), takes place in the region where she was born. Here in a small farming community near Winchester, young Willa spent the first nine years of her life. The town was at that time named Back Creek but was later renamed in honor of Willa's great-aunt, Sidney Cather Gore, a strong, independent widow who managed a farm after her husband's death, taught school, and became the local postmistress.

Willa was very close to her maternal grandmother, Rachel Boak, on whom she modeled "Old Mrs. Harris," in the short story by the same name, and the strong-willed Rachel Blake in *Sapphira*. Willa's grandmother lived with the family in both Virginia and Nebraska and was Willa's first teacher, teaching her to read and write and inspiring her love of books. She was also the unofficial town nurse, who, Cather later wrote, "served without recompense, from the mere love of it." Rachel Boak managed the Cather household at Willowshade, cooking and cleaning and performing other domestic duties.

In *Sapphira*, the most autobiographical of Cather's novels, the novelist wrote affectionately of the Willowshade kitchen as the "pleasantest room in the house—the most interesting. The parlor was a bit stiff when it was not full of company, but here everything was easy." Edith Lewis, Cather's life companion, later stated that Cather was deeply bereft at having to leave Back Creek, her "familiar earth," where her ancestors had farmed for generations. But the family made the decision to move west to a drier climate after one of the Cather children died of tuberculosis. Willa was distraught from homesickness her first few weeks in Nebraska. "I would not know how much a child's life is bound up in the woods and hills and meadows around it," she remembered in a 1913 interview, "if I had not been jerked away from all these and thrown out into a country as bare as a piece of sheet iron." (*See also* Red Cloud, Nebraska.)

RICHMOND

Pre-Stonewall hangouts

In an article in *Southern Exposure*, Bob Swisher identifies two white gay bars in Richmond in the segregated pre-Stonewall era. *Marroni's*, on the ground floor of the *Capitol Hotel*, opened in the years right after World War II, a small space where only whites were permitted. *Sepul's* opened in the early 1950s diagonally across the street from Marroni's and was also whites-only. Sepul's was run by a couple, Benny and Maria, who operated a straight restaurant called Sepulveda in front. The back room, equipped with booths and a jukebox, was reserved for gays, and dancing was permitted. But Benny and Maria allowed drag only on Halloween, demanding decorum from their gay clients. "If we sat in the front part [the restaurant]," one gay client recalled, "we had to behave ourselves."

After closing time at the bars, gay revelers would race to *Oriental Restaurant, Fifth and Grace Streets (SE corner)*, which, though not a gay space, became an ad hoc cruising place. One gay man remembered everyone making a dash for the booths that faced Grace Street, then hanging out the windows screaming at other gays on the street.

From the collection of the author

IV

MIDWEST

ILLINOIS

CALUMET CITY

Patch
201 155th Street
This is one of the oldest continuously operating lesbian bars in the country. Tocci, a local lesbian who left home at age seventeen, has owned gay bars in the Chicago area since 1963. Her earlier ventures were called the 307 Club and Tocci's Hideaway. She opened Patch in 1971, and it continues to attract women who grew up in the conservative region and still live there. "You could never have windows in a gay bar here," Tocci has noted, since the windows of one of her bars were broken years ago by a local homophobe. "It's hard to come out here."

Another lesbian bar from the early 1960s was called *The Club,* located at *706 State Line* in Calumet City. By 1968, its name had changed to *Our Place.*

CEDARVILLE

Jane Addams birthplace
425 North Mill Street
Social reformer Jane Addams (1860–1935) was born at this address into a comfortable, middle-class family, the daughter of a prosperous mill owner. In her autobiography, *Twenty Years at Hull-House* (1910), she described a peaceful and privileged childhood, where she rarely came face-to-face with the misfortune of others. But when she did, it left a lasting impression. At age seven, Addams later wrote, "I had my first sight of the poverty which implies squalor. . . . I remember launching at my father the pertinent inquiry why people lived in such horrid little houses so close together."

Addams's family wanted her to "come out" into society and marry according to her class, but she strenuously resisted. While attending Rockford Seminary, a private college for women, she met Ellen Starr, with whom she had her first serious relationship. Whenever they were apart, Addams placed Starr's picture "where I can see you almost every minute."

Addams went on to study medicine in Philadelphia, but ill health forced her to abandon her medical studies. It was on a trip to Europe with Starr in 1887 that she encountered the full-scale horrors of urban poverty and observed the workings of the experimental settlement house Toynbee Hall in London—an experience that would compel her to want to make a greater contribution to society. Addams decided to leave her family and its restricting ideas behind and move to Chicago with Starr to found their own settlement house, Hull-House (*see* Chicago, Illinois). "Let's love each other through thick and thin," Addams wrote to Starr, after they devised their plan, "and work out a salvation." It was, Addams noted, "the comfort of Miss Starr's companionship" that allowed her to embark on her grand experiment.

After her death in 1935, Addams was buried in a family plot about twelve hundred feet from the house where she was born, which is privately owned. Many historical items associated with Addams and her family are now housed at the *Stephenson County Historical Society, 1440 South Carroll Street*, in Freeport.

CHICAGO

Gay Horizons
3225 North Sheffield

Founded at this address, Gay Horizons has been Chicago's gay social service organization and community center since 1973 and is one of the oldest centers of this type in the country. Its major programs and services include a lesbian and gay help line, an antiviolence project with a twenty-four-hour crisis line, psychotherapy and counseling, a speakers' bureau, legal services, and support groups. Now called *Horizons Community*

Services and located at *961 West Montana Street*, the organization has grown exponentially over the years and currently has a staff of eighteen full-time people and six part-time. This first office of Gay Horizons was also the birthplace of the Gerber/Hart Library and Archives (*see next entry*).

Gerber/Hart Library and Archives
3225 North Sheffield

When it was founded in 1981, Chicago's gay and lesbian archives was first housed here, at the offices of Gay Horizons, the community's social service organization (*see previous entry*). Originally called the Midwest Gay and Lesbian Archive and Library, the organization changed its name after three months to honor two local activists—Henry Gerber (1892–1972), the guiding light behind the Society for Human Rights in the 1920s, and Pearl M. Hart (1890–1978), a pioneering civil rights attorney who defended gay rights throughout her life. The Chicago Gay and Lesbian History Project, headed by Gregory Sprague, was the force behind the establishment of the archives. In its first decade, Gerber/Hart resided in several locations before relocating to 3352 *North Paulina*, where it has been since 1991.

Since its founding, Gerber/Hart has been run entirely by volunteers, and most of the books and periodicals in the lending library have been donated by individuals. The archives house such items as handbills, posters, and buttons, as well as significant collections of research material. For example, the records of the Lesbian Community Center, which operated from the mid-1970s until 1983, and of the lesbian-run Metis Press, which folded in 1989, are located there.

Lorraine Hansberry home
5330 Calumet Avenue

The South Side of Chicago was the first home of playwright Lorraine Hansberry (1930–1965). Hansberry later described the black ghetto as having "scrubbed porches that sag and look their danger. Dirty gray wood steps. And always a line of white and pink clothes scrubbed so well, waving in the dirty wind of the city."

When Hansberry was a young child, her father, a prosperous businessman, moved his family to a middle-class white neighborhood of Chicago,
where their house was surrounded by an angry white mob and a brick was
thrown through the window. It was the difficulty of blacks seeking better
housing in traditionally white neighborhoods that Hansberry placed at the
center of her celebrated play *A Raisin in the Sun* (1959). *Raisin* was the
first play by an African-American woman to be produced on Broadway.

Hansberry was committed to the discussion of social injustice. After
college, she moved to New York City, where she worked for Paul Robeson's
journal, *Freedom*, and studied African history with W. E. B. Du Bois.
Hansberry also became an ardent feminist. Though she married Robert
Nemiroff in 1953, they separated amicably a few years later, when Hansberry began the process of coming out as a lesbian. A subscriber to the
early lesbian magazine *The Ladder*, she wrote several letters to the editor—
signed "L. H. N.," for Lorraine Hansberry Nemiroff—in 1957 in support
of lesbian rights and feminism.

Sadly, Hansberry died of cancer at the young age of thirty-four, with
plans for many more plays than she was able to write. Her contribution as
an African-American woman to literature is recognized at the *Lorraine
Hansberry branch, Chicago Public Library, 4314 South Cottage Grove
Avenue.*

I'm glad as heck that you exist. You are obviously serious people and I
feel that women, without wishing to foster any strict *separatist* notions,
homo or hetero, indeed have a need for their own publications and organizations. Our problems, our experiences as women are profoundly
unique as compared to the other half of the human race. . . . I feel that
THE LADDER is a fine, elementary step in a rewarding direction.
　　—extract from Lorraine Hansberry ["L. H. N."] letter to the editor,
The Ladder, May 1957

Hull-House
800 South Halstead Street

In 1889, Jane Addams and Ellen Gates Starr, intimate companions since their college days, founded one of the most famous social experiments in this country's history, Hull-House. It was their intention, Addams wrote later, "to rent a house in a part of the city where many primitive and actual needs are found, in which young women . . . might learn of life from life itself."

The house they located was built in 1856 for Charles Hull, a prominent Chicagoan. Addams described the building as "a fine old house standing well back from the street, surrounded on three sides by a broad piazza which was supported by wooden pillars of exceptionally pure Corinthian design and proportion." It stood, she noted with amusement, "between an undertaking establishment and a saloon." Though the house was being used for offices and storerooms for a neighboring factory, Addams and Starr were able to rent the second floor and a downstairs drawing room, and the following year, they obtained the lease on the entire building. They furnished it with "a few bits of family mahogany" and items from their travels abroad and officially took up residency at "Hull-House" in September 1889.

In an era when foreigners were feared and xenophobia was rampant, Addams, Starr, and the women who came to work with them offered immigrants (mainly Italians) education, medical care, guidance, and child-care facilities. Expanding to thirteen buildings over the years, Hull-House became a model for settlement houses across the country. It was also a training ground for numerous reformers, including Julia Lathrop and Florence Kelley.

Addams's biographers have generally ignored her personal life, assuming that she didn't have one because she wasn't attached to a man. Yet, though her intimacy with Ellen Starr had waned by the early 1890s, Addams shared a forty-year relationship with Mary Rozet Smith, who was one of the many idealistic young women from a wealthy background who came to work at Hull-House. Smith routinely accompanied Addams on her lecture tours, and Addams was always sure to wire ahead to the hotel where they were staying for a room with a big double bed.

Lesbian-feminist Chicago

During the 1970s and early 1980s, many major U.S. cities were equipped with a network of women-only spaces created by the lesbian-feminist movement to provide for women's social, political, health, and cultural needs. These were designed as alternatives to the bars, which were usually not women-owned or -operated. Examples of women-only spaces included community centers, coffeehouses and restaurants, bookstores, learning centers, art galleries, performance spaces, offices and meeting spaces, and archives. Such spaces provided lesbians with access to other lesbians and their ideas for the purposes of organizing at the grass-roots level, forming political ideology, and meeting friends and lovers. A few of the women's spaces in second-wave feminist Chicago included the following:

Blue Gargoyle Coffeehouse, 5655 South University: This ivy-covered building was host to the Third Annual Lesbian Writers Conference in 1976, attended by almost two hundred women. The conference included workshops, panels, readings, and musical performances. "In 1976," said one attendee, a lesbian-feminist editor, "speaking to women may be the ultimate political action."

Lesbian Community Center, 1226 West Grace: One of the first grass-roots women's centers in the city, the Lesbian Community Center opened in 1978 as a social center for lesbians. The center offered a hot line and newsletter, as well as support groups, cultural events, and parties. After years of struggle with its finances and a move to 3435 *North Sheffield*, the LCC closed its doors in 1983, leaving (as one patron put it) "a big hole in Chicago's lesbian life."

Lesbian Feminist Center, 3523 North Halsted: The ad for the center in the local lesbian newspaper *Lavender Women* proclaimed in no uncertain terms, "Women only!" Among the services sponsored by and housed at the center were a bookstore, the New Alexandria Library for Lesbianwomen, resources and referrals, and a monthly calendar of events.

Mama Peaches Restaurant, 3059 North Sheffield: This lesbian-owned vegetarian restaurant opened in 1976. It was here that planning for the creation of the *Lesbian Community Center (see above)* took place.

Metis Press, 825 West Wrightwood: Founded in 1976 by Arny Christine Straayer and Chris Johnson, Metis billed itself as "a printing and publishing collective" that sought to train lesbians in publishing. They were still publishing sporadically in the late 1980s. Some of their titles included *A Book of One's Own: A Guide to Self-Publishing; Hurtin' and Healin' and Talkin' It Over;* and *Bernice: A Comedy in Letters.*

Mountain Moving Coffeehouse, 1655 West School Street: Opened in 1975, this Saturday-night-only coffeehouse was run by a collective of lesbians who saw "the need for inexpensive entertainment and gathering space in an all-woman environment" and an alternative to the bars. The collective showed films of interest to lesbians and booked musical performers, charging one to three dollars for admittance. On opening night, a classical guitarist and harpsichord player entertained the women-only audience. In addition to entertainment, the coffeehouse served up baked goods, coffee, and teas to "womyn only and their children."

Little Review office
Fine Arts Building, Room 917
410 South Michigan Avenue

The *Little Review* was a monthly literary and art magazine founded at this office address by Margaret C. Anderson in 1914. She chose the Victorian-era Fine Arts Building because she considered it "one of the most delightful buildings in the world." At that time, the building was also a locus of Chicago's literary movement.

In 1914, Anderson was only in her early twenties and was working as a book reviewer and editor. Moving in Chicago's literary circles, she frequently attended the swank soirees of Floyd Dell, the literary editor of the *Chicago Evening Post.* At one of Dell's parties, Anderson met a man she referred to in her memoirs only as "Dick," whom she coaxed into financing an experimental and cutting-edge magazine, which she planned to edit.

"Practically everything the *Little Review* published during its first years," Anderson later wrote, "was material that would have been accepted by no other magazine in the world at the moment." Early contributors included Dell, Vachel Lindsay, William Butler Yeats, and Sherwood Anderson. The *Little Review* is perhaps best known for serializing James Joyce's *Ulysses* at a time when no one else would touch it.

Anderson was a lesbian, and one of her lovers, Jane Heap—whom Anderson called "the world's best talker"—worked with her on the *Little Review*. At the time, Heap was a schoolteacher who was living at 8 *St. James Place* in Chicago. After their relationship fizzled, Anderson moved to Paris, and Heap took over as editor of the *Little Review* until its demise in 1929. In Paris, Anderson met another lover, Georgette Leblanc, to whom she dedicated her memoirs, *My Thirty Years' War* (1930). She was also briefly involved with Solita Solano, lover of Janet Flanner.

Recently, Mathilda Hills, a professor of English, discovered Margaret Anderson's unpublished lesbian novel, *Forbidden Fires*, after years of trying to track it down. The novel was finally published in 1996 by Naiad Press, with an introduction by Hills describing her detective work in the United States and in Europe.

Maxine's
79th and Langley Streets

Maxine's was a pre-Stonewall gay bar that served a mostly lesbian clientele. It was located on the site of an earlier lesbian bar of a different name. Patrons from the mid-1960s remember that loud music blasted from the jukebox and that no dancing was allowed. Early in 1968, Maxine's was raided by the police, and everyone present at the time was taken into custody. Owner Maxine—who wasn't on-site—personally made bail for all of her employees and customers.

Public homosexuality

Beginning in the early 1900s, *Washington Square (or Bughouse Square)*, the city's oldest park, located near the wealthy Gold Coast district, was a

OTHER CHICAGO LESBIAN BARS FROM THE MID-1960s

Front Page Lounge
Chicagoan Hotel
530 North Rush Street

Lost and Found
2959 West Irving Park

popular male cruising area, particularly for trade in search of gay sex. As a member of the vice squad reported after a sweep of the park, "These guys [trade] tell their wives they're just going down to the corner for the evening paper. Why, they even come down here in their slippers!"

In the lakefront area, *Grant Park* was a spot where, in 1925, the director of the Juvenile Protection Agency of Chicago noted that a group of homosexual men and boys had "their headquarters . . . publishing a paper of their own, using a vocabulary which no one outside the group could easily understand."

In the 1920s, lesbians had several areas of the city that they frequented, primarily the furnished room districts. One of Ma Rainey's queer songs of the early 1920s claimed that *State Street* on the South Side of Chicago was a lesbian domain (*see box*). Box-Car Bertha, who wrote an autobiography, *Sister of the Road*, about her experiences as a hobo during the 1920s, reported that "several tea shops and bootleg joints on the near north side . . . catered to lesbians" (no locations given).

Goin' down to spread the news
State Street women wearing brogan shoes. . . .
There's one thing I don't understand
Some women walkin' State Street like a man.

—Ma Rainey, 1924

Society for Human Rights
1710 Crilly Court

In December 1924, at a cost of ten dollars, the Society for Human Rights incorporated as a not-for-profit organization, listing its business office at this address (which was the home of its secretary, Henry Gerber, and Henry Teacutter, one of its trustees). In doing so, it went into history as the first homosexual rights organization in the United States. The objective the Society stated in its charter, however, was so fraught with code words that the state clerk who filed the papers could not have suspected what the organization's real purpose was (*see box below*).

Henry Gerber, one of the leading forces behind the Society, had been to Germany as part of the Army of Occupation after World War I, and he had seen the early homosexual rights movement there firsthand. Gerber's dream was to initiate a homosexual emancipation movement in this country, and he drafted a Declaration of Purpose for a new organization, which borrowed its name from a German counterpart. Through lectures and publications, Gerber and his colleagues hoped to educate legislators and law enforcement officials about the "problem" of homosexuality and the "folly" of prison terms for sex offenders.

The Society published two mimeographed issues of *Friendship and Freedom*, written by Gerber, before having to give up the endeavor for lack of money. "The most difficult task," Gerber later wrote, "was to get men of good reputation to back up the Society." Fear of recrimination by the authorities kept many from donating funds or placing their names on the Society's mailing list. Finally, the organization was forced to disband after less than a year, when one member's wife reported the group to a social worker, who in turn notified the police. Gerber and two of his colleagues were arrested; the police confiscated Gerber's typewriter, diaries, notary public diploma, and all the literature of the Society. The judge who heard the case dismissed the charges when it was discovered that the police had not obtained warrants for the arrests, and Gerber and the others went free. But after the scandal was reported in the local newspaper, Gerber was dismissed from his post office job.

Gerber continued fighting for homosexual rights throughout his life. In 1932, he published an essay pseudonymously called "In Defense of Homosexuality" in a journal called *The Modern Thinker.* Two years later, Gerber was listed as circulation manager of a literary magazine called *Chanticleer,* for which he wrote a dozen articles and reviews on the subject of homosexuality under his own name. His concise history of the Society for Human Rights appeared in *ONE* magazine in 1962. Today, the lesbian and gay archives of Chicago, founded in 1981, is called the Gerber/Hart Library and Archives in the gay rights pioneer's honor.

The object for which it is formed is to promote and to protect the interests of people who by reasons of *mental and physical abnormalities* are abused and hindered in the legal pursuit of happiness which is guaranteed by the Declaration of Independence, and to combat the public prejudices against them by dissemination of facts according to *modern science* among *intellectuals of mature age.* The Society stands only for law and order; it is in harmony with any and all general laws insofar as they protect the rights of others, and does in no manner recommend any acts in violation of present laws nor advocate any matter inimical to the public welfare.

—from the charter of the Society for
Human Rights, 1924 [*emphasis added*]

EVANSTON

Frances Willard home
"Rest Cottage"
1730 Chicago Avenue
Frances Willard (1839–1898) left her hometown in Wisconsin to attend Evanston College for Ladies (*see* Janesville, Wisconsin). After a teaching career at various women's colleges, she became president of her alma mater in 1871 and then dean of women at Northwestern University when

the schools merged two years later. In 1874, with the founding of the Women's Christian Temperance Union, Willard resigned her post at the university to become the WCTU's corresponding secretary. Five years later, as WCTU president, Willard led a national movement for "Home Protection." Her temperance campaign was a direct reaction against the violence (both physical and emotional) perpetrated on women and children by alcohol-abusing men, and it eventually led to the enactment of prohibition in 1919.

In her autobiography, *Glimpses of Fifty Years*, Willard included a chapter titled "Companionships." In it, she outlined her passionate relationships with women over the years, including one in Evanston with "Mary B., for whom my attachment was so great that when she very properly preferred my brother . . . the loss of her was nothing less than a bereavement, a piteous sorrow for a year and more, as my journals testify, one of the keenest of my life." She referred to her relationships with women as "attachments, so much less restful than friendships."

For thirty-three years, Willard's "live-in private secretary" was Anna Gordon, also a devoted temperance worker. Willard called Gordon "the rarest of intimate friends" and by the pet name "Little Heart's-ease."

ASIDE-STEP

In 1837, the young lawyer Abraham Lincoln rode into Springfield, Illinois, looking for a place to stay, and inquired at Joshua Speed's general store about lodgings. Speed quickly offered, "I have a very large room and a very large double bed in it, which you are perfectly welcome to share with me if you choose." Lincoln took his saddlebags upstairs—and stayed four years! The romantic friendship ended when Speed returned to his hometown of Louisville, Kentucky, to settle his father's estate and was pressured by family members into marriage. When Speed left Springfield, Lincoln pronounced himself "the most miserable man living."

Gordon stayed on in the house they shared after Willard's death, becoming president of WCTU herself in 1914.

Willard and Gordon's restored home in Evanston is open to the public, appearing much as it did when they lived there. On exhibit are many memorabilia of Willard's years as a temperance warrior.

WINNETKA

Rock Hudson home
719 Center Street

For much of his early childhood, Roy Scherer, Jr. (better known as Rock Hudson, 1925–1985) lived at this address with an extended family of six adults and five children. The house, which had only one bedroom, belonged to his maternal grandparents, who slept on the sunporch. Young Roy occupied the bedroom with his parents, and an uncle and his family lived in the converted attic. With no privacy, Roy learned early on how to hide his sexual orientation, of which he claimed to be conscious at age nine. He became even more conscious of it when he left Winnetka at age eighteen to enlist in the navy. (*See also* Los Angeles, California.)

INDIANA

BLOOMINGTON

Kinsey Institute
Indiana University
Alfred C. Kinsey (1894–1956), a professor of biology at Indiana University, initiated the now legendary Kinsey Report because his students were inundating him with questions about sex and sexuality. "They came to him," the official report explained, "because they hoped that he as a scientist would provide factual information which they might consider in working out their patterns of sexual behavior."

With the support of the university, the staff of the Institute for Sex Research (the Kinsey Institute) undertook a massive study of human sexuality beginning in 1938. Their initial report, "Sexual Behavior in the Human Male," was published in 1948 and followed in 1953 by "Sexual Behavior in the Human Female." Kinsey's researchers established a simple numerical scale from 1 to 6 to classify sexual behavior, with "1" indicating exclusive heterosexuality and "6" exclusive homosexuality.

Based on a survey of approximately eight thousand men, the Kinsey Report knocked everyone's socks off with its finding that one in ten identified as exclusively homosexual, a percentage that continues to be contested today by conservative researchers. Even more "shocking" was Kinsey's assertion that over one-third of the men surveyed had had at least one adult same-sex experience and that fully half admitted having erotic responses to other men. The figures for women were slightly lower but carried the same wallop.

Though not intended as such, the Kinsey Report—both studies were instant best-sellers—was a milestone in gay and lesbian history. For gay people, it gave scientific credence to the idea that "we are everywhere," and for Americans in general, it paved the way for a more open discussion of human sexual desire.

FAIRMOUNT

James Dean childhood home
Winslow farm
7184 South 150th Road East
After his mother's death in 1940 (*see* Santa Monica, California), young James Dean (1931–1955) was sent back to his native Indiana by his father to be raised by relatives. From age nine until he graduated from high school, young Jimmy Dean lived on the Winslow farm with an aunt and uncle whom he soon came to call Mom and Dad. The house, a thirteen-room frame farmhouse with an L-shaped front porch, dates from 1904 and is still standing. There was a nearby barn and pond where people fished in summer and skated in winter.

Jimmy went to local public schools, and at Fairmount High in the 1940s he became active in the school's dramatic productions. It was in high school that he also developed his passion for motorcycles and for driving as fast as he could. By age sixteen, Jimmy had already had several affairs with older men—one a minister with a penchant for teenage boys.

Dean left Indiana in 1949 for southern California and an acting career. Over the next six years in Hollywood and New York, he established himself as one of the leading young actors of his day, the embodiment of angry youth—the "rebel without a cause." According to his biographer, Paul Alexander, Dean's primary sexual relationships were with men, though his name was linked romantically with many of the most glamorous actresses in Hollywood in the early 1950s. His life was cut short in an automobile accident on September 30, 1955.

At the *Fairmount Historical Society, 203 East Washington*, the James Dean Room commemorates the life of the town's most famous resident. On exhibit are Dean's first motorcycle, a gift from his uncle when he was fifteen years old; the boots he wore in *Giant*; his baseball and basketball letter sweaters from high school; and, gruesomely, a replica of the Porsche he was driving when he was killed. Also on display is his 1949 high school yearbook photo. (*See also* Marion, Indiana.)

James Dean grave
Park Cemetery
County Road 150E

James Dean (1931–1955) was buried in his hometown at Park Cemetery (along with other Deans, including his great-great-grandfather) after his fatal car crash in California. Three thousand people attended his funeral. His gravestone is simply engraved with his name and dates (it was stolen briefly in 1987 as a prank but recovered near a dumpster in Fort Wayne). Every year on the anniversary of Dean's death, fans gather for a three-day celebration of his short, fast life and career, which is called Museum Days/Remembering James Dean. The event includes a parade, a lookalike contest, a screening of Dean's three movies, and a memorial service at Park Cemetery. As many as thirty thousand people have attended in recent years.

INDIANAPOLIS

Janet Flanner birthplace
952 North Delaware

In a fashionable neighborhood of large houses and wide avenues, journalist and novelist Janet Flanner (1892–1978) was born into a solidly middle-class family. Her father was a mortician, who co-owned a funeral home, ambulance service, and the state's only crematorium; her mother was a published poet and producer of amateur theatricals. Though his family was embarrassed by his profession, Frank Flanner's social position in Indianapolis was suggested by a notice in a local newspaper: "A newcomer to our fair city asked what she might do to become adjusted socially and correctly in our city. The reply was join the Riviera Club, send your children to Mrs. Gates' Dancing School, and be buried by Flanner and Buchanan."

Sadly, when Janet was twenty years old, her father poisoned himself in his own mortuary. The scandal rocked Indianapolis, and gossip-mongers blamed everyone from his wife to his business partner to his mother. In her novel *The Cubicle City* (1926), Janet Flanner based the idealistic, yet suicidal, real estate broker, James Poole, on her own father.

Flanner became a journalist after a brief stint at the University of Chicago. After a few years in New York mingling with the literati and married to a man she didn't love (*see* New York City, New York), Flanner spent most of her adult life abroad, following her first love, journalist Solita Solano, there in 1921. The two women settled in Paris, becoming part of the American artists' community. Flanner was a regular at Natalie Barney's salon, and she and Solano were so well known among expatriate lesbians that they appeared as "Nip and Tuck" in Djuna Barnes's lesbian roman à clef, *Ladies Almanack*.

Flanner is perhaps best remembered for the column "Letter from Paris" on French culture and personalities, which she wrote for *The New Yorker* from 1925 to 1975. As her pen name, *New Yorker* publisher Harold Ross suggested "Genet," possibly a Gallicized "Janet." The best of her letters were later collected in the volume *Paris Was Yesterday* (1972).

MARION

James Dean birthplace
South McClure and East Fourth Streets (southwest corner)
Now a parking lot, this was once an apartment building called the Seven Gables, and one of its cramped apartments was the first home of actor and pop icon James Dean (1931–1955). Shortly after his birth, Dean's parents moved to nearby Fairmount (*see above*), where the family changed addresses several times over the next year, mostly living with Dean relatives. For three generations, the Dean family had lived and farmed in Grant County.

Dean's mother, Mildred, encouraged a love of the arts in her young son, Jimmy, and early on enrolled him in dance classes at the *Marion College of*

Dance and Theatre Arts on East Third Street. But young Jimmy's lessons were cut short when his father, a dental technician, got a job offer in Los Angeles that he couldn't refuse. (*See also* Santa Monica, California.)

PERU

Cole Porter grave
Mt. Hope Cemetery
He lived at elegant addresses in Manhattan, Beverly Hills, and the Berkshires, but Cole Porter (1891–1964) chose to be buried in his hometown of Peru. At the nearby Marion Conservatory of Music, young Cole first studied violin and piano and performed at recitals dressed like Little Lord Fauntleroy in a velvet suit with lace cuffs. Though his biographer claims Porter was "no prodigy," he played with a vigor and zest that stole the show. (*See also* Los Angeles, California; New Haven, Connecticut; and Williamstown, Massachusetts.)

IOWA

CHARLES CITY

Carrie Chapman Catt house
2397 Timber Avenue

Born in Wisconsin, Carrie (Lane) Chapman Catt's (1859–1947) family moved to Iowa after the Civil War, when Carrie was only seven years old. Originally from the East, Carrie's mother had disliked the desolation of rural Wisconsin, though it is hard to imagine that Charles City (with a population at that time of only five hundred) was much less isolated. Still, the town at least had a railroad station, and the Lanes built themselves an urban-style brick house instead of a clapboard farmhouse. Carrie attended the local one-room school, where, as one of the brightest and most responsible students, she often helped the teacher attend to the younger pupils.

Her teaching skills paid off later. Carrie's father, who owned a modest farm, could afford to pay only twenty-five dollars a year toward the college education of his daughter (and he also believed it a "waste" to educate girls). Carrie earned the rest of her tuition and board at Iowa State Agricultural College (now Iowa State University in Ames) by washing dishes, working in the college library, and teaching school during summers and other breaks. (Today, the Carrie Chapman Catt Center for Women and Politics at Iowa State is named for the school's distinguished alumna.) A teaching offer after her graduation in 1880 brought her to Mason City, a prairie town, where she met her first husband, Leo Chapman, with whom she shared the editorship of a local newspaper.

Carrie married twice (and was widowed twice), and both husbands were men with strong feminist beliefs. Her second husband, George Catt, a successful engineer, encouraged her to develop her public speaking skills on the lecture circuit and funded her reform and suffrage work. Carrie began her participation in the suffrage movement as a local organizer in Floyd County, Iowa (where Charles City is located), but her leadership abilities eventually took her all the way to the presidency of the National American Woman Suffrage Association. Her hectic schedule of speaking on behalf of votes for women meant that she and George rarely lived together, and her constant companion was one of her suffrage "lieutenants," Mary Garrett (Molly) Hay. When George died, Catt immediately began cohabiting with Hay, who remained her intimate companion for the next twenty-three years. (*See also* The Bronx, New York, and New Rochelle, New York.)

DAVENPORT

Alice French house
321 East 10th Street
Alice French (1850–1934) was a popular and highly paid writer at the turn of the twentieth century, but today she is virtually unknown. In fact, her only biography is titled *Journey to Obscurity.* She published under two pseudonyms, using Frances Essex for her early stories and essays and the androgynous Octave Thanet for her novels. A regionalist, French's fiction was highly descriptive of the two areas she knew best—Iowa, where she was raised and lived most of her life, and Arkansas, where the successful writer "wintered" with her life partner, Jane Crawford (*see* Clover Bend, Arkansas).

French and Crawford met when the two were young girls in Davenport. Jane left town to be married, much to French's dismay, but she returned a few years later after her husband's mysterious death. The two women proceeded to spend their lives together, living most of the year in this comfortable residence, which has now been converted to apartments. Due to her great financial success, French was able to write full-time, while Jane managed the house and nurtured her partner. They remained inseparable until French's death in 1934.

Kansas

Independence

William Inge Collection
Independence Community College
College Boulevard
Included in this collection are books, tapes, and records from the private cache of playwright William Inge (1913–1973). Inge is best known for four successful Broadway plays that were subsequently made into successful films—*Come Back, Little Sheba* (1950), *Picnic* (1953—winner of the Pulitzer Prize), *Bus Stop* (1955), and *The Dark at the Top of the Stairs* (1957). Also a screenwriter, Inge won an Academy Award in 1961 for the original script of *Splendor in the Grass*.

Inge was born and raised in Kansas, and all of his plays took that state as their setting. His work often focused on the repressed sexuality and stultifying social norms that he must have experienced in his own life. A closeted gay man and an abuser of alcohol, Inge included characters who were gay stereotypes in a few of his lesser-known plays, written in the 1960s after his success had faded. His one-act "The Boy in the Basement" dealt with a man's discovery of his homosexuality and was Inge's only play to address the topic in a direct manner. Sadly, Inge's inner demons led him to suicide in 1973.

^   ^   ^

LAWRENCE

Langston Hughes home
732 Alabama Street

Langston Hughes statue
Elizabeth Watkins Community Museum
1047 Massachusetts Street

Poet Langston Hughes (1902–1967) was born in Joplin, Missouri, but his earliest memories were of living at his grandmother's house in Lawrence after his parents' marriage fell apart. One of Lawrence's most celebrated residents, a statue of Hughes at age thirteen stands in a local museum. Hughes spent most of his childhood in his grandmother's simple two-bedroom house with a wood shed and outhouse in the back, plus a pump for water. Occasionally, his grandmother rented out a room to make money, and sometimes she rented out the entire house, moving herself and Langston to the home of friends James and Mary Reed, who lived at *731 New York Street.* Later, Langston remembered "the mortgage man . . . always came worrying my grandmother for the interest due."

Langston endured a solitary boyhood in a mostly white Lawrence neighborhood; he did not play with many other children and felt his loneliness like "a dull ache." One of his favorite pastimes was visiting the morgue at the nearby University of Kansas, where he sneaked in and watched, fascinated, as students worked on cadavers. Langston attended predominantly white schools, and though he rarely studied, he was always near the top of his class.

Langston's grandmother died in 1915, and he lived briefly with the Reeds. When his mother remarried, he moved with her to Lincoln, Illinois, where her new husband had secured work. It was in Lincoln, Langston later said, that he first started writing poems and was chosen class poet in eighth grade, where he was again one of only a few black students. "My classmates," he recalled, "knowing that a poem had to have rhythm, elected me unanimously—thinking, no doubt, that I had some, being a Negro." (*See also* Cleveland, Ohio, and New York City, New York.)

MICHIGAN

ASHTON

Anna Howard Shaw Monument
Frayer Halladay Park

Born in England, suffragist Anna Howard Shaw (1847–1919) came to Michigan with her family in 1859 and grew up in the town of Paris in a log cabin built by her father. In her autobiography, *Story of a Pioneer*, Shaw described the crudely made house as "achingly forlorn and desolate." At that time she was simply Anna Shaw; she added the "Howard" when she entered public life and faced prejudice as an unmarried woman.

Anna began teaching at a frontier school in 1862, at the tender age of fifteen. But it was after hearing a woman preach in nearby Big Rapids (*see below*) that she became determined to be a minister. She preached her first sermon in Ashton in 1870, and a stone monument at this location marks the spot where she preached. Shaw was officially licensed to preach the following year.

Shaw went on to study theology and was ordained by the Methodist Church in 1880, the first woman ever to do so. An ambitious go-getter, she also earned a medical degree at Boston University. Shaw was an ardent social reformer who worked first in the temperance movement and then for women's suffrage, tirelessly delivering about ten thousand speeches in her lifetime. Though dedicated to her career and to the cause of women's rights, she lived with and shared her life with a partner, Lucy Anthony, the niece of the great suffragist Susan B. (*See also* Moylan, Pennsylvania.)

BAY CITY

Madonna's birthplace
Mercy Hospital
100 Fifteenth Street

The "Material Girl," a gay and lesbian icon for over a decade, was born Madonna Ciccone at this location in 1958 (the site is now Bradley Retirement Home). Her mother died when Madonna was small, and she and her five siblings were raised by their father. Madonna dropped out of the University of Michigan after two years and moved to New York City to pursue a career in dance, her first love.

Though teasingly ambiguous about her own sexuality—remember when she crashed the Cubbyhole, a New York lesbian bar, posing as lovers with pal Sandra Bernhard?—Madonna's public relationships have all been with men. Still, she has been a vocal supporter of gay rights and of AIDS charities; her brother/manager, Christopher, is openly gay. From a queer standpoint, Madonna is also enormously quotable; one of my personal favorites is, "Every straight guy should have a man's tongue in his mouth at least once."

BIG RAPIDS

Anna Howard Shaw statue
Corner of Michigan and Oak Streets

There are several monuments to Michigan suffragist and minister Anna Howard Shaw (1847–1919) in this town, because it was here that she heard a sermon delivered by a woman, which convinced her to study to be a minister. In addition to this statue, a marker at the Big Rapids Intermediate School calls Shaw a "World Citizen" and praises her for cutting "a path through tangled underwood of old traditions out to broader ways." (*See also* Ashton, Michigan, and Moylan, Pennsylvania.)

^ ^ ^

LANSING

Michigan Women's Historical Center Hall of Fame
213 West Main Street
On permanent display here are tributes to some of Michigan's heaviest female hitters. Included is Anna Howard Shaw (1847–1919), suffrage leader, orator, and minister, who grew up in a log cabin in Paris, Michigan, and first preached in Ashton. Shaw was inducted in 1983. (*See also* Ashton, Michigan, and Big Rapids, Michigan, and Moylan, Pennsylvania.)

MT. PLEASANT

We Want the Music Collective
1501 Lyons Street
First located at this address, WWTMC still runs the herstoric Michigan Womyn's Music Festival, which has taken place each August since 1976 on one hundred and sixty wooded acres of women-owned land in *Hesperia*. The philosophy behind the outdoor music festival continues to be "the creation and affirmation of women's space." At the first festival, over a thousand women enjoyed performances by Maxine Feldman, New Harmony Sisterhood Band, Margy Adam, Holly Near, Teresa Trull, Linda Tillory, and Meg Christian. One visitor recalled that the first festival was embued with "a sense of beauty and strength that comes from being in a total womon environment." For a generation of dykes, "going to Michigan" was a rite of passage.

Over the years, the festival has come under attack for the strident politics of its organizers and attendees. In the 1980s, women with small boy children were hounded away from the site by radical separatist campers who called the boys "baby pricks." Even more recently, festival staff have sought to exclude transgendered people from the festival, limiting attendance to "womyn-born womyn." (Hmm—do they ask for a birth certificate at the gate?) In response, "Camp Trans" was established in spontaneous protest in 1993 across from the main festival gate by a handful of transsexual women ("humyn-born humyns"), who were later joined by about two hundred supporters.

ASIDE-STEP

Novelist Isabel Miller (born Alma Routsong, 1924–1996) was originally from Traverse City, Michigan. Miller's most famous book is the historical novel *Patience and Sarah* (originally titled *A Place for Us*), one of the first lesbian-themed novels to be published by a mainstream house. *Patience and Sarah* is based on the story of Miss Willson and Miss Brundage, two lesbians who made a home together in upstate New York in the early nineteenth century. (*See also* Greenville, New York.)

MINNESOTA

GRAND RAPIDS

Judy Garland home
727 Second Avenue, NE
This house in Grand Rapids was the birthplace of Frances Gumm/Judy
Garland (1922–1969), the singer/actor/dancer who was every drag queen's
dream and whose death has occasionally been credited with setting the
flame that ignited the Stonewall Rebellion. Garland's father was reportedly
gay, as was her second husband, director Vincente Minnelli, and there
have been rumors about her own membership in the club.

The Gumms owned the *New Grand Theater* on Pokagama Avenue in
Grand Rapids in the 1920s. Baby Gumm gave her first public performance
there at age two, singing "Jingle Bells" with her two older sisters. When
she was four, her parents moved the family to California to pursue their
show business ambitions—and also apparently to escape the rumors of
Frank Gumm's sexual inclinations.

Judy's best-loved and -remembered role is undoubtedly as Dorothy
Gale in the 1939 classic musical *The Wizard of Oz*. Every June since 1975,
Grand Rapids has celebrated its most famous resident with a Judy Garland
Festival, complete with bands and floats. In 1989, the fiftieth anniversary
of the movie, the town dedicated its very own Yellow Brick Road, a path-
way of five thousand bricks, about one-fifth of which have been engraved
with personal messages (at an average cost of about fifty dollars per brick).

The Yellow Brick Road leads to the *Central School, 10 Fifth Street, NW*,
an 1895 structure that is home to the Itasca County Historical Society.
What is billed as "the world's largest Judy Garland collection" is on exhibit
there, including family items and photographs and plenty of *Wizard of Oz*
memorabilia.

MINNEAPOLIS / ST. PAUL

Amazon Bookstore
1612 Harmon Place
Founded in 1970, Amazon was one of the first lesbian-feminist bookstores
to open in the United States, and it is amazingly still going strong when so
many others have failed. It remains a center of the local lesbian community
and the best place to find out about cultural events of interest to women.

Quatrefoil Library
1619 Dayton Avenue, #105-107
Quatrefoil Library, a lending library of books and materials related to sexual minorities, takes its name from the 1951 novel by James Barr, *Quatrefoil,* which was one of the first to depict gay characters positively. In the
mid-1970s, David Irwin and his partner, Dick Hewetson, each began collecting gay books. When they moved in together in 1977, they combined
their collections and kept them in the linen closet of their condo, which
was soon overflowing with volumes. The two men incorporated their
holdings as Quatrefoil Library in 1983. Though their relationship ended
the following year, their important collection of gay literature was able to
live on.

The library grew exponentially during its first years and found much-
needed space at this address, a former school renovated to house the offices of various organizations. Relocating to its new quarters in 1987—"a
cozy set of rooms," according to one reporter—Quatrefoil boasted a collection of over four thousand volumes and three hundred periodicals. Today,
Quatrefoil collects not only books and magazines, but memorabilia, audio-
and videotapes, games, newspaper clippings, and historical erotica relating
to sexual minorities dating back to the 1950s. Quatrefoil exists, according
to the board chair, because, even though "the public library is starting to
have more material like this . . . it's still not a comfortable place." At a cel-
ebratory event in 1991, *Quatrefoil's* author, James Barr, was the library's
special guest.

310 East 38th Street

The building at this location has been an ad hoc gay community center since the 1980s. Located here are the offices of *Equal Times* (Room 207), the area's gay and lesbian newspaper, and the Gay and Lesbian Community Action Council (Room 204), which, among other things, operates a gay switchboard and referral service.

Missouri

St. Louis

Josephine Baker homes
1526 and 1534 Gratiot Street

The child who would become Josephine Baker (1906–1975), the toast of the Folies Bergère, was born in the Female Hospital of St. Louis. Her mother was an unmarried twenty-year-old who never revealed her child's father's identity. Young Josephine's first home was a third-floor railroad flat at 1534 Gratiot, the apartment of her maternal grandparents, who had been born in slavery.

When Josephine was four years old, her mother married, and the new family moved a few houses down the street to No. 1526. There in 1910 a three-room apartment with a stable rented for $6.50 a month. From the apartment on Gratiot, the stagestruck Josephine often went to the *Booker Washington Theater, 23rd and Market Streets*, for a vaudeville show and the movies. So enamored was she of the theater that she even played hooky to go to the Booker, where ushers and performers sheltered her from the school truant officer. Sometimes she performed on the cobblestone street in front of the theater for people passing by.

Married twice (the first time at the tender age of thirteen), Josephine took the name "Baker" from her second husband. But it was Clara Smith—a singer with the Russell-Owens Company, a traveling vaudeville troupe that often performed at the Booker—who got Josephine her start in the business. Clara, who was advertised as the South's "favorite coon shouter," mentored Josephine, taking her on as both protégée and lover, and convinced the head of the company to hire her.

From small-town vaudeville, Josephine eventually went on to New York City, where she costarred with Florence Mills in Eubie Blake's *Shuffle*

Along. Spotted by Caroline Reagan, a producer, the nineteen-year-old Josephine was given her big break, which she jumped at—the chance to headline Reagan's "La Revue Nègre" in Paris. Within a year, Josephine had achieved such phenomenal success in Paris that she was able to open her own nightclub. Josephine never lived in the United States again and in 1937 became a naturalized French citizen.

William S. Burroughs home
4664 Pershing Avenue

In 1914, author William S. Burroughs was born on this quiet, tree-lined street. The large, three-story, red-brick house belonging to his family is still standing. Burroughs was named for his paternal grandfather, who, in 1885, invented the adding machine and amassed a small fortune.

Young Burroughs began writing at age eight, and his first effort was a ten-page "novel" entitled "The Autobiography of a Wolf." From that time on, he wanted to be a writer, and he penned everything from westerns to adventure to horror. As a teenager, he became obsessed with true crime and began writing his own gangster stories.

In his teens he also first experimented with drugs and formed a romantic attachment with another boy at his boarding school. Drug addiction and homosexuality would also become the primary themes of his fiction. Living off a monthly stipend from his parents, he became addicted to heroin in the mid-1940s in New York, where he and pals Jack Kerouac and Allen Ginsberg formed the core of the Beat Generation. Burroughs was arrested for possession of narcotics and tried to start a new, clean life as a cotton farmer in Texas. But he was on and off junk and in and out of rehab, and when he was arrested a second time, he and his wife, Joan, decided to relocate once again, this time to Mexico. There, in 1951, he accidentally shot and killed Joan during a drunken imitation of William Tell. He lived much of the rest of his life in self-imposed exile in Europe and Tangier.

Burroughs later claimed that his wife's tragic death "motivated and formulated" his writing, but Kerouac and Ginsberg—who considered him a genius—were instrumental in spurring him on. Ginsberg (Burroughs's occasional fuck-buddy) helped get his first novel, *Junkie* (1953), a confessional account of his recurring battle with addiction, published. Burroughs's most famous novel was *Naked Lunch* (1959), a title suggested by Kerouac. *Naked Lunch* was a surrealistic account of an addict's life, which was banned in Boston and was at the center of a famous censorship trial. In all of his work, Burroughs drew on the genres that had fascinated him as a child writer in St. Louis—detective fiction, westerns, thrillers, sci-fi—and transformed them, creating his own distinctive and subversive brand of literature.

Harriet Hosmer home
34 Eighth Street

Originally from Watertown, Massachusetts, Harriet Hosmer (1830–1908) applied to study anatomy—as preparation for sculpting the human body—at Boston Medical School and other eastern schools and was refused admittance. Wayman Crow, the father of one of her school friends, got her into the Missouri Medical College in St. Louis, and Hosmer lived with his family at this address while she was a student. Crow, a prominent St. Louis businessman, became a lifelong benefactor of Hosmer, and his influence helped obtain important commissions for her. Among her public sculptures in the city are the *Senator Thomas Hart Benton statue, Lafayette Park*, and *"Beatrice Cenci"* at the *Mercantile Library, 510 Locust Street*.

Back in Boston, Hosmer ran with a lesbian crowd, including Charlotte Cushman, the actress and art patron, and her lover, sculptor Emma Stebbins. While touring the country, Cushman was invited to visit the Crows, Hosmer's second family, and became infatuated with Emma Crow, Wayman's daughter, addressing her in letters as "my darling little lover," much to Wayman's dismay. When Cushman traveled to Rome, Hosmer went with her to study sculpture, writing to her worried benefactor: "I shall keep a sharper lookout on Miss Cushman and not allow her to go on in this serious manner with Emma—it is really dreadful and I am really jealous." Knowing Wayman would disapprove, Hosmer used the convenient excuse of "keeping a lookout" on Cushman to justify living with her in Rome.

Throughout her life, Hosmer claimed that all she wanted to do was get married, but she never did. In a letter to Wayman, she joked, "I have been searching vainly for Mr. Hosmer." In 1858, Nathaniel Hawthorne and his wife visited Hosmer at her studio in Rome, and the writer gave a telling description of her: "She had on a male shirt, collar, and cravat. . . . She was indeed very queer." (*See also* Cambridge, Massachusetts.)

Hosmer Hall
Washington Boulevard and Pendleton Avenue

Named for lesbian sculptor Harriet Hosmer, this girls' secondary school was founded in 1884 by two intimate "friends," Miss Martha Mathews and Miss Clara Shepherd. At a time when serious academic training for women was in its infancy, the founders of Hosmer Hall stressed scholastic achievement, offering a full range of college preparatory subjects, including French, German, and Latin. Taught by graduates of the leading women's colleges, Hosmer Hall students were routinely excused from taking college entrance exams because of the school's excellent reputation. The school's most famous alumnae include playwright Zoe Akins and poet Sara Teasdale (*see below*), class of 1903, both of whom won the Pulitzer Prize during their careers. In 1917, the school moved to Clayton, Missouri, and then closed its doors in 1936.

International Shoe Company
1509 Washington

In 1931, Tennessee Williams's father, Cornelius, secured his son a summer job as an office clerk at the shoe company where he himself was a sales manager. Later, when the Depression leveled the family's finances and Cornelius withdrew his son from the university, Tennessee lived at home and eventually worked full-time as a clerical worker at the company's warehouse during 1934 and early 1935. Because he hated it and dreamed of being a writer, Williams later exaggerated his employment time there, saying it dragged on for three or four years. He wrote after work and late into the nights at the kitchen table, existing mostly on cigarettes and coffee.

At International Shoe, there was a brawny worker named Stanley Kowalski, a "ladies' man," who became Williams's closest companion, though they were completely different in style and temperament. According to Williams's biographer, Donald Spoto, there is no evidence that the two men had a homosexual relationship, but it is clear that Tennessee was infatuated with his coworker, much as Blanche DuBois was drawn to the other Stanley Kowalski of *A Streetcar Named Desire*.

According to Spoto, Williams's employment records list "ill health" as the reason for his resignation from International Shoe in the spring of 1935. Suffering from anxiety attacks that felt like cardiac arrest and which were probably part homosexual panic, Williams was sent to recuperate with his grandparents in Memphis. (*See also* Memphis, Tennessee.)

Tearooms

In 1970, a writer named Laud Humphreys (who went to great lengths to thank his wife and kids in the acknowledgments) published a book called *Tearoom Trade,* a sociological study about the sexual activity of men in public rest rooms. Humphrey's research was reportedly based on his "observations" of public gay sex in the rest rooms of Washington University—most notably the basement bathroom (now closed) of Duncker Hall—and also in the city's Forest Park, which had long been a cruising ground for closeted (often married) gay men.

Sara Teasdale home
3668 Lindell Avenue

The poet Sara Teasdale (1884–1933) was born in an elegant old mansion at this address to wealthy parents. Teasdale's mother designed and planned the home herself with the help of an architect. The house was later razed to make way for new buildings for St. Louis University.

Because her parents were in their forties when she was born and her siblings were considerably older than her, Sara grew up sheltered and alone, having what her biographer calls a "strong inner life." Surrounded by adults, she learned to amuse herself with stories she created in her active imagination. Teasdale received her primary education from her mother. Later she attended private schools, including the girls' academy Hosmer Hall (*see above*). An honors student who was too shy to make a commencement speech, Teasdale instead wrote her class song in 1903.

After graduation, Teasdale and several of her friends started a monthly literary magazine called *The Potter's Wheel*, in which she published her early poems. Sara was influenced early by the poetry fragments of Sappho, though she ignored the eroticism of them. Her first collection was called *Sonnets to Duse and Other Poems* (1907), a tribute to Eleanora Duse, the famous Italian actress. By age thirty, Teasdale had become one of the most famous women writers of her day. Her collection *Love Poems* won the Pulitzer Prize in 1919. But she was plagued by ill health, disappointment in love, an unsuccessful marriage, and emotional despair, and she committed suicide at age forty-eight.

Teasdale had several romantic attachments to men but was notably unfulfilled by them. In 1915, the year after her marriage, she was already wondering why there was "no ecstasy" in the relationship. Teasdale's primary relationships were all with women, though they were probably not sexual. The last of her intimate companions was Margaret Conklin, a young college student who wrote her a fan letter in 1926. In the years that followed, Teasdale wrote passionate poems for Conklin, some of which were published after her death.

Tennessee Williams home
4633 Westminster Place

Born in Mississippi, Thomas Lanier "Tennessee" Williams (1911—1983) spent most of his childhood and young manhood in St. Louis, after his father, a shoe salesman, secured employment there. But Williams's father often drank or gambled away his paycheck, forcing the family to live in a variety of crowded, rented rooms, moving a dozen times in just a few years.

In 1921 this small, dark apartment, with only two rooms for a family of five, was home. A rear window was blocked by a fire escape, allowing only minimal light into the rooms. Williams's parents were openly hostile to each other, and his mother was increasingly unhappy to be so far removed from the genteel life she had known as a southern minister's daughter.

Williams set his first successful play, the autobiographical *Glass Menagerie* (1945), here on Westminster Place, though the actual events he depicted in that play happened at a later time in another apartment in St. Louis (*see next entry*). According to Williams's stage instructions, the building in which the Wingfields/Williamses lived was "one of those vast hive-like conglomerations of living-units that flower as warty growths in overcrowded urban centers of lower middle-class population." This building was later named "The Glass Menagerie Apartments," in recognition of its place in theatrical history.

Tennessee Williams home
6254 Enright Avenue

During his last years of high school, Tennessee Williams and his family moved to five small rooms at this address. Though Williams went off to the university in Columbia in 1929, he returned here for summers and to live in 1932, when his father could no longer afford to finance his education. It was events at this address that Williams depicted in *The Glass Menagerie*. His older sister, Rose, who suffered from phobias and hysteria and had twice been hospitalized, was living at home and retreating more and more into herself. The social call that is at the heart of *The Glass Menagerie* occurred in 1933, when Tennessee's mother tried unsuccessfully to set Rose up with one of her son's college friends, Jim O'Connor. Williams's younger brother, Dakin, later recalled that "The events of *The Glass Menagerie* are a virtually literal rendering of our family life at 6254 Enright Avenue."

^   ^   ^

YMCA
201 South 20th Street

Now a moderately expensive hotel called the Drury Inn, located just north of the city's Union Station, this building was originally St. Louis's YMCA. Since the first YMCAs were constructed in the 1910s, they traditionally have been gathering places for transient gay men, particularly service members. During World War II, the St. Louis Y was reportedly hopping with soldiers looking for gay sex. Later, during the 1950s, the basement of the building housed a gay bar called Martin's.

WEATHERBY LAKE

Naiad Press
7800 Westside Drive

This was the first location of the oldest, still-operating lesbian publisher in the country. Founded in 1973 by life partners Barbara Grier and Donna McBride, Naiad was started "for the purpose of publishing realistic lesbian fiction—happy, positive, accurate views of lesbians and their lives." Naiad made its name and its money primarily publishing lesbian romances and mysteries and by reprinting lesbian pulp novels from the 1950s, particularly the Beebo Brinker series by Ann Bannon. Their authors have included Pat Califia, Katherine V. Forrest, Jane Rule, Diane Salvatore, Sarah Schulman, and Ann Allen Shockley.

For almost ten years, Grier and McBride worked full-time jobs, and then came home to do Naiad's work, putting in eighty-hour workweeks. Beginning in 1982, they were finally able to pay themselves salaries (but continued to work long hours!). Naiad is now located in Tallahassee, Florida.

Nebraska

Omaha

Montgomery Clift home
2101 South 33rd Street
Handsome, brooding Montgomery Clift (1920–1966) was born at this address (he was a twin) in a fashionable neighborhood. But his father was a wealthy investment banker who traveled often, and the family didn't stay in Omaha or anywhere else for very long. "We lived all over," his mother, Ethel, recounted to Clift's biographer, Robert LaGuardia. "It was unusual for us to live in one place longer than eight months."

Young Monty first became interested in the stage at age eight, when he began accompanying his mother to plays. A few years later, when the family was living in Sarasota, Florida, thirteen-year-old Monty approached the head of a summer theatrical company and asked to be given a part in a play. His first role was in an amateur production called *As Husbands Go.* The following summer, when the family had moved within a few miles of Stockbridge, Massachusetts, Monty's father helped him win his first serious role in *Fly Away Home*, a play that was in a pre-Broadway run. The play went to New York the following year with Monty in it, and he impressed both the critics and the audiences. He continued to dazzle New York until 1947, when he went to Hollywood to make his first feature film, *Red River*, and to become one of the biggest stars of the 1950s.

Attractive to both men and women, Monty knew he was gay from his teenage years but was always secretive about it for fear that it would hurt his acting career. As one friend remembered, "I never felt that Monty was disturbed about the homosexuality itself. . . . I think it was just the fact of having to pretend, to make people think he was someone he wasn't, that bothered him." (*See also* Brooklyn, New York.)

RED CLOUD

Willa Cather home
Third and Cedar Streets

Willa Cather (1873–1947) set six of her best-loved novels and several short stories in Red Cloud, the town of twenty-three hundred residents in which she lived from age nine to seventeen. "My deepest feelings were rooted in this country," Cather later wrote of the region where she grew up, "because one's strongest emotions and one's most vivid mental pictures are acquired before one is fifteen." Even after she left the area to attend college and start her career, Cather repeatedly returned to Red Cloud to visit. Though she lived most of her adult life in New York City, Cather's small-town roots continued to feed her creative work.

The Cather family home is a modest frame structure built in 1879, which Cather depicted lovingly and realistically in her novel *The Song of the Lark*. It was restored in the 1950s. So faithful were Cather's descriptions of the house that today guides there read from Cather texts as they escort visitors through the various rooms. The most interesting part of the tour is Cather's attic room, which was sealed off for years and has remained virtually untouched since the late nineteenth century when Cather occupied it. Cather's siblings lived in a separate, dormitory-style room, but as the oldest child, she rated her own space. The room is still papered with the wallpaper ("small red and brown roses on a yellowish ground," she wrote in *Lark*) that Cather purchased herself with her earnings from working at Cook's Drug Store in Red Cloud, and appointed with the shabby, secondhand furniture she sketched in such detail in *Lark*.

A National Historic Landmark, Cather's home is often featured in magazines such as *Historic Preservation* and *National Geographic Traveler*. None of the articles, however, broach the topic of her sexuality. And you won't learn on your tour that it was at this home at age fourteen that the budding lesbian created her male persona, William Cather, Jr., a role she enacted throughout her teen years, trimming her hair to a crew cut and donning boys' clothes. For that information, you'll have to turn to Sharon

O'Brien's insightful biography of the writer, which examines her life and work with an eye to her sexual orientation.

Willa Cather Pioneer Memorial and Educational Foundation
326 North Webster

Red Cloud abounds in sites mentioned in the fiction of its most famous resident, and this foundation offers a walking tour of the town that uncovers many of those depicted, especially in *My Ántonia*—the train depot, the Catholic church, the houses of the main characters. The foundation also sponsors driving tours: one that includes a tour of the graves of many Cather characters, such as Ántonia's father, the man whose suicide lies at the heart of the story; and another tour that focuses on the Divide, the area between the Little Blue and Republican Rivers where the Cathers first lived when they moved to the area and which provided the setting for *O Pioneers!*

In addition, the foundation manages another Cather-related site in Red Cloud, the 1889 Farmers' and Merchants' Bank Building. Inside is an exhibit of Cather memorabilia, including a painting of a Russian sleigh pursued by wolves, which may have been a source of inspiration for *My Ántonia*.

WILLA CATHER FICTION SET IN OR AROUND RED CLOUD

O Pioneers! (1913)
The Song of the Lark (1915)
My Ántonia (1918)
One of Ours (1922)
A Lost Lady (1923)
"Old Mrs. Harris" (1931)
Lucy Gayheart (1945)
"The Best Years" (1945)

Willa Cather Memorial Prairie
U.S. 281 (five and a half miles south of town)
"The red of the grass made all of the great prairie the color of wine-stains,"
wrote Willa Cather. If you travel just south of Red Cloud, you can glimpse
the grandeur of the plains that Cather cherished—a real, honest-to-
goodness prairie, which has been conserved by an organization called The
Nature Conservancy and named for the woman who immortalized the
wide-open spaces of her childhood home.

OHIO

CLEVELAND

Langston Hughes home
11217 Asbury Avenue

Langston Hughes (1902–1967) grew up in Kansas and Illinois but moved with his mother and stepfather to Cleveland during his early high school years, when his stepfather, Homer Clark, found work as a machinist in a Cleveland steel mill. The move was Langston's first encounter with urban life, and it fueled his lifelong passion for cities. The family lived in a neighborhood that had once been white and upscale, but the large homes had been subdivided to accommodate the great migration of African Americans from the South. Rents were high, and the black district was crowded. "We always lived, during my high school years," Hughes later recalled, "either in an attic or a basement, and paid quite a lot for such inconvenient quarters. White people on the east side of the city were moving out of their frame houses and renting them to Negroes at double or triple the rents they could receive from others."

As in his other schools, Langston was one of few black students. Central High School was one of Cleveland's best and boasted John D. Rockefeller as an alumnus. At Central, Langston joined the editorial staff of the *Monthly*, in which his first story was published in 1918. Tired of moving around, Langston remained in Cleveland to finish high school when his mother and stepfather took off for Chicago. He rented an attic room at *2266 East 86th Street*, where he ate boiled rice and hot dogs every night for dinner, the only food he knew how to prepare for himself. "Then I read myself to sleep," he remembered. After graduation, Langston joined his biological father for a year in Mexico. While he was there, the poem that secured literary recognition for him, "The Negro Speaks of Rivers," was published in *The Crisis* in 1919. (*See also* New York City, New York, and Lawrence, Kansas.)

EARLY GAY COMMUNITY CENTERS STILL IN OPERATION IN THE MIDWEST

Women's Resource and Action Center (founded 1971)
130 North Madison Street
Iowa City, Iowa

Horizons Community Services (founded 1973)
961 West Montana Street
Chicago, Illinois

Dayton Lesbian and Gay Center (founded 1976)
665 Salem Avenue
Dayton, Ohio

The United (founded 1978)
14 West Mifflin Street, Suite 103
Madison, Wisconsin

Stonewall Community Center (founded 1981)
1160 High Street
Columbus, Ohio

Up the Stairs Community Center (founded 1983)
3426 Broadway
Fort Wayne, Indiana

Gay and Lesbian Resource Center (founded mid-1980s)
414 East 5th Street
Des Moines, Iowa

Lesbian/Gay Community Service Center
1418 West 29th Street
Founded in 1975, the Center offers a smorgasbord of services and programs, including a hot line, a youth program, a drop-in and referral center, a speakers' bureau, and a program for those who are HIV-positive. In addition, meeting space is available for local gay and lesbian groups. This is the oldest continuously operating center in the state.

Pre-Stonewall bars
According to John Kelsey's study "The Cleveland Bar Scene in the Forties," most of the city's gay bars at that time were seedy joints owned by heterosexuals and were little more than "cleared-out storerooms" attached to straight bars or nightclubs. One notable exception was the *Cadillac Bar, East 9th Street and Euclid Avenue*, which was well-lit, clean, and furnished with blond leatherette booths, with murals of tropical scenes painted on the walls. Mrs. Gloria Lenahan, the owner, ran the tightest ship in town. If a patron talked too loud or too crudely, he was made to leave. Mrs. Lenahan also enforced a strict dress code of jackets and ties.

A far cry from the Cadillac Bar was *Mac & Jerry's* (M & J's) on *Superior Avenue across from the Cleveland Hotel*. Not a gay bar per se, M & J's was a hangout for rough trade, and "rough" is a fair description of it. Kelsey reports that several murders and near-fatal beatings were the result of pickups made at M & J's. This bar was reportedly a favorite of Sumner Welles, Franklin Roosevelt's undersecretary of state, a married man whose gay comings and goings were carefully scrutinized by J. Edgar Hoover's FBI. At M & J's, the story goes, Welles was discovered by detectives, who kindly escorted him to the Cleveland Hotel across the street. But an hour later, Welles was back at the bar. Welles resigned his office in 1943 before his homosexual proclivities could be made public. (*See also* District of Columbia.)

^   ^   ^

Phillis Wheatley Center
4450 Cedar Avenue

In 1905, Jane Edna Hunter (1882–1950) came to Cleveland right out of nursing school. Her search for decent housing was full of frustration and rejection—YWCAs were not yet open to black women, and Hunter was forced to let a dingy and uncomfortable room in an unsafe area. Women were viewed as undesirable roomers, and though they earned less than men (primarily in jobs as domestic workers), they were charged extra for "amenities" such as bathtubs or cooking gas. Loneliness and despair marked Hunter's first years in the city, and hers was a common experience for African-American women.

In 1911, Hunter gathered a group of disillusioned domestic workers to discuss the establishment of a Working Girls' Home Association. Patterned after the all-white YWCA, the Association would provide housing, recreation, training, and employment opportunities, as well as safety for African-American women. The group pledged that each member would raise a nickel a week and gather as many new recruits as possible. Hunter also persuaded white donors to contribute, based on the assumption that she would be training black women to be "loyal" domestics.

The Phillis Wheatley Home, named for the slave poet, was one of the most successful social service programs for blacks in Cleveland. Founded at a twenty-three-room house at *2265 East 40th Street* in 1913, it moved to its present eleven-story structure fourteen years later. Hunter served as its director, at the same time earning her law degree and passing the Ohio bar exam. Nine additional houses similar to the Wheatley Center were established in cities across the country.

Hunter's own home was located just behind the Wheatley Center and named Elli-Kani, an African tribal name that translates as "house of faith." Her home served as a retreat for visiting African-American celebrities, who could not stay in the segregated all-white hotels in town. Hunter married once, briefly, but preferred to live her life in a women-centered atmosphere. Whether or not she was a lesbian, she was a strongly woman-identified woman.

DAYTON

Natalie Clifford Barney birthplace
Fifth and Wikinson Streets, southwest corner

Born to a successful businessman and a free-spirited artist, poet Natalie Clifford Barney (1876–1972) was one of the most famous—and wealthiest—lesbians of her day. Both of her parents inherited sizable family estates, and Natalie was raised in the lap of luxury. When Natalie was two years old, her family relocated to Cincinnati, and when she was in her early teens, they took up residence in the nation's capital, where they moved in the top social and diplomatic circles (*see* District of Columbia). Throughout her youth, Natalie often traveled with her mother, the painter Alice Pike Barney, to Europe for extended stays. It was in Paris that Natalie finally decided to settle at age twenty-four, the heir of her own substantial fortune.

Barney published numerous poetry collections and plays in French during her lifetime, noted for their openly lesbian content, and also penned several volumes of memoirs. Her tempestuous affair with poet Renée Vivien and her long-term relationship with painter Romaine Brooks are frequently written about. But it is as the host of a celebrated Friday afternoon literary salon at 20 rue Jacob that she is perhaps best remembered. Barney's salon was the center of the French avant-garde and of queer expatriate Paris for fifty years, frequented by such literati as Marcel Proust, Colette, Gertrude Stein, Djuna Barnes, Oscar Wilde, Radclyffe Hall, Janet Flanner, and André Gide. Djuna Barnes's roman à clef, *Ladies Almanack* (1928), spoofed both the salon and its best-known members.

Historian Shari Benstock has shown, however, another side of the over-romanticized Barney. Benstock's research has revealed that Barney was in fact a Nazi sympathizer during World War II, a point rarely discussed by contemporary lesbians looking for openly gay foremothers.

OBERLIN

Oberlin College

Founded in 1832, Oberlin College is situated in a small Ohio town that was a center of antislavery work in the decades preceding the Civil War. Within three years of its founding, Oberlin began accepting the enrollment of African Americans. Among its early black students was Edmonia Lewis (1845–1909), who later rose to prominence as a sculptor.

Lewis, part African, part Chippewa, had been born and raised near Albany, New York, and was orphaned at a young age. She came to Oberlin in 1859, where she resided with twelve other girls in the home of the Reverend John Keep. In a bizarre incident in 1862, she was charged with poisoning two white female students by doctoring some wine with Spanish Fly, an aphrodisiac. Though acquitted after a sensational trial, Lewis became the target of white vigilantes who abducted and beat her. Shortly after the "spiced wine" incident, Lewis left Oberlin for good.

Lewis later made her home in Boston, where she studied sculpture and became a well-known neoclassical sculptor. Her themes were often drawn from African-American and Indian history. Specializing in portrait busts, she sculpted Maria Weston Chapman, an abolitionist, and Robert Gould Shaw, the Civil War leader. After her works were displayed at the Philadelphia Centennial Exhibition in 1876, she acquired many wealthy white patrons, such as Ulysses S. Grant and William Lloyd Garrison.

Lewis traveled in the same lesbian social circle as Charlotte Cushman, the actress and art patron, whose other members included sculptors Harriet Hosmer and Emma Stebbins. Like Cushman and Hosmer, Lewis is buried in Mt. Auburn Cemetery in Cambridge. (*See also* Cambridge, Massachusetts.)

South Dakota

Fort Meade

When the Seventh Cavalry was stationed here in the "Dakota Territory" in the early 1870s, the company laundress, "Mrs. Corporal Noonan," was a popular midwife, seamstress, cook, and nurse. She had three soldier husbands between the years 1868 and 1878, the last of whom was John Noonan, an orderly. According to historian Jim Wilke, General George Armstrong Custer's wife, Elizabeth, also employed Mrs. Noonan privately, praising the woman's handiwork: "When she brought the linen home, it was fluted and frilled so daintily that I considered her a treasure."

But Mrs. Noonan also had a well-kept secret. Elizabeth Custer remembered that the laundress "kept a veil pinned about the lower part of her face." When Mrs. Noonan died in 1878, the women at the post who had the task of preparing her body for burial discovered that she was in fact a man. Her husband would have undoubtedly been court-martialed and sent to the penitentiary, but the unfortunate corporal committed suicide before he could be prosecuted, just a month after his wife's death.

WISCONSIN

APPLETON

Edna Ferber home
218 North Street
Born in Kalamazoo, Michigan, Edna Ferber and her family moved to this house in Appleton when she was a child. Ferber (1887–1968), who was unable to attend college because of family financial difficulties, began her writing career at the tender age of seventeen as a newspaper reporter for the *Appleton Daily Crescent*. She later worked for newspapers in both Milwaukee and Chicago.

But it was here in Appleton, recovering from a prolonged illness, that Ferber began writing her first novel, *Dawn O'Hara* (1911), the story of an intrepid female reporter. Ferber's novels are all marked by their feminist content and their portrayal of strong and independent women—much like Ferber herself. Her novels were enormously popular, and one (*So Big*, 1924) won the Pulitzer Prize. Later works such as *Show Boat* (1926), *Cimarron* (1930), *Saratoga Trunk* (1941), and *Giant* (1950) were best-sellers that were also made into successful Hollywood movies. With George S. Kaufman, Ferber scripted a number of plays during the 1920s and 1930s, including the classic *Dinner at Eight* (1932) and *Stage Door* (1936).

Early in her career as a novelist, Ferber moved to New York City, where she moved in stylish literary circles, including the Algonquin Round Table. She was a famous cross-dresser, and her habit was to appear at functions in full male drag. At a party at director George Cukor's in Hollywood, Ferber and Noël Coward reportedly both showed up wearing double-breasted suits. Coward said, "You almost look like a man." Without missing a beat, Ferber shot back, "So do you." When asked in 1939 about being fifty-something and unmarried, Ferber quipped, "Being an old maid is like death by drowning—a really delightful sensation after you cease to struggle."

JANESVILLE

Frances Willard home
1720 South River Road
Temperance pioneer Frances Willard (1839–1898) came to Wisconsin from New England with her family in a covered wagon in 1846. The site of their home in Janesville is marked, but the actual building has been relocated to another place. Educated by her mother, Willard was a tomboy who preferred to be called "Frank." Her infatuations and passionate friendships with women and girls from an early age are chronicled in her autobiography, *Glimpses of Fifty Years*. (*See also* Evanston, Illinois.)

MADISON

Thornton Wilder birthplace
"Kerr House"
Langdon Street
Thornton Wilder (1897–1975) was born at this location when Madison was a town of only eighteen thousand residents—the typical sort of "our town" that the playwright later celebrated and immortalized. The Wilder family also enjoyed a summer cottage on nearby Lake Mendota.

However, financial difficulties (Thornton's father was part-owner of an unsuccessful newspaper) drove Wilder, Sr., to seek a new, more lucrative career, and in 1906, he succeeded in persuading President William Taft, an old college friend, to appoint him consul general of Hong Kong. The family moved there briefly, but Thornton's mother didn't like life abroad and moved back to the United States with her children within a few months. Thornton spent the rest of his adolescence in Berkeley, California—another small town— taunted by classmates for being a "freak" and self-identifying as "queer" at a young age. (*See also* Berkeley, California, and Hamden, Connecticut.)

Ripon

Carrie Chapman Catt birthplace
324 Spaulding Avenue
Carrie Lane (1859–1947), the girl who would become Carrie Chapman Catt, one of the greatest activists for U.S. women's suffrage, was born on a

Aside-step

In 1914, Ralph Kerwinieo was working at a factory in Milwaukee. He had recently left his companion of thirteen years, Marie White, and married Dorothy Klenowski before a justice of the peace. Possibly angry at being thrown over for another woman, Marie White revealed a secret that brought her former lover up on charges of "disorderly conduct"—that Ralph was, in fact, Cora Anderson and had been passing as a man for over a dozen years.

According to contemporary newspaper accounts, Marie White and Cora Anderson had studied nursing together in Chicago, and then set up housekeeping in Cleveland and later Milwaukee. But Cora, who was Native American, had difficulty finding work free from sexual harassment and began passing as a man in order to support herself without hassle. Sporting suits and derbies, Ralph found work first as a hotel bellboy and later at a manufacturing company. The news reports were careful to skirt the issue of lesbianism and insisted that the "marriage" with Klenowski was never "consummated." After a hearing, Kerwinieo/Anderson was released and ordered to wear women's clothing. She spoke of her years of passing in a Chicago newspaper, asserting that she had done it because "this world is made by man—for man alone."

family farm in Wisconsin and lived there the first seven years of her life. By her own description, she was "an ordinary child in an ordinary family on an ordinary farm." But even at a tender age, Carrie was an ardent supporter of her sex. As a youngster on the school playground, she once boldly slapped the face of the leader of a group of boys who were making fun of a girl whose hoopskirt had slipped down. "They had more respect for girls after that!" the suffragist remembered years later. After the Civil War, Carrie's family moved to a farm in Iowa, which, with a total of five hundred people, seemed like a thriving metropolis after Ripon! (*See also* Charles City, Iowa, and New Rochelle, New York.)

V

WEST

Arizona

Phoenix

Gay pride march

Arizona's very first lesbian and gay pride march took place in Phoenix on June 27, 1981, the twelfth anniversary of the Stonewall riots in New York City. The march stepped off at *Patriot's Park*, and then continued down *Washington Street to the State Capitol*, a distance of about two miles. The day ended with a rally on the capitol grounds. Keynote speakers for the historic occasion were Leonard Matlovich, the Air Force sergeant who won reinstatement after being discharged for being gay, and Arlie Scott, a pioneering lesbian-feminist who was the author of the famous NOW position paper on lesbian rights that was adopted at the national conference in 1971.

Aside-step

Located in the desert just outside of Benson, Arizona (forty miles off the main highway), was the Sri Ram Ashram, the site of the first gathering of the Radical Faeries in 1979 at a Labor Day weekend retreat organized by gay rights pioneer Harry Hay. Over two hundred gay men assembled to reclaim their spirituality through healing circles, blessings, and chants. The event that most participants remembered best was a spontaneous mud ritual. Fifty naked Faeries carried water to a dry riverbed near the ashram and mixed it with fine clay to make mud, in which they then covered themselves. The weekend was the beginning of a new movement of paganism for gay men.

TOMBSTONE

Nellie Cashman businesses

You won't find it anywhere in print that Nellie Cashman (1851–1925) was a lesbian, but you can make up your own mind. Cashman was a gold miner, a restaurant and boardinghouse owner, and a philanthropist. From the 1870s on, Cashman, a native of Ireland, moved from one mining camp to the next, setting up businesses and looking for quick money. In the early 1880s, Tombstone, a center of frontier violence at that time, was her base. Some of her ventures included the following:

Allen and Fifth Streets: At this address, Nellie Cashman and her "business partner," Jennie Swift, started Cashman & Swift, a store that specialized in importing fresh produce from southern California. Swift had followed Cashman from Los Angeles to Arizona in 1879. An ad in the June 1880 Tucson *Arizona Daily Citizen* stated: "The Misses Nellie Cashman and Jennie Swift, who have been here long enough to become most favorably known to the people of Tucson, intend to open a provision and fruit store in Tombstone. We wish these ladies unlimited success for their new home and business place." What happened between Cashman and Swift is not known, but after a short time Nellie bought out her partner and started other businesses in the area.

Russ House, Fifth and Toughnut Streets: Established in 1881, Cashman's restaurant and hotel was in the heart of Tombstone's business district, not far from the Milt Joyce's Oriental Saloon, of which law enforcer Wyatt Earp was part owner. Cashman printed her menus in the Tombstone papers and was known for her good food, fair prices, and generosity. "If a fellow has no money," one miner noted, "Miss Nellie gives him board and lodging until he makes a stake." Her beneficence earned her the nickname the "Miners' Angel." A devout Catholic, Cashman was also known for raising funds to build churches and hospitals.

Cashman eventually struck out for Alaska, where she made a fortune mining and was known as "a small figure in mackinaw, trousers, boots and fur cap." One female acquaintance gave as her guess why Nellie never married, "Seen too much o' the worst side of men, I guess." Cashman herself always brushed aside questions about why she remained a spinster. "I've been too busy," she stated, "to talk about such things."

VAIL

Nourishing Space
Cave Canyon Ranch

Thirty miles southeast of Tucson, a collective of lesbian separatists founded Nourishing Space, "a place for women and children only," in 1975. Nourishing Space consisted of one hundred and sixty acres of desert land in a canyon near the Coronado National Forest, with two houses, a garden, and a tool shed. The retreat was designed as a place for women to learn about what the collective called the "nourishment process"—"how we energize or drain ourselves, . . . how we empower or disempower ourselves, . . . new ways to create our revolution." The women tried to support the venture through fundraising events such as workshops and potluck dinners and by renting camping space to other women. But the income was too small and the expenses too great (including a $1,000 a month mortgage) to make ends meet, and Nourishing Space folded within a few years.

CALIFORNIA

BAKERSFIELD

Robert Duncan childhood home
1908 Verde Street

Queer poet Robert Duncan (1919–1988) was born in Oakland but was put up for adoption when his mother died in childbirth. Adopted by Edward and Minnehaha Symmes of Alameda, he grew up in this lower middle-class neighborhood in Bakersfield. As an adolescent, he received the nickname "Sissie Symmes" at Bakersfield Junior High, but the gifted student and future poet didn't let it deter him. Editor of the school journal, the *Emersonian*, he boldly listed the epithet "Sis" directly after his name in the 1932 graduation issue. As a young adult, he began using the surname Duncan, which had been the family name of his birth parents.

BERKELEY

New Athens Roundtable/Robert Duncan home
2029 Hearst Street

Robert Duncan lived at this address in the mid-1940s, after he published his groundbreaking essay "The Homosexual in Society" in the journal *Politics*. Here he started the New Athens Roundtable in 1946. The table was simply a round plank of wood painted with automobile lacquer. Most nights of the week, a dozen or more "bohemians" would gather for dinner and conversation, followed by poetry readings and storytelling. One participant recalled later that "there was always a lot of laughter and the pitch and tone of the conversation would rise as the meal went on." The fame of Duncan's roundtable spread through the arts community, and the cultural evenings attracted such visiting celebrities as E. M. Forster, who came to see "where the poets live."

The roomy Hearst Street house had a garden with a fishpond and fountain. Duncan's second-story room was "the second room from the street," his writing desk situated in an alcove with a large window. After he had an affair with Janie O'Neill—one of his housemates whose husband also lived there—Duncan moved out, and the New Athens came to an abrupt end. According to his biographer, the affair with O'Neill was the last heterosexual relationship of Duncan's life.

Duncan subsequently lived at *2208 McKinley Street* with his lover, Gerald Ackerman, a student at Berkeley, and several other housemates, including writer Philip K. Dick. Duncan and Ackerman shared a spacious pine-paneled room, where the poet would often give readings for friends. The couple later moved to their own apartment on Adeline Street (now a subway station), where in 1949 Duncan found Ackerman in bed with Paul Goodman, the writer and social critic who became a guru of the 1960s counterculture. (*See also* Bakersfield, California, and Woodstock, New York.)

Thornton Wilder family home
2350 Prospect Street

Born in Wisconsin, playwright Thornton Wilder (1897–1975) spent much of his early youth in northern California. Before moving with his family to this address in 1913, young Wilder attended Thacher School, a boys' boarding school in the Ojai Valley, where he was taunted by classmates as a "freak." At Thacher, Wilder discovered his love of the theater and delighted in the school's dramatic club. But when he was cast as Lady Bracknell in Oscar Wilde's *The Importance of Being Earnest*, Wilder's father—fearing the meaning of his son's effeminate ways—stepped in and forbade him to play female roles. Painfully aware of his difference from other boys, Wilder early on described himself as "a queer pupil" with a "queer walk."

As a teenager in Berkeley, Wilder began writing stories and plays. He confessed dramatically in his notebook that if he wasn't writing he had "no right to breathe." In college, Wilder continued to pursue both writing and the theater, first at Oberlin, where he wrote poetry to a favorite professor, and then at Yale, where he became infatuated with a young actor, Gareth Hughes, whom Wilder described as "sheer genius and poetry. . . . And when his glasses are off the divinest thing to look upon that I have ever seen." Despite a deep, lifelong attraction to men, Wilder never enjoyed more than brief, meaningless homosexual affairs. But he did succeed in winning three Pulitzer Prizes. (*See also* Hamden, Connecticut.)

CORONADO

Hotel del Coronado
1500 Orange Avenue
A beautifully maintained landmark from the Victorian age (built 1888), the Hotel del Coronado is perhaps best remembered as the resort in the Billy Wilder movie *Some Like It Hot.* On display is an exhibit about the 1958 filming of the classic movie, which starred Tony Curtis, Jack Lemmon, and Marilyn Monroe. Curtis and Lemmon are two musicians who accidentally witness the St. Valentine's Day massacre in Chicago in the 1920s, and then don female drag and join an all-girl band to escape the gangsters who want to kill them. A millionaire vacationing at the hotel, played by Joe E. Brown, pursues Lemmon's female counterpart, Geraldine. When Lemmon doffs his blonde wig at the end to show why Geraldine can't marry her suitor, Brown simply shrugs and says, "Nobody's perfect." The film is not only a masterpiece of comedy but a drag-positive tour de force. If you haven't seen it since you came out, you owe yourself the treat.

LODI

De Force Avenue

This street is named for Laura de Force Gordon (1839–1907), a suffragist with a laudable string of accomplishments to her name, who owned a farm just outside of Lodi. A Stockton newspaper owner, one of the first two women admitted to the state bar, a women's rights litigator, and a stunning orator sometimes called the "Daniel Webster of Suffrage," Gordon was also a woman-loving woman. When a one-hundred-year-old time capsule was unearthed and opened in San Francisco in 1979, a pamphlet written by Gordon on California geysers was found inside. On the flyleaf she wrote: "If this little book should see the light after its 100 years of entombment, I would like its readers to know that the author was a lover of her own sex and devoted the best years of her life in striving for the political equality and social and moral elevation of women."

LOS ANGELES

Dorothy Arzner home
2249 Mountain Oak Drive

While doing research for a study of film director Dorothy Arzner (ca. 1900–1979), Professor Judith Mayne discovered boxes of material relating to Arzner in the UCLA research collection. Inside one box was a photograph of the atrium of Arzner's opulent home in the Hollywood Hills, with an annotation in Arzner's own handwriting: "Home of Marion Morgan and Dorothy Arzner/1930–1951." "That moment of discovery was thrilling," Mayne later wrote in *Directed by Dorothy Arzner*, "for here was evidence of a home and a life shared by two women."

Starting as a script typist and working her way up to film editor on such silent movies as *Blood and Sand*, Arzner progressed to directing in 1927. With credits including *The Wild Party*, *Working Girls*, *Christopher Strong*, *Dance, Girl, Dance*, and *The Bride Wore Red*, the butchy Arzner was the only successful female director in Hollywood during its golden age. (Even today, directing remains a predominantly male domain.) It was on the set of her first movie, *Fashions for Women*, that Arzner met Marion Morgan, a vaudeville dancer with her own performance troupe and a busy career choreographing movie dance sequences. After working together on several movies, the two women set up their home together in 1930, and they remained devoted to each other until Morgan's death forty years later.

Also among the boxes Mayne discovered were numerous snapshots of Arzner and Morgan entertaining guests (among them, Marlene Dietrich) at their elegant, quintessentially Hollywood home. The photos of the house's lush atrium suggest a love of natural light and greenery. After Arzner's retirement from directing in 1943, she and Morgan traveled the world extensively, and in 1951, they moved to a new home in La Quinta, a community in the southern California desert. There Arzner was an avid gardener whose correspondence made frequent and proud mention of her roses. But even in her retirement, Arzner continued to keep a hand in directing, teaching at UCLA's film school, producing plays, and directing Pepsi-Cola commercials for Joan Crawford.

George Cukor home
9166 Cordell Drive

The film director George Cukor (1899–1983) resided at this elegant address for the last fifty years of his life. Arriving from Broadway to direct films in 1930, Cukor spent his first years in Hollywood living in hotels. Finally, in 1932, he purchased this six-acre estate for only ten thousand dollars and remodeled and landscaped it as an Italian villa a few years later. Besides the main house, there were three cottages on the grounds, one of which was home to Cukor's friend Katharine Hepburn when she was working in Hollywood. During the 1940s, Spencer Tracy occupied one of the other cottages, in order to be closer to Hepburn.

Cukor—who directed such screen classics as *Dinner at Eight* (1933), *Camille* (1936), *The Philadelphia Story* (1940), and *My Fair Lady* (1964), plus the gender-bending cult film *Sylvia Scarlett* (1935)—was flamboyantly homosexual and famous for the "gay" parties he threw at his estate.

For years, Cukor and Cole Porter held competing soirees on Sundays, each trying to outdo the other. They were known as the rival queens of Hollywood.

"George was really queen of the roost," Joseph Mankiewicz later said of Cukor's parties. His dinners were elegant, his luncheons informal but still carefully "directed." Cukor's guests included movie stars, stage personalities, foreign film notables, famous writers, and royalty. Though not all the guests were homosexual, Cukor's was definitely one of the premiere places to mingle with the queer elite of Hollywood. At one of Cukor's affairs, the story goes, Edna Ferber and Noël Coward both showed up wearing double-breasted suits. "You almost look like a man," Coward said. "So do you," Ferber said.

Cukor's house was formally decorated by William Haines, a silent film star and one of Cukor's friends, and was crammed with expensive pieces of art by Matisse, Renoir, and Picasso. Mixed in with the antique furniture and modern art was a collection of show-business memorabilia, plus displays of Cukor's own awards and commendations. Over the years, Cukor made few changes in the house, except for some cosmetic touches, and at his death it remained the same as it had been during the 1930s, a memorial to Hollywood's golden age. In 1983, it sold for just under one and a half million dollars.

First Universalist Church
Ninth and Crenshaw Streets
This church was the site of a definitive convention of the Mattachine Society (*see* "Harry Hay home" *below*). A gathering of Mattachine members was called in April 1953, and five hundred gay men showed up to debate the future of the organization, convening the first large public gathering of homosexuals in the history of the United States.

A split had been forming between the radical Mattachine founders who formed the group's steering committee—Harry Hay, Bob Hull, et al.—and the more conservative, middle-class element that had become strong within the organization. Hay, who identified as a Marxist, was thought to be pulling the Mattachine Society in a partisan direction; a congressional committee was on the verge of investigating the Society for its Communist leanings, part of the McCarthy red-baiting that was taking place at that time. The members Hay called "the status quo types" were less interested in changing society than in fitting into it; at the convention, they began discussions to create a separate organization. Hay and the other founders, recognizing that a congressional investigation would uncover their Communist Party ties and fearing that this would spell the end of the Mattachine Society, withdrew from the organization, leaving it to be run by the more conservative faction. As a result, Hay has noted that "the Mattachine after 1953 was primarily concerned with legal change, with being seen as respectable," rather than the more idealistic original purpose "to unify, to educate, and to lead."

Gay Community Services Center
1614 Wilshire Boulevard

Probably the first gay community center in the country (though the center in Albany also claims this distinction), the L.A. Center got off the ground at this location in 1971, finally adding the word "lesbian" to its name in 1980. (It is now called the Los Angeles Gay and Lesbian Community Services Center and its executive director is a woman.) It changed locations several times over its twenty-five-year history—first to *1213 North Highland* and later to its current site at *1625 North Shrader Boulevard* (formerly Hudson Boulevard). From its humble origins, the Center grew to become the largest gay community center in the United States, with a budget of about fourteen million dollars and a staff of two hundred. The Center provides employment training and placement, mental health services, recovery services, youth services, a homeless shelter, an HIV/AIDS clinic and anonymous HIV testing, a lesbian health clinic, and a computerized AIDS information network.

∧   ∧   ∧

OTHER EARLY GAY COMMUNITY CENTERS STILL IN OPERATION IN CALIFORNIA

The Gay and Lesbian Community Services Center of Orange County (founded 1972)
12832 Garden Grove Boulevard, Suite A
Garden Grove

The Lesbian and Gay Men's Community Center (founded 1973)
3916 Normal Street
San Diego

Gay and Lesbian Resource Center (founded 1976)
126 East Haley Street, Suite A17
Santa Barbara

Gay and Lesbian Community Services Center of Long Beach (founded 1978)
2017 East 4th Street
Long Beach

Santa Cruz Lesbian, Gay, Bisexual and Transgendered Community Center (founded 1980)
1328 Commerce Lane
Santa Cruz

Billy DeFrank Lesbian and Gay Community Center (founded 1981)
175 Stockton Street
San Jose

Gay and Lesbian Resource Center of Ventura County (founded 1983)
363 Mobil Avenue
Camarillo

Cary Grant/Randolph Scott home
2177 West Live Oak Drive

Though he married five times, movie star Cary Grant (1904–1986) enjoyed several homosexual relationships during his early career in New York and Hollywood. One of his most famous romances was with fellow actor Randolph Scott (1898–1987), the rugged star of numerous Hollywood westerns. Grant and Scott met at Paramount Studios in 1932 and were immediately attracted to each other. Soon after, they moved in together, sharing this house in the Los Feliz area near Griffith Park. The move was disguised by P.R. agents at the studio as a way for the two actors to "cut costs" and share expenses, even though both made ample salaries and could afford their own homes. Even after Grant's marriage to Virginia Cherrill, the two men continued cohabiting; Cherrill simply moved into the Los Feliz house!

Between liaisons with other men and women, Grant and Scott's relationship persisted, well known to their colleagues in the industry. (If you haven't seen it, don't miss the two as costars in the hilarious movie, *My Favorite Wife*.) In the late 1930s, Grant and Scott occupied a Santa Monica beach house at *1019 Ocean Front* (now renumbered 1039). In fan magazines, they were often photographed together in domestic bliss, wearing aprons and cavorting poolside or on the patio. According to Grant's biographer, they believed that public flamboyance—instead of damning them—would in fact raise them above suspicion. They must have been right, because Grant enjoyed a screen career as a suave "ladies' man" for the next thirty years.

Graumann's Chinese Theater
6925 Hollywood Boulevard

Now called Mann's Chinese Theater, this delightfully gaudy movie palace dating from the golden age of the Hollywood studios is a must-see for most tourists in Los Angeles. I visited the site for the first time as a wide-eyed, twelve-year-old dyke-in-the-making who had no inkling that there was anything queer about Joan Crawford, Cary Grant, Rock Hudson, or Barbara

Stanwyck. If only I'd known! It's fun and campy to visit it again as an out gay person and to literally walk in our ancestors' footsteps (or totter in their high-heel prints).

Griffith Park

Long a cruising spot for gay men, especially the area known as Horseshoe Bend, Griffith Park was the target of numerous police sweeps in the pre-Stonewall era. Rangers routinely tipped off the vice squad to homosexual activity in the scenic hillside park, but the threat of entrapment and arrest did not deter gay men looking for quick sexual encounters. "You won't change fairies," one park habitué was quoted in *The Advocate*, ". . . if you close the park to them, they'll go someplace else." Another L.A. park known at that time for cruising (and for police harassment) was *Barnsdall Park*, located off Hollywood Boulevard.

Griffith Park was also the site of the first Los Angeles Gay-In on March 17, 1968. Two drag queens, "The Duchess" and "The Princess," organized a flamboyant gay picnic at the infamous Horseshoe Bend. "There were lavish pants, fluffy sweaters, fur hats, beads, earrings, and flowers everywhere," reported *The Advocate*. Along the main road in clear view of all park visitors the queens boldly posted signs reading, "This Way, Girls!" Festivities included volleyball (the "Nells" versus the "Butches"), dancing, and skateboarding. "The Duchess" ("the Pearl Mesta of Griffith Park") told *The Advocate* reporter that she had instructed several queens to spray-paint the area fuchsia and had hired a plane to drop sequins over the party, but that those arrangements fell through. *The Advocate* pronounced the affair "Los Angeles's first major Homosexual Love-In."

Harry Hay home/The Mattachine Society
2328 Cove Avenue

This three-story split-level house located in a private cul-de-sac in the Silver Lake section of Los Angeles was home to Harry Hay and his wife, Anita, beginning in 1943. The living room boasted a grand piano and a view of the lake that was the Hays' "pride and joy." In those days, Hay was a member of both the Communist Party and the folk music movement, and his home was the site of numerous meetings and soirees.

But even while married, Hay began acting on his homosexual desires, becoming lovers in 1950 with Rudi Gernreich, future designer of the topless swimsuit. Because Hay had a wife and Gernreich lived with his mother, the lovers met clandestinely at the home of a friend at *313 Alta Vista Drive* in Hollywood to be together and have sex. Hay later said that he and Rudi formed a "society of two" that later became the Mattachine Society.

It was at Hay's Cove Avenue residence that he, Gernreich, and two of their friends, Chuck Rowland and Bob Hull, began meeting every week to discuss homosexuality and homosexual disenfranchisement. Hay discovered the name "Mattachine" in his research into folk songs. The Mattachines had been all-male troupes of jesters during the Middle Ages in western Europe, who, though officially outlawed, boldly dressed as women and performed songs and dances throughout the countryside for the poor and oppressed.

The Mattachine Society meetings of the early 1950s were always secret. If a guest were invited, he would meet a member in public and be driven around to disorient him before being taken to Hay's home. Eventually, as the group grew in size, other more public meeting sites were used. In 1953, at a Mattachine convention at the *First Universalist Church, Ninth and Crenshaw (see above)*, a rift in the membership of the Mattachines forced out Hay and the other founders and brought in a more conservative leadership. The group became less political and eventually disbanded in Los Angeles, resurfacing in a new form a few years later in San Francisco. Other Mattachine Societies sprouted up in other cities across the country.

Hollywood Memorial Park
6000 Santa Monica Boulevard

Several queer movie stars are buried at this location, and an illustrated map available at the park directs visitors to the grave sites. Among them are Clifton Webb, who, according to Vito Russo, specialized in portrayals of "sissies." Webb's most memorable screen sissies were the murderous Waldo Lydecker in *Laura* (1944) and the aging, pathetic Elliott Templeton in *The Razor's Edge* (1946). Webb's sexual orientation was well-known in Hollywood, and the rumor was that he gave many of his handsome young paramours their start in the industry.

Also buried here is heartthrob Tyrone Power, who started as a stage actor and switched to films in 1936. That year, the movie *Lloyds of London* made him a star, and he continued to be a major box-office draw into the 1950s. Though he married three times, Power reportedly also enjoyed affairs with songwriter Lorenz Hart and actor Errol Flynn, among others.

If you're interested in more queer graves, at the equally campy *Forest Lawn Memorial Park, 6300 Forest Lawn Drive,* are the final resting places of Errol Flynn and Liberace, among others.

Rock Hudson home
"The Castle"
9402 Beverly Crest Drive

Situated on a ridge overlooking Beverly Hills, The Castle was home to actor Rock Hudson (1925–1985) from 1962 until his death. At the height of his career, Universal Studios purchased it for him as part of his contract renewal. Made of Spanish-style stucco with a red-tile roof, the house was protected by a massive gate in the front and high cliffs on three sides, which ensured the closeted actor's privacy. Oddly, though, the gate to the house and the front door were never locked. A friend explained, "He liked the excitement of the unknown."

In his authorized biography, Hudson gave a detailed description of the house he loved and meticulously restored for twenty-three years. The interior included two living rooms, a steam room and gym, a theater with stage and footlights, and four fireplaces. Hudson liked to name the rooms of the house, and he christened his bedroom "the blue room" because it was carpeted in a rich royal blue. His bed was an immense wooden four-poster carved with a nude male figure. One of his favorite spots was the "playroom," or theater, which originally had been a garage. It housed a vast collection of films and all the best in projection equipment. A collection of rare records filled one wall. On the wooden stage, he rehearsed upcoming roles.

The Castle was decorated in what one of Hudson's friends termed "early butch"—dark wood, pewter candlesticks, zebra skins, and an assortment of wrought iron. On the red-tiled patio stood sculptures of naked boys. The patio led to a forty-foot pool with jacuzzi and lion's head fountain, and a twenty-foot barbecue that could cook enough meat to feed a hundred people. Also on the three and a half acres of grounds was a greenhouse overflowing with orchids.

For most of his years at The Castle, Hudson lived alone with his female housekeeper and seven dogs. But occasionally, he had a live-in lover. When he did, he was careful to maintain two separate phone lines for "appearances" and to make sure he was never photographed with the other man.

After his death from complications of AIDS, Hudson's memorial service was held at The Castle, attended by several hundred guests who were treated to chili, margaritas, and a mariachi band. If Hudson's life in Beverly Hills had screamed ostentation, then so did his death.

Lesbian-feminist Los Angeles

Following the Stonewall Rebellion in 1969 in New York, lesbians and gay men around the country were energized to make local gay rights movements happen. Los Angeles was no exception. The city had already seen the founding in the 1950s of homophile organizations such as the Mattachine Society and ONE, Inc., but after Stonewall the number of gay activist groups in southern California increased exponentially. The Gay Liberation Front (GLF), like its counterpart in New York, was L.A.'s first gay political action group, with both male and female members. But by 1971, women who experienced sexism within the coed movement began to break away from GLF to form their own distinctive lesbian liberation movement, which would continue to grow through the next two decades, with services for a diverse population of lesbians. The following are just a handful of the spaces and sites associated with the heyday of lesbian feminist activism in Los Angeles.*

Gay Women's Service Center, 1542 Glendale Boulevard, was one of the first social services centers for lesbians anywhere in the country (the Lesbian Resource Center in Seattle was founded about the same time). The center was founded by Del Whan and other women from the Gay Liberation Front (GLF) in 1971.

Lesbian Feminists, a group founded by women from GLF, met regularly at the *Women's Center, 1027 Crenshaw Boulevard,* beginning in 1972. It was, according to former member Yolanda Retter, "a high energy group." Lesbian-feminists lobbied NOW in support of the "lesbian resolution" passed in 1971, hosted a weekend coffeehouse, supported antirape projects, and participated in the First National Lesbian Kiss-In in 1973 in front of the L.A. County Museum of Art.

Lesbian Tide, 8855 Cattaragus Avenue, was founded in 1971 with Jeanne Cordova as its publisher. Published bimonthly, within a few years *LT* had a subscriber list of almost seven thousand. *Lesbian Tide*'s publisher and editors identified as "radical feminists," as opposed to socialist, Marxist, or separatist. Coverage included local and national current events; book, film, and music reviews; herstory; poetry; and personal testimony.

CatchOne, 4067 Pico Boulevard, which opened in the early 1970s, self-described as a bar with a "multiracial clientele." Though lesbians of color participated in all the early feminist groups and projects mentioned here, there were few physical spaces in the city that were specifically for them. Besides being a place to socialize and hang out, CatchOne was also used as a meeting, organizing, and fundraising space for women of color.

Sisters Liberation House, 745 South Oxford Street, opened in 1972 under the sponsorship of the Gay Community Services Center (*see above*). It provided both housing and meeting space for lesbians.

*My thanks to Yolanda Retter for her help and generosity in identifying these sites, which she has been documenting with careful detail. For more information, visit the L.A. Lesbian History Project on-line at http://www-lib.usc.edu/~retter/main.html.

Sisterhood Bookstore, 1915-3/4 Westwood Boulevard (then 1351 Westwood), opened its doors in 1972 and lasted into the 1990s selling publications, music, and jewelry by women.

Women's Building, 743 South Grandview, was a feminist space founded in 1973 with a strong lesbian presence. It later moved to *1727 Spring Street.* It was at the Women's Building that the historic Great American Lesbian Art Show (GALAS) was held in 1980. The building closed in 1991.

Connexxus Women's Center/Centro de Mujeres, 9054 Santa Monica Boulevard, was started in 1984 with the largest financial base of any L.A. lesbian organization, and it aimed to help rectify the lack of women-of-color spaces in the city. Connexxus set up support groups for Latinas, which still continue in East L.A. It also sponsored the first Latina Lesbian Mental Health Conference and funded a Latina lesbian photography project. In addition, Connexxus sponsored the June Mazer Lesbian Collection's move from Oakland to southern California in 1987. Connexxus folded in 1990.

June Mazer Lesbian Collection, 2969 Raymond Avenue, moved from Oakland to Los Angeles in 1987. (In Oakland, it was known as the West Coast Lesbian Archives.) This was its first location, but it later moved to its current site at *626 North Robertson.* Open by appointment, the Mazer Collection houses books, journals, videos, photographs, lesbian pulp novels, buttons, and tapes and albums.

ONE *magazine*
232 *South Hill Street*

Founded in January 1953, *ONE* magazine is usually credited with being the first homophile publication in this country. (In the 1920s, however, Henry Gerber's Society for Human Rights published two issues of *Friendship and Freedom. See* Chicago, Illinois.) A project of ONE, Inc., an educational group organized in 1952, *ONE* magazine took its name from a Thomas Carlyle quote, which the editors printed on the first page of every issue: ". . . a mystic bond of brotherhood makes all men one." A leading organ for homophile rights, the magazine operated from a post office box for several months, but by late 1953 had moved to offices at this address in downtown Los Angeles (now a parking lot), where the staff worked out of two rooms with one window and no phone. "Visitors are heartily welcome," the magazine announced, "and invited to bring any office furniture they'd like to contribute."

Over the course of its history, *ONE* experienced a number of setbacks with the United States postmaster in Los Angeles, beginning in its first summer when an issue was delayed for "inspection" by the post office. The following year, the Los Angeles postmaster seized copies of *ONE* magazine and refused to mail them, labeling them "obscene, lewd, lascivious and filthy."

ASIDE-STEP

Cole Porter first came west in 1935 to write the score for *Born to Dance*. He rented a house on Sunset Boulevard in Beverly Hills, but in the late 1930s began renting a house in Brentwood on Rockingham Place. According to one of his biographers, the glamorous Hollywood life brought out his more flamboyantly homosexual side, to his wife's dismay.

It was in Brentwood that Porter held his celebrated Sunday afternoon parties in the years following World War II, cultivating a rivalry with director George Cukor, with whom he was professionally friendly. Porter's parties were more informal than Cukor's, with parlor games and soft music playing in the background. According to Cukor's biographer, Patrick McGilligan, each man saw himself as "the center of this unique homosexual universe" and maneuvered to have the most handsome men at their soirees. While each had a devoted following, some guests party-hopped. "I had lunch at Cole's and dinner at George's," one guest later remembered, "but you never told one about the other." (*See also* New Haven, Connecticut, and Williamstown, Massachusetts.)

Though *ONE* editors challenged the postmaster's actions, a federal district judge upheld the postal service's action in 1956, and an appeals court reduced the magazine to "cheap pornography" in 1957. In 1958, however, the U.S. Supreme Court reversed the rulings of the two lower courts in what *ONE* described as a "legal and publishing landmark." Indeed, the historic ruling ensured that homophile publications would not suffer from further post office censorship. Despite its rocky times with the post office, *ONE* continued publication until the 1960s.

ONE Institute of Homophile Studies started in 1956, offering lectures and forums and maintaining a library devoted to gay publications. ONE was the first to offer classes in Homophile Studies, predating current gay and queer studies by nearly thirty years. Today, the ONE, Inc., Archives is a treasure trove of material on the movement for gay rights in this country.

OAKLAND

Gertrude Stein home
"Stratton House"
Thirteenth Avenue and Twenty-fifth Street

The first six years of Gertrude Stein's life (1874–1946) were nomadic. Born in Pittsburgh, she and family relocated several times before settling in Oakland in 1879. They spent their first year renting rooms at Tubbs Hotel before moving to a more permanent space, Stratton House.

Oakland at that time was half-country and half-city. For fifty dollars a month, the Steins rented a ten-acre farm at this site with a rambling house and an orchard. What Gertrude remembered most about the farm was the preponderance of reading materials. "Most of all," she wrote later, "there were books and food, food and books, both excellent things." She and her brother, Leo, were inseparable, playing and writing together, particularly after the death of their mother when Gertrude was just fourteen years old.

Gertrude left Oakland to attend college in the East, but she returned for a brief visit during her American lecture tour in 1935 to see the home where she had grown up. Sadly, she found the farm gone and the house no longer standing, having been replaced by a group of much smaller houses. Her famous observation was that there was "no there there."

Women's Press Collective
5251 Broadway

In the 1970s, the ideological concept of "Lesbian Nation" sprung up around the country. As Lillian Faderman writes, lesbian-feminists of the 1970s "wanted to create entirely new institutions and to shape a women's culture that would embody all the best values that were not male." A popular saying of the time was, "The power of the press belongs to those who own the presses," and lesbians set out with a vengeance to build a separate media network—newspapers and magazines, printing presses, publishing houses, and bookstores. "Existing institutions and channels for communication have ceased to meet the growing needs of the women's struggle," the editorial collective of the newspaper *off our backs* theorized in 1970.

Founded in 1970, this feminist collective dedicated itself to publishing and distributing books by women. Women's Press Collective not only published poetry chapbooks, it printed them, too. Included among its members was the poet Judy Grahn. Grahn's well-known collections *Edward the Dyke and Other Poems* and *A Woman Is Talking to Death* were first published by WPC, along with the poetry of Willyce Kim, Pat Parker, and Martha Shelley, among others.

PASADENA

Site of Bayard Rustin's arrest
Raymond Avenue and Green Street

A Quaker pacifist, Bayard Rustin (c. 1910–1987) was a major figure in the black civil rights movement in this country. One of the movers and shakers behind the Montgomery bus boycott in 1956, he became a trusted adviser to Dr. Martin Luther King, Jr., and went on to be the chief organizer of the historic 1963 March on Washington for Jobs and Freedom.

Rustin was also gay, a fact well known to King. Some black community leaders feared that his homosexuality would be used to discredit King or tarnish the march, so labor leader A. Philip Randolph was installed as titular head of the action, while Rustin did the behind-the-scenes organizing work as his "deputy."

But two weeks before the march, with the help of FBI director J. Edgar Hoover, archconservative Strom Thurmond revealed from the floor of the Senate (and in the *Congressional Record*) that Rustin had been arrested ten years earlier in Pasadena on "suspicion of lewd vagrancy," having been found in a parked car at this spot with two younger men. Rustin was sentenced to two months in the county jail. Rustin later called the arrest "an absolute setup"; he had been organizing for civil rights as far back as the early 1940s and was known as an agitator. At the time of his arrest, he had been leading demonstrations in southern California against discrimination in public places.

Newspapers across the country carried stories on their front pages about the purported scandal. To their credit, black religious and labor leaders stood firmly behind Rustin, as did King. "We have absolute confidence in Bayard Rustin's integrity and ability," read their public statement. The march brought a quarter of a million people to Washington and is now viewed as one of the most significant events in the civil rights movement in this country, the scene of King's immortal "I Have a Dream" speech.

ASIDE-STEP

Literary critic F. O. Matthiessen (1902–1950) was born in Pasadena and lived there until his parents divorced in 1915. Matthiessen is known as the scholar who coined the term "American Renaissance" to describe the flowering of literature in the mid-nineteenth century, his area of expertise. He was lovers with painter Russell Cheney for twenty years and, sadly, committed suicide after Cheney died.

SAN DIEGO

Balboa Park
This park was a well-known cruising area for gay men in the 1950s and 1960s, and one often staked out by police. In 1968, a three-week sweep of the park and nearby beaches by police led to the entrapments and arrests of seventy-five gay men.

Las Hermanas
4003 Wabash Street
In the late 1970s, this was a coffeehouse and an ad hoc cultural center for lesbians in the San Diego area. Besides dinners and brunch, Las Hermanas ("The Sisters") also offered concerts, dancing, workshops, and meetings for groups such as AA.

SAN FRANCISCO

Is there any place on Earth as gay as San Francisco? Even the city's unofficial theme song, "I Left My Heart in San Francisco," was written in 1954 by two gay men, Douglass Cross and his lover, George Cory, who had moved to New York and were homesick for the "City by the Bay."

World War II was a transformative event for queer people, one that threw them together in same-sex situations and fostered the beginnings of gay community. After the war, many gay servicemen and -women remained in port towns like San Francisco, looking for new lives and loves outside the confines of their hometowns. Today, San Francisco has one of the largest percentages of gay people in the general population of any city in the country. For a fascinating and informative overview of San Francisco's gay past and present, see Susan Stryker and Jim Van Buskirk's *Gay by the Bay* (Chronicle Books, 1996).

Babe Bean birthplace
806 Green Street

Babe Bean, a passing woman who lived on a houseboat moored in scenic McLeod's Lake near Stockton, became famous in the fall of 1897, when she was detained by police in Stockton for wearing men's clothing. The Stockton newspaper published her picture (in men's tie and hat) and a series of sensational feature stories about her. "As a man," Bean said to justify passing, "I can travel freely, feel protected and find work." After a brief stint as a newspaper reporter in Stockton, Bean, under the alias Jack Garland, enlisted in the army during the Spanish-American War. Later, Bean moved to San Francisco and became known as a caretaker of the poor and homeless. In 1936, Bean/Garland died suddenly of a heart attack and was revealed to have once been Elvira Virginia Mugarrieta. She had been born in 1869 at this San Francisco address, the daughter of José Marcos Mugarrieta, the Mexican consul.

Black Cat Cafe
710 Montgomery Street

Like many early gay bars, the famous Black Cat didn't start out that way. Just a few blocks from the center of North Beach, the Black Cat was first distinguished as a bohemian hangout (it billed itself as "Bohemia of the Barbary Coast") and provided the backdrop for part of Jack Kerouac's *On the Road*. Following World War II, when gay men and lesbians thronged to San Francisco after service in the Pacific, the Black Cat assumed a "gayer" personality. The poet Allen Ginsberg, who knew it in the 1950s, described it as an enormous bar with a honky-tonk piano that "everyone" went to: "All the gay screaming queens would come, the heterosexual gray flannel suit types, longshoremen. All the poets went there."

At a time when homophile organizations like the Mattachine Society were largely conciliatory to the police and to city officials, the Black Cat was noteworthy as a site of resistance. Its owner, Sol Stoumen, refused to pay off the police for protection against harassment, and his bar was routinely raided and fined in the 1940s through the early 1960s. During the

1950s, the Black Cat's flamboyant drag performer, José Sarria, sang campy parodies of torch songs, giving them political twists, and finished each set by leading the bar's patrons in his rendition of "God Save Us Nelly Queens," even when members of the vice squad were present. His brand of activist theater made him extremely popular among gays, and in 1961 Sarria decided to campaign for city supervisor, knowing that he had no chance of winning. Though he received only a few thousand votes, Sarria said later that his intention had been to show his peers that a gay man had the right to run, whether he won or lost.

The Black Cat was closed for good in 1963. Said the attorney for the club, "That place is like an institution. This is like closing the cable cars or the Golden Gate Bridge."

California Hall
625 Polk Street

The New Year's Ball of 1965 was held here on the first of January. The ball was a "respectable" event, organized by six homophile organizations to raise money for the newly formed Council on Religion and the Homosexual, which was designed to open communication between the established church and the city's gay community. Though council members met with police in advance to ensure a smooth-running event without incident, the police didn't hold up their end of the bargain. (Surprise!) As intimidation, they took photographs of each person entering the fundraiser and parked paddy wagons outside the hall. Several attorneys were arrested for arguing with a policeman at the entrance.

Despite the deliberate police harassment, five hundred people attended the ball, gay and straight, lay and clergy. Outrage against the police interference ran high after the event and led to a greater politicization of the homophile community, which demanded certain changes in police dealings with gays. Concessions ultimately obtained from the city included having a police liaison to the gay community, a hot line for minority groups against police brutality, and a National Sex Forum to educate officials and police about human sexuality.

A FEW OTHER PRE-STONEWALL GAY HANGOUTS IN SAN FRANCISCO

> *Finocchio's, 506 Broadway (at Kearny Street):* This world-renowned bar opened its doors as a speakeasy in 1929 and was legalized in 1933 with the end of Prohibition. Finocchio's has catered to a gay and lesbian clientele for years because it has specialized in female impersonation, billing itself as "America's most unusual nightclub." During World War II, it was declared off-limits to military personnel.

> *The Old Crow, Market Street:* At this location from 1935 to 1980, this bar attracted older men and had a stringent policy of excluding women.

> *Sailor Boy Tavern, Howard Street:* Opened in 1938, this was only a block from the Embarcadero YMCA and catered to a (you guessed it) navy crowd.

Daughters of Bilitis/The Ladder
693 Mission Street

Started in 1955 as a social group providing an alternative to the bars, the Daughters of Bilitis, the first U.S. lesbian organization, expanded rapidly into a lesbian rights organization (*see box below*). The name "Bilitis" was taken from a poem by Pierre Louys about a lesbian of Sappho's time.

Launched in 1956, DOB's magazine, *The Ladder*, started with a post office box number but by its fourth issue gave this Mission Street address as its publication office. Its masthead listed Phyllis Lyon as editor and Del Martin as assistant editor. (Lyon and Martin, who later wrote *Lesbian/Woman*, were a couple, and they are still together forty years later.) Early issues of *The Ladder* contained such articles as "A Citizen's Right in Case of Arrest" and the regular column, "Lesbiana," which briefly reviewed books of interest to lesbians. *The Ladder*'s subscription coupon specified that it cost "$2.50 a year, mailed in a plain, sealed envelope."

The Ladder also included a monthly calendar of DOB events. In the

PURPOSE OF THE DAUGHTERS OF BILITIS

A women's organization for the purpose of promoting the integration of the homosexual into society by:

1. Education of the variant, with particular emphasis on the psychological, physiological and sociological aspects, to enable her to understand herself and make her adjustment to society in all its social, civic and economic implications—this to be accomplished by establishing and maintaining as complete a library as possible of both fiction and non-fiction literature on the sex deviant theme; by sponsoring public discussions on pertinent subjects to be conducted by leading members of the legal, psychiatric, religious, and other professions; by advocating a mode of behavior and dress acceptable to society.

2. Education of the public at large through acceptance first of the individual, leading to an eventual breakdown of erroneous taboos and prejudices; through public discussion meetings aforementioned; through dissemination of educational literature on the homosexual theme.

3. Participation in research projects by duly authorized and responsible psychologists, sociologists and other such experts directed towards further knowledge of the homosexual.

4. Investigation of the penal code as it pertains to the homosexual, proposal of changes to provide an equitable handling of cases involving this minority group, and promotion of these changes through due process of law in the state legislatures.

—from *The Ladder*, 1956

early months, DOB business meetings were routinely held at *1030-D Steiner Street*, while discussion meetings took place at *465 Geary Street*. Discussions featured guest speakers on topics such as "Fear and Human Emotions," "Self-Acceptance," "The Sexual Impulse," and "The Legal Status of DOB." Occasionally, DOB held a joint meeting with its brother organization, the Mattachine Society, which had offices at *1830 Sutter Street*.

By 1958, DOB membership and *Ladder* subscribers had grown exponentially, forcing the organization to seek new quarters at the *Department Store Center Building, 165 O'Farrell Street*. (Did they know that O'Farrell Street had once been home to that infamous dyke Alice B. Toklas before she went to Paris and met her Gertrude?) There, DOB maintained office hours three times a week and operated a lending library of lesbian titles, which could be borrowed for thirty days.

The Ladder enjoyed continuous publication until the early 1970s, though by that time, DOB had moved to an office at *1005 Market Street*. Today, complete sets of the magazine can be found at various lesbian and gay archives across the country.

Isadora Duncan birthplace
501 Taylor Street (at Geary)

The birthplace of dancer and free spirit Isadora Duncan (1878–1927) is commemorated by a plaque at this site, which reads: "Daughter of California Pioneers, America's Genius of Dance. . . . She created a new art form, liberating the dance as an expression of life." Young Isadora lived here only briefly, though. Her parents separated when she was a baby, and her mother moved the family to Oakland. She supported her four children by teaching piano.

All four children were natural performers, learning to dance and staging their own plays. As teenagers, Isadora and her sister opened their first dance school in Oakland and then a second in San Francisco. They favored classical music as accompaniment and wore flowing Grecian tunics as they matched their movements to "the rhythm of the waves." It was a style that broke with tradition, and Isadora Duncan is often credited with being the first proponent of modern dance.

A lover of both men and women, Duncan led an enigmatic, wandering life, touring the world to give performances and to open schools for teaching her naturalistic dance philosophy. Her life and her death—strangled by her own flowing scarf, which got caught in the wheel of her car while she was motoring through southern France—have been highly romanticized. (Another "free spirit," Vanessa Redgrave, portrayed her in the 1967 film *Isadora*.) Today, the Temple of Wings in Berkeley still teaches her theory of dance.

Full Moon Coffee House and Bookstore
4416 Eighteenth Street (at Eureka)

Advertised as a "worker-owned, consensus collective," Full Moon opened on March 7, 1974. In addition to selling books, records, posters, and cards, a weekly coffeehouse featured musical performances and poetry readings. That year, from a low platform that comprised the "stage," visitors could hear Cris Williamson sing and play on a donated piano for a $1.50 cover. On another evening, Rita Mae Brown was on hand to "rap." As Deborah Goleman Wolf described it in her book *The Lesbian Community*, "The coffeehouse itself is a long, rather narrow room, running the length of the building. . . . The overall impression is one of comfort, a cozy place in which one can spend several hours pleasantly."

Run by a collective and staffed by shifts of volunteers who considered the coffeehouse/bookstore their "real work," Full Moon's space was also available for theatrical productions, meetings, and workshops—in short, whatever would "serve the women's community." Bulletin boards ran announcements for events, services, jobs, and housing. Women were encouraged to bring in and display their artwork. As did many women's and lesbian bookstores across the country, the space functioned as an ad hoc community center.

Elsa Gidlow home
150 Joice Street

Originally from Montreal, poet Elsa Gidlow (1898–1988) was a pioneering lesbian writer. In 1917, she started a salon in her parents' home that attracted other queer writers and artists, one of whom, Roswell George Mills, a gay man, wrote an advice column in a local newspaper under the pseudonym Margaret Currie. Mills and Gidlow became close friends, attending concerts together, sharing their writing, and talking about favorite readings by Havelock Ellis and Edward Carpenter, two early sexual reformers. Gidlow's salon also included an unhappily married middle-aged woman named Marguerite Desmarias, with whom Gidlow had an affair.

The salon expanded, dubbing itself "Les Mouches fantastiques," and started a literary magazine by the same name. With the support of her friends, Gidlow began publishing poetry in several Canadian journals and launched her writing career. In 1923, her collection *On a Grey Thread* became one of the earliest volumes of explicitly lesbian poetry published in North America.

After the breakup of her second lesbian relationship, Gidlow moved with Mills to New York City, where they shared a flat in Greenwich Village. In 1926, Gidlow migrated to San Francisco, and to pay the rent, she worked as an editor for a variety of trade journals. Always first and foremost a poet, she was well known in the city's queer and bohemian subcultures. In 1940, she relocated to Marin County, where her home attracted many prominent writers and intellectuals. Writing a total of fifteen books, including an autobiography, she continued to publish even in old age and to mentor younger lesbian writers. Her volume *Sapphic Songs* was an early title from the lesbian-feminist publisher Diana Press (*see* Baltimore, Mary-

> Every lesbian personality I have knowledge of is in some way creative. . . . The lesbian has sought wholeness within herself, not requiring, in the old romantic sense, to be 'completed' by an opposite.
>
> —Elsa Gidlow, 1977

land). Gidlow's papers reside at the Gay and Lesbian Historical Society of Northern California.

Macondray Lane

Macondray Lane was the model for Barbary Lane, the Russian Hill street made famous by Armistead Maupin's *Tales of the City*. In 1976, Maupin's story began as a daily serial in the *San Francisco Chronicle*, relating the adventures of an eclectic group of residents at 28 Barbary Lane. When it was published as a book in 1978, *Tales* was an immediate best-seller. Maupin followed a community of friends and lovers, straight and gay, through six volumes, ending with *Sure of You* in 1989. His chronicle of Barbary Lane proved a keenly observant satire of the 1970s and 1980s.

Harvey Milk home and Castro Camera
Castro Street (between 18th and 19th Streets)

Harvey Milk (1930–1978) is probably the most famous gay politician of our time. Originally from Brooklyn, Milk moved to San Francisco in 1968, where he worked as a financial analyst and eventually owned a camera shop in the Castro district. This Victorian storefront (now home to "The Skin Zone") was the site of Castro Camera, which Milk opened with his lover, Scott Smith, in 1972 and operated for four years. The couple didn't care that they knew little about cameras—Milk wanted to own a real neighborhood store, like his family back in Brooklyn had. The roomy store had a hand-painted shingle on the door that read "Yes, We Are Very Open." Harvey and Scott lived upstairs.

As Milk became increasingly active in local politics, Castro Camera functioned as an ad hoc community center, and Milk was the "unofficial mayor of Castro Street." Signs in the store's large picture windows advertised demonstrations, protests, and neighborhood meetings; camera and film sales became secondary to politics (the store's sorry financial picture led the couple to close it in 1976). At night, Milk transferred the addresses from every check written to the store into his own political mailing list.

Milk became involved in organizing gay voter registration drives, helping to establish the first Castro Street Fair, speaking out against Anita Bryant's antigay campaign, and working against the Briggs initiative, a proposal to bar lesbians and gay men from teaching in California public schools. During the mid-1970s, he made several bids for public office, all of which proved unsuccessful. His goal, he once told a friend, was to be mayor of San Francisco.

Then the election of the liberal, gay-supportive mayor George Moscone in 1975 paved the way for Milk's election to the San Francisco Board of Supervisors in 1977, making Milk the first openly gay elected official in the city's history. Sadly, both he and Moscone were gunned down by the radically conservative supervisor Dan White the following year. White's lawyer pleaded the infamous "Twinkie defense"—that eating too much junk food had diminished White's ability to reason. White went to jail anyway, but on the charge of manslaughter rather than murder one. After he was released in 1985, he committed suicide.

"Cruisin' the Castro" is a walking tour of the Castro district, led by a local historian, that includes stops at many sites associated with Milk, including the camera store; reservations can be made by calling 415-550-8110.

Julia Morgan office
Merchants Exchange Building
465 California Street, 13th floor

Julia Morgan (1872–1957) enjoyed a successful fifty-year career as an architect, designing over seven hundred buildings. A native Californian, she received an engineering degree from Berkeley, and then became the first woman ever admitted into the architecture program at the Ecole des Beaux Arts in Paris. The 1906 earthquake created a desperate need for architects, enabling Morgan to open her own office, first at her family home in Oakland, and then shortly after at this location. The name on the front door of the suite read simply, "Julia Morgan, Architect."

The main drafting room of the office seated nine or ten designers in good times. Morgan's office was a separate twelve-by-fourteen room lined with bookcases, holding over five hundred books on architecture. One employee remembered, "You worked when you were in Julia Morgan's office. You worked from eight to five and you didn't stop and you didn't take time off." Though she may have pushed her employees hard, Morgan also shared the profits from the business with them, which was highly unusual for architectural firms.

A SAMPLE OF CALIFORNIA STRUCTURES DESIGNED BY JULIA MORGAN

Berkeley
> Berkeley City Club (1919–1920)
> Delta Zeta sorority house, University of California (1923)

Los Angeles
> *Herald Examiner* Building (1915)
> Hollywood Studio Club (c. 1925)

Oakland
> Chapel of the Chimes (1926–1930)
> First Baptist Church (1907)
> Mills College structures—Margaret Carnegie Library (1905–1906); "El Campanil" bell tower (1903); college gymnasium (1909)
> Ming Quong Chinese Girls School (1924–1925) (now Alderwood Center, Mills College)

Pacific Grove
> Asilomar Conference Center (1913)

San Francisco
> Chinese YWCA (c. 1920) (now Chinese Community Center)
> Katherine Delmar Burke School (1916)

San Simeon
> Hearst Castle (1919–1942)

Many of Morgan's projects were women's organizations, primarily YWCAs, and schools for girls and young women (*see box above*). Her buildings were distinguished by their use of light and color, and she became expert at designing pools. But her most famous and ambitious design was San Simeon, the estate of publishing mogul William Randolph Hearst. Morgan developed a close rapport with Hearst, and the twenty-three-year design and construction project was a collaboration between the unlikely pair (*see* San Simeon, California).

Morgan's biographers have little to say about her private life, except that she never even considered marriage. Tiny in stature and weight, Morgan favored tailored "mannish" suits and French silk shirts. Was she a lesbian or simply an independent career woman? Modest and intensely private, Morgan was virtually anonymous outside of her circle of clients, never writing articles or entering contests. When she retired and closed her California Street office in 1951, she destroyed all her files, blueprints, and drawings, rationalizing that her clients had copies and the public had no use for them. She spent her last four years living alone as a recluse in her remodeled Victorian home on Divisidero Street.

Palace Hotel
Market and New Montgomery Streets (southwest corner)

This seven-story Victorian hotel is where Oscar Wilde stayed in April 1882 on his yearlong lecture tour of North America. In Wilde's day, the hotel boasted a central court with potted palms, rocking chairs, and spittoons. The Palace was noteworthy for withstanding the great earthquake of 1906—its exterior iron bolts were insurance against collapse.

Wilde arrived first in New York City from England in January, telling a customs official, "I have nothing to declare but my genius." Wilde gave lectures in many major cities across the United States and Canada and was wined and dined by leading Irish Americans. In San Francisco, Wilde lectured on Irish poets and poetry, emphasizing the influence of Celtic myths on European literature.

One of Wilde's other stops was a visit to the aging Walt Whitman at his brother's home in Camden, New Jersey. The old poet and the young playwright talked for several hours, sipping homemade elderberry wine. "If it had been vinegar," Wilde later wrote, "I should have drunk it all the same, for I have an admiration for that man which I can hardly express."

Society for Individual Rights (SIR)
83 Sixth Street

The Society for Individual Rights, a homophile organization, was founded in 1964 and listed its office at this address. Started by activist gay bar owners who were fed up with police harassment, SIR differed significantly from earlier homophile organizations in that it took for granted from its inception the worth of homosexuals and their right to public expression of their sexual orientation. SIR leaders set out to foster a sense of community among gay men in the city, offering varied social events and establishing the country's first gay community center in 1966. Membership quadrupled in just two years. On the political front, SIR members did voter registration drives and sponsored evenings when candidates for local office could meet and address the gay constituency. SIR also undertook a campaign to educate gay men about the risks of venereal disease, and it led demonstrations that brought a halt to police harassment of the city's gay bars. Also among the group's significant accomplishments was the publishing of *Vector*, a monthly magazine sold on newsstands across San Francisco, which featured a mixture of articles about gay rights, book and theater reviews, gossip, and glossy photographs.

Alice B. Toklas home
922 O'Farrell Street

In 1877, Alice Babette Toklas was born at this address, the home of her maternal grandparents, the Levinskys. Her biographer, Diana Souhami, describes this block of O'Farrell Street as "solid bourgeois housing in a fashionable part of town." In *The Autobiography of Alice B. Toklas*, Gertrude Stein had Alice reminisce about her early years, "I led in my childhood and youth the gently bred existence of my class and kind."

When Alice was thirteen years old, her father moved the family to Seattle to be closer to his mercantile business ventures (*see* Seattle, Washington). In her youth, Alice was a serious student of the piano, but she abruptly gave it up as a young woman. Gertrude wrote in the *Autobiography*, "I studied and practiced assiduously but shortly then it seemed futile . . . there was no real interest that led me on." After her mother became ill with cancer, Alice returned to San Francisco with her father and brothers, and when her mother died, the family moved in with Alice's grandfather again. Alice took care of the household and served as hostess—a role she would repeat later on with her life companion.

In 1907, Alice made the acquaintance of Gertrude Stein's brother and sister-in-law, who were visiting from their home in Paris and who told intriguing stories about the art and culture they enjoyed there. The following year, Alice decided to see Paris for herself using money inherited from her grandfather, and while she was abroad looked up her acquaintances, the Steins. They, in turn, introduced her to Gertrude, who had moved to Paris a few years earlier trying to forget a soured love affair (*see* Baltimore, Maryland). The rest, as they say, is herstory.

Valencia Street

Many of the physical sites of 1970s and early 1980s lesbian-feminist San Francisco grew up on or near Valencia Street in the Mission District and included the following:

Amelia's, 647 Valencia Street: A bar opened by Rikki Streicher in the early 1980s, who also ran the historic Maude's Study (*see box below*).

Artemis Cafe, 1199 Valencia Street: Opened in 1977, Amelia's had a variety of veggie sandwiches and quiches, lesbian entertainers on the weekends, and a wealth of information on their community bulletin board. It is now called the Radio Valencia Cafe.

Old Wives Tales Bookstore, 1009 Valencia Street: Founded in 1976 and still going strong.

The Women's Building, 3543 Eighteenth Street: Organized in 1970, the Women's Building still operates at this address, now owning its building.

A Few Other Pre-Stonewall Lesbian Bars in San Francisco

> *Mona's (Club 440), 440 Broadway:* In the 1930s, the celebrated 250-pound cross-dressing lesbian Gladys Bentley used to perform here.

> *Hula Shack, 979 Folsom Street:* This was listed in the 1963 guide *The Lavender Baedeker.*

> *Maud's Study, 937 Cole Street:* Rikki Streicher opened Maud's Study in 1966 and kept it going until 1989, making it at that time the city's oldest continuously operating lesbian bar. Its history and ultimate closing were the subject of the documentary *Last Call at Maud's* (1993).

The center offers bilingual referrals and information, workshops, fairs and other cultural programs, and rental space for women's groups.

The Whoo Cares?
782 Haight Street

An article in the September 1, 1958, edition of the *San Francisco Chronicle*, titled "That Was No Lady, That Was . . . ," gave a rare picture of a tough dyke bar from the heyday of butch-femme. On the preceding evening, a straight man named Roberto Lopez dropped into The Whoo Cares? and learned the hard way that he had wandered into a lesbian bar. He noticed "couples dancing" and proceeded to ask a few women to dance. An argument ensued, and "he was jumped by about eight women wielding broken beer bottles," some of whom were wearing men's clothing. Lopez's injuries required minor surgery. In the official police report, it stated that The Whoo Cares? "is frequented by many sexual degenerates, lesbians and homosexuals."

SAN SIMEON

Hearst Castle
750 Hearst Castle Road

Designed by the architect Julia Morgan, whose sexual orientation we can only guess (*see* San Francisco), San Simeon was her largest and most famous commission, occupying much of her time from 1919 to 1942. Morgan had designed several homes for Phoebe Apperson Hearst, the mother of newspaper magnate William Randolph Hearst, and in 1915, she won the commission of designing the *Herald Examiner* building in Los Angeles for Hearst himself. He was so pleased by her work that he awarded her the plum of designing his own personal "castle."

At the time San Simeon was being designed and constructed, Hearst was living in New York City, so the collaboration over the design that occurred between him and his architect was all accomplished by telegram and letter. Morgan traveled from her office in San Francisco to the one-hundred-and-thirty-seven-acre site almost every weekend for approximately eighteen years, overseeing an army of artisans and an array of details. There were a main building and several guest houses with one hundred twenty-seven rooms in all, including dozens of bedrooms and baths, fourteen sitting rooms, an eighty-foot assembly hall, two libraries, a movie theater and billiard room, and two sumptuously tiled pools. The main building was designed to look like a church in southern Spain that was a favorite of Hearst's, and it was adorned with treasures he had brought back from his many travels. The expenditures for the twenty-three-year project were just under five million dollars.

SANTA MONICA

James Dean home
1422 Twenty-third Street

This was the childhood home of actor James Dean (1931–1955). Though Dean was born in Indiana, he and his parents moved to California in 1936 so his father could pursue an attractive job offer in a dental laboratory. When his mother died four years later, Dean was rejected by his father and sent back to Indiana to live with relatives. He returned to California in 1949 as a young actor trying to break into movies. (*See also* Fairmount, Indiana, and Marion, Indiana.)

Greta Garbo / Mercedes de Acosta meeting place
165 Mabery Road

In 1931, when she was living just blocks away at *1717 San Vincente Boulevard*, the young Swedish film sensation Greta Garbo met and fell for Mercedes de Acosta, a dramatic-looking writer with pale skin and raven black hair who habitually sported white flannel trousers, silk shirts, berets, and boyish haircuts. Both women had been invited to tea at this address on Mabery Road, which was the home of their friend Salka Viertel. A playwright and stage manager for Eva LeGallienne (who was also her lover), de Acosta had come to Hollywood from New York two years earlier to write a treatment for Pola Negri.

After de Acosta and Garbo met, the proverbial sparks flew, and they spent six weeks sequestered at Silver Lake, swimming naked and walking in the mountains. There they "honeymooned" on an island in the middle of the lake, in a small log cabin that belonged to actor Wallace Beery.

Garbo later credited de Acosta with giving her the "foundation" on which she based the wonderfully androgynous character Queen Christina. While lovers with de Acosta, Garbo began her habit of wearing trousers in public. The two women would stroll boldly down Hollywood Boulevard in similar attire, flaunting their relationship. The same year that they met, the lovers moved to adjoining homes on North Rockingham Road in Brent-

She used to climb ahead of me, and with her hair blown back, her face turned to the wind and sun, she would leap from rock to rock on her bare Hellenic feet . . . looking like some radiant, elemental, glorious god and goddess melted into one.

—Mercedes de Acosta, writing about her
1931 "honeymoon" with Greta Garbo

wood. Over the years, their relationship ran hot and cold, each taking numerous lovers. (De Acosta was with Marlene Dietrich for a while.) In 1960 came the final split, when Garbo—the queen of privacy—became upset by the publication of de Acosta's "tell-all" memoir, *Here Lies the Heart*.

SOQUEL

Charley Parkhurst polling place
Soquel Firehouse
4747 Soquel Drive
A plaque at this location honors the memory of Charlotte "Charley" Parkhurst (1812–1870), a passing woman. As a young girl, Parkhurst escaped from an orphanage in the East by donning boys' clothing and learning how to drive a six-horse team. Heading west, she made her living as a stagecoach driver, beginning in the years of the California gold rush. On November 3, 1868, Parkhurst marched into this polling place and cast her vote in the presidential election, fifty years before women were granted suffrage. The plaque notes that she "shot and killed at least one bandit." Like so many other passing women, Parkhurst's birth sex was discovered only after her death. (*See also* Watsonville, California.)

WATSONVILLE

Charley Parkhurst grave
Pioneer Cemetery
Freedom Boulevard

A grave marker commemorates Charlotte "Charley" Parkhurst, a passing woman, as "One-eyed Charley . . . noted whip of the Gold Rush Days." An able stagecoach driver who knew the dirt roads around Watsonville like the back of her hand, Parkhurst acquired her nickname because she had lost an eye shoeing one of her horses. She was believed to be a man until her death in 1870. (*See also* Soquel, California.)

COLORADO

COLORADO SPRINGS

Pikes Peak

With a height of 14,110 feet, Pikes Peak is a formidable challenge for any climber, but in 1893, a young English professor named Katharine Lee Bates (*see also* Falmouth, Massachusetts, and Wellesley, Massachusetts) made it to the summit. At Wellesley, Bates earned only four hundred dollars a year and was forced to accept frequent guest lectureships in order to make ends meet. During the summer of 1893, Bates took a teaching position at Colorado College, though it meant several lonely months away from her intimate companion, Katharine Coman. After scaling Pikes Peak and admiring the breathtaking view of "spacious skies" and "purple mountains' majesty," she was inspired to write the poem "America the Beautiful" in just one day, penciling four verses quickly into her notebook. Bates recalled that she was disappointed with her effort, but when the poem was published in 1895, it became an instant hit with the public and was later set to music. Today, a plaque at the summit of Pikes Peak carries the first two verses of the poem Bates at first called "disheartening."

DENVER

Big Mama Rag
1724 Gaylord Street

Big Mama Rag was a lesbian-feminist monthly news journal that began publishing in 1973 at *1000 East 23rd Street*, and its office moved to this site the following year. At the start, it cost a mere twenty-five cents per copy. *BMR* self-defined as "socialist oriented," with a fervent support of the Mental Patients Liberation Movement. Though its primary focus was on local and national news, it also included features about women's health and work, book reviews of publications from women's presses, interviews, classified ads, and occasional poetry. Like many newspaper collectives, *BMR* suffered from chronic money problems and internal political conflicts (all collective members had to agree on every story) and struggled for a decade before folding.

Denver Lesbian Center
1895 Lafayette Street
In the 1970s, the Denver Lesbian Center was an active component of the local women's community. The center sponsored consciousness-raising groups of a variety of types, a lending library, and a weekend coffeehouse at the *First Unitarian Church, 14th Avenue and Lafayette*, which cost a mere quarter for admission. DLC also provided information on local resources of interest to lesbian-feminists.

Feminist bookstores
The Denver women's community enjoyed several bookstores/ad hoc community centers in the 1970s. Among them were the following:
Woman to Woman Feminist Center, 2023 East Colfax Street, carried books, records, posters, and newspapers. In addition, the store/center provided a lending library of lesbian books, meeting space for groups, and a bulletin board of local information.
The Woman's Voice, 673 South Pearl Street, sold books and other feminist items and provided space for art exhibits. In 1973, the store stated as its long-term financial goals to provide alternative job opportunities for local feminists and to put money back into the community in the form of an abortion-counseling service and a group meeting space.

Pre-Stonewall hangouts
In an article in *Social Science Journal*, Thomas Jacob Noel locates several gay bars operating in Denver in the pre-Stonewall era. *Moses Home, Fifteenth Street near Larimer*, was a saloon in the late nineteenth century,

when Denver was a frontier town, that may have been an early homosexual hangout. The first exclusively gay bar in the city opened in 1939 and was called *The Pit,* on Seventeenth Street in the heart of downtown Denver. During World War II, *Mary's Tavern,* located on Broadway, was a favorite with servicemen. A group of gay soldiers from Denver's Lowry Air Force Base began frequenting Mary's, camping it up and getting thrown out at first. But when they kept coming back, the straight clients started to leave, and Mary's metamorphosed into a gay hangout.

The city's *Chessman Park* has long been a cruising ground for gay men. After the Stonewall rebellion, the park was the site of a "Gay-In" in 1974, the city's first gay pride event.

The Three Sisters, 3358 Mariposa, located in a roomy adobe building, is reportedly the oldest women's bar in the country that is still in operation. It is unique in that it has always been (according to one ad) "owned by women—run by women—for women." Its nickname is "Six Tits."

HAWAII

HAWAII ISLAND

KAILUA-KONA

Ahuena Heiau
Palani Road (adjacent to King Kamehameha's Kona Beach Hotel)
Located on the Kona coast, these restored thatched-roof structures comprised the royal living compound of King Kamehameha I (1758–1819), the Hawaiian monarch who unified the islands by force in 1810. The powerful six-foot-six Kamehameha "the Great" originally ruled from Lahaina on Maui (*see below*) but moved his residence here in 1812. He had several wives, but he also had an *aikane*, or male lover, named Kuakini, a high chief who later became governor of the Big Island. Kamehameha also died at this royal site, and his body was prepared for burial in the traditional way—the flesh was burned and buried, while the bones were taken away and hidden. This was to preserve the king's *mana*, or spiritual power. (*See also* North Kohala, Hawaii Island, and Lahaina, Maui Island.)

In 1824, Kamehameha the Great's youngest son, Kamehameha III (1815–1854), became the ruler of the islands at age nine. The boy received a Christian education under the Reverend Hiram Bingham but remained steadfastly Hawaiian in his beliefs throughout his life. Like his father, Kamehameha III enjoyed the company of an *aikane*, a man named Ka'omi. When the Reverend Bingham pressured Kamehameha III to marry, the king took his own sister as his wife.

According to historian Lilikala Kame'eleihiwa, before the storming of Hawaii by white Christian missionaries in the late eighteenth and early nineteenth centuries, native Hawaiians were very tolerant of homosexual intimacy, and it was common for male chiefs to take male lovers. Little, however, is known about relationships between women.

KAPA'AU

Keokea Beach County Park
Highway 270
In the tiny village of Kapa'au, there is a statue of the celebrated King Kamehameha I (*see above*), the queer ruler who unified the islands. A boulder in this local park is known as Kamehameha Rock, because it was reportedly the mammoth stone that the future king lifted as a teenager to prove his kingly *mana*, or spiritual power.

KILAUEA CALDERA

Halema'una'a Crater
Chain of Craters Road
The most famous of Hawaiian goddesses is Pele, the Volcano or Fire Goddess. By legend, Pele first landed in Kauai but was pursued by her vengeful sister from island to island until she came to settle on the Big Island. Native Hawaiians believe that Pele resides in Halema'una'a Crater, a sacred site in this region of many volcanoes. A strong-willed, fiery-tempered Amazon and a lesbian icon, Pele has reputedly been seen in the region of the crater in many forms, most often as a long-haired young woman or an old crone, always disappearing just as observers come too close to her. Chain of Craters Road is periodically closed due to violent volcanic eruptions—the temper tantrums of a goddess! Visitors are warned not to remove any rocks or sand from the region, which offends Pele and can bring bad luck and misfortune. Pele's presence here, some believe, is the reason women on the Big Island won more equal footing with men sooner than women on all the other islands.

NORTH KOHALA

Mookini Heaiu
Highway 270
The remains of this fifth-century temple consist of moss-covered rocks on a bluff with a clear view of the island of Maui. Just a few hundred yards away, a low-walled foundation marks the reputed birthplace of King Kamehameha I in 1758 (*see above*), the same year as Halley's Comet. The royal baby was taken to the ancient Mookini temple for birth rituals, and then secreted away to be raised in the Waipi'o Valley (off Highway 240).

MAUI ISLAND

LAHAINA

Brick Palace
Lahaina Harbor
The first royal capital of the Hawaiian Islands, much of the town of Lahaina has been given National Historic Landmark status. Facing the scenic harbor is the Brick Palace, which was the first royal residence of Kamehameha I (the Great), Hawaii's queer king. All that's left now are the foundations of what was once a western-style structure, a modest two-story brick building. In the mainstream guidebooks, the story is that Kamehameha located his capital here to be close to the grave of his beloved first wife. But since he also had a beloved *aikane*, or male lover, we might wonder how much of the story has been "straightened out" by history. (*See also* Kailua-Kona, Hawaii Island, and North Kohala, Hawaii Island.)

^   ^   ^

Oahu Island

Honolulu

Kamehameha Schools
Kapalama Heights

Named for the great kings of the Hawaiian islands, these schools were founded in 1887 with a bequest from the female high chief, Bernice Pauahi Bishop, granddaughter of Kamehameha the Great. Though they had wives, queer research has shown that both Kamehameha I and his son, Kamehamcha III, also had male lovers (*see above*). These schools for children of Hawaiian descent began with just a few dozen students and today enroll more than 3,000.

IDAHO

RUBY CITY

It's just a ghost town now, but in the late 1800s this mining camp in the southwestern corner of the state was the home of Joe Monahan, the inspiration for the feature film *The Ballad of Little Jo* (1993). Joe was born Johanna (in the film, Josephine) and migrated west for reasons unknown. The film speculates that Jo/Josephine was kicked out of her eastern home for having an illegitimate child and that she cross-dressed to protect herself on the frontier after an attempted rape. Unfortunately, the film "straightens out" history by making Jo devotedly heterosexual, with a Chinese male lover on the side.

The facts of Joe Monahan's life are, in fact, obscure, though it is known that after coming to Ruby City in 1868, he built a successful cattle ranch and lived a celibate life. His birth gender was discovered only at his death in 1903. Though sometimes frustrating, the fictionalized film is still worth renting (if only to see Suzy Amis in male drag!).

BOISE

Boise Valley Traction Company
Seventh and Bannock Streets

Even a community as small as Boise in 1920—with a total of about twenty thousand residents in a state of fewer than a half-million people—had its share of same-sex activity. According to a recent article by historian Peter Boag, the public men's room of the Traction Company building, located at this corner in downtown Boise, was a "particular hot spot" of homosexual activity in the early decades of the century. Boag reports that, in the summer of 1920, Traction Company officials discovered a two-and-a-half-inch hole drilled in the partition between two adjoining toilet stalls. Suspecting that men were engaging in oral sex in the stalls, company officials tried to block the holes first with plates and then with 2 x 4s, but someone kept removing the barriers. As a last resort, the general manager placed a spy to observe the lavatory's users through a hole in the ceiling. After weeks of "periodic and frustrated observation," the spy, a company electrician named A. C. Sutton, finally caught a threesome in the act. Two of the men involved, E. E. Gillespie and W. E. Danner, were tried, convicted, and sentenced to a minimum of five years in the Idaho State Prison. (How the third man escaped punishment is unknown.)

During the trial, it became evident that the Traction Company "tearoom" was not the only public spot where men in Boise could and did engage in sexual relations with each other. Other cruising places included hotel lavatories, barbershops, pool halls, and streets and alleys outside of saloons. Gillespie, one of the accused, had faced a similar charge a year earlier for public sex at the city's Mitchell Hotel, but he had not been convicted at that time.

Boag notes that, sadly, consensual sex between men is still illegal in Idaho today, regardless of whether it takes place in a tearoom or in a private home.

Montana

Butte

Mary MacLane home
419 North Excelsior Avenue
In 1902, the little town of Butte became a household word with the publication of *The Story of Mary MacLane*. The diary of MacLane (1881–1929), a twenty-year-old originally from Canada, revealed her shockingly passionate thoughts and desires. The diary was an instant hit even by today's standards, selling eighty thousand copies in its first month alone.

What made MacLane's diary such a hot ticket? In it, she wrote of her passion for the "anemone lady," the only person in the world of any importance to her. The "lady" was in fact MacLane's English teacher at *Butte High School (southwest corner of Idaho and Park Streets)*, Fannie Corbin, and MacLane proclaimed that she loved Corbin "with a peculiar and vivid intensity, and with all the sincerity and passion that is in me." MacLane wondered why she could not have been born a man, so that she could love Corbin in the way she wished. "Do you think a man," wrote MacLane, "is the only creature with whom one may fall in love?"

When the book was published, MacLane was living at this address. (Fannie Corbin lived at *117 North Montana Street.*) MacLane left Butte after her meteoric rise to celebrity and spent the rest of her days living a bohemian life in Chicago. Despite her early literary success, she died poor and obscure in a small hotel room. "I don't know whether I am good and sweet . . . or evil and untoward," MacLane wrote in her diary. "And I don't care." How's that for lesbian pride!

GLACIER COUNTY

Blackfeet Reservation
Glacier International Peace Park
In 1916, a white man, James Willard Schultz, published an account called *Blackfeet Tales of Glacier National Park*, concerning his experiences among the Native Americans of northwestern Montana. Schultz gave a detailed account of a girl from the tribe named Running Eagle. Because she rejected traditional female activities, she was known as sakwo'mapi akikwan, or in English "boy-girl."

From an early age, Running Eagle wished to be a boy. "But if I cannot be one," she said, "I can at least do a boy's work." She joined her father in hunting, and when he was killed by members of the Crow tribe, Running Eagle dressed in men's clothes and joined the war party that avenged his death. By age twenty, she had achieved the name "Girl Chief."

As an adult, Running Eagle kept her own lodge and took a "wife" named Suya'ki, a woman "who wanted nothing more to do with men." According to Schultz, her lodge was "a visiting place for many girls, young married women, and not a few old women." Honored and respected for her achievements, elders of the tribe were still recalling her exploits in oral history a hundred years after her death in 1840.

I am someway the Lesbian woman. . . . All women have a touch of the Lesbian: an assertion all good non-analytic creatures refute with horror, but quite true: there is always the poignant intensive personal taste, the *flair* of inner-sex, in the tenderest friendships of women.
—Mary MacLane, *The Story of Mary MacLane* (1902)

NEW MEXICO

ABIQUIU

Georgia O'Keeffe home and studio

Anyone in the tiny pueblo of Abiquiu can direct you to the house on the edge of town where artist Georgia O'Keeffe (1887–1986) lived and worked from the late 1940s to her death. The entire town—situated on top of a mesa—consists of only twenty-five or thirty buildings.

O'Keeffe first came to New Mexico (which she called "the Faraway") in 1934 at the invitation of Mabel Dodge Luhan (*see* Taos *below*). About fifteen miles north of Abiquiu off Highway 84, O'Keeffe discovered a dude ranch called Ghost Ranch, where she spent most summers for the rest of her life. In 1940, she bought the house that she had been renting for six years. (It is still standing, and Ghost Ranch is now a religious retreat.) But O'Keeffe found the logistics of living at Ghost Ranch difficult. It was in a remote spot where it was difficult to get supplies and services, and the land was too dry and arid for raising her own vegetables.

In 1945, she found a house on three acres of land right in Abiquiu. The house, which dated from the early 1800s, was in ruins, and O'Keeffe reportedly bought it from the local Catholic church for ten dollars. She fell in love with its location, since it was built on the curve of the mesa with a view of the mountains. Completely surrounded by an adobe wall, the U-shaped house had its own well and a patio "with the bright sky overhead." On one of the patio's walls was an intriguing black door that captured O'Keeffe's attention and which she painted many times over the following years.

Though O'Keeffe's most celebrated relationship was with her husband, photographer Alfred Stieglitz, she was a bisexual who also enjoyed the company of a number of young women over the years. The renovation of the Abiquiu house was overseen by Maria Chabot, a writer who began living with O'Keeffe in 1941 in an intimate friendship—"a tall handsome young woman," as O'Keeffe described her. Maria planned all the details of the renovation, including the location of the fireplaces, and studied Hopi architecture in order to duplicate its designs. The adobe bricks were all made by hand on the property. The interior walls, made of smooth, dark gray adobe brought from one hundred miles away, were finished by a team of female artisans. O'Keeffe wrote to a friend that the walls were "the soft warm adobe one always wants to touch—or one sometimes feels it too fine to touch."

In all, the renovation took almost four years. It included the design and planting of an East Coast–style vegetable garden, complete with an expensive irrigation system. The house—which exudes O'Keeffe's spirit—is marked by a purity of design and decoration, with a color scheme of white, black, and natural adobe. A handful of O'Keeffe's paintings provide the only bursts of vibrant color. Some might call it austere, but O'Keeffe preferred its bare aesthetic. The artist's bedroom contains a narrow bed with fine white linens, and a fireplace, furniture, and shelves built directly into the walls. A simple hand-of-Buddha sculpture projects out from one wall. Only the living room is crowded with modern, 1940s-style furniture and a variety of natural objects, such as skulls, stones, shells, and rattlesnake skins—the very items she most loved to paint. Her studio, with a wall of windows looking out over the edge of the mesa, was formerly a livestock shelter. "It is so large it is like being outdoors," O'Keeffe wrote when it was completed.

The O'Keeffe compound, which appears exactly as she left it at her death and is maintained by the Georgia O'Keeffe Foundation, is open to groups of six visitors at a time by appointment only. The hour-long tours are booked several months in advance. Unfortunately, no photographs are allowed.

∧   ∧   ∧

ALBUQUERQUE

Pre-Stonewall bars

In her article "Differences and Identities: Feminism and the Albuquerque Lesbian Community," Trisha Franzen outlines a number of popular lesbian and gay bars that were operating in the decades before the Stonewall Rebellion. Most, according to Franzen, were located on Central Avenue (the old Route 66) about two miles east of downtown Albuquerque and just east of the university (where many gay people still live). Some of these bars were:

The Newsroom: In the 1950s, this was a smoky, sleazy, predominantly lesbian bar often subject to police harassment. Fights, Franzen notes, added to the "risk and excitement."

Old Heights: This was a gay bar opened around 1958 by a male couple, which was similar in style to The Newsroom. In the early 1960s, its successor, *New Heights*, opened at the same location, as part of an elegant restaurant, and was an improvement over the earlier bars. The crowds at both the Old and New Heights were mixed, gay men and women, and reflected the solidarity between lesbians and gay men at that time.

Cricket's, 5511 Central Avenue: Owned by a Native American woman, this lesbian bar opened in the mid-1960s as a private club, since that was the only legal way to have a bar that served only women. It is still in operation today, though it is no longer private and now serves gay men as well.

SANTA FE

La Fonda Hotel
100 East San Francisco Street

La Fonda was a new hotel and Santa Fe was a rural town when Willa Cather and her life partner, Edith Lewis, vacationed there during the summer of 1925. Situated on the southeast corner of Santa Fe's plaza, the adobe hotel was built on the same spot as an earlier inn that served travelers at the end of the Santa Fe Trail. La Fonda looks down San Francisco

Street toward St. Francis Cathedral, with its adjacent bishop's residence and gardens—the inspiration for Cather's novel *Death Comes for the Archbishop* (1927).

Cather had long wanted to set one of her novels in New Mexico, since she had first visited the territory in 1914. While staying at La Fonda, Cather began reading about Bishop Jean Lamy and Father Joseph Machebeuf, the Roman Catholic priests who first organized the diocese of New Mexico. In their story she found the novel she wanted to write, and she began absorbing information and local color while visiting Mabel Dodge Luhan (*see* Taos *below*). Cather's manuscript was completed the following summer, when she and Lewis returned to Santa Fe and stayed with their friend, writer Mary Austin, at her home, "*Casa Querida,*" 439 *Camino del Monte Sol.* Unfortunately, Bishop Lamy had not been the noble hero Cather depicted, but a racist who had ruthlessly trampled on the Indian and Spanish cultures of the region, and Austin was reportedly angered by Cather's romanticized portrayal of him.

TAOS

Mabel Dodge Luhan home
"Los Gallos"
Luhan Lane

Born to a wealthy family, Mabel Ganson (1879–1962) made a name for herself in early-twentieth-century New York City as Mabel Dodge, a patron of the arts and the host of a weekly salon at her apartment. She married four times and enjoyed numerous heterosexual affairs, but her memoirs, *Intimate Memories* (1932), also chronicle her early passions for women.

Dodge first saw New Mexico on a trip in 1916. She fell in love with the area, moving there in the 1920s and marrying Tony Luhan, a Pueblo Indian. They settled in this adobe home in Taos, which at that time was a dusty village with few white inhabitants. She helped promote an artists' colony in Taos, bringing artists and writers such as Georgia O'Keeffe and D. H. Lawrence to the area.

In 1925, while visiting Santa Fe, Willa Cather received an invitation to call on the Luhans (*see above*). Taken with the beauty of the region and determined to write a novel set there, Cather accepted the offer, and she and her partner, Edith Lewis, spent two weeks with the Luhans. They stayed in "the Pink House," which had been decorated by a drawing of a phoenix by its last resident, D. H. Lawrence. Tony Luhan graciously acted as tour guide, driving Cather and Lewis through the countryside and showing them sites that would later become incorporated into Cather's New Mexico novel, *Death Comes for the Archbishop*.

ZUNI

Zuni Pueblo
Route 53 (off U.S. 40)
On the border of New Mexico and Arizona is the Zuni Pueblo, which was once home to one of the most famous two-spirited people, We'wha (1849–1896). Today, Zunis still relate stories about We'wha, an accomplished weaver and potter who was one of the first Zunis to sell wares for cash. Anthropologist Mathilda Coxe Stevenson described We'wha as "the strongest character and the most intelligent of the Zuni tribe." In 1886, We'wha spent six months in Washington as Stevenson's guest, becoming the hit of the capital's social scene and being generally accepted as an "Indian princess" (*see also* District of Columbia).

In Zuni culture, We'wha was a *lhamana*, an individual who combined male and female work and social roles and often dressed in women's clothing. (Among whites, such individuals were commonly known as *berdaches*, a French colonialist word meaning "slave boy.") A *lhamana* was neither exclusively female or male; of We'wha, they said, "She is a man." Gay historians disagree about whether or not the *lhamana* role was exalted or lowly. Some contend that *lhamana* were holy people—priests and artists—while others say their role was one of humiliation and passivity.

As a child, We'wha lost both parents and was adopted into the family of an aunt. In many photographs at the Smithsonian Institution, We'wha can be seen weaving in front of the family dwelling, which was located in the southeast corner of the Zuni Pueblo. The pueblo is open to visitors every day until dusk, but no photography is permitted "until further notice."

OREGON

ASTORIA

Founded by trader John Jacob Astor in 1811 as a trading post and fort, it was here that white explorers first came into contact with the woman they called the Kutenai berdache. "Berdache" is a French term for those whom Native Americans call "two-spirited," individuals who subverted traditional gender roles. Whereas reports of male berdaches had been fairly common among whites, stories of female berdaches were much less frequent. This cross-dressing woman, known as Ko-come-ne-pe-ca, was a Native American guide, courier, and interpreter, who appeared at Fort Astoria in the year of its founding as a peace mediator, accompanied by her "wife." She in fact had several "wives" over the course of her lifetime and was, as one observer put it, a "bold adventurous amazon" who passed as a man "to travel with more security." Her travels took her to Montana, Idaho, and up into British Columbia. A white trader reported in 1837 that she was murdered by a Blackfoot Indian ambush. Accounts of her adventures were preserved orally in her tribe well into the twentieth century. Jonathan Ned Katz's *Gay American History* reprints many of the details of her life and exploits from contemporary white sources.

GRANTS PASS

Womanshare Women's Land Retreat
1531 Grays Creek Road
Located on twenty-three forested acres of land in southern Oregon, the Womanshare lesbian land collective has been around since 1974. By its own definition, Womanshare "is a home and family of lesbians involved and committed to caring for the land, personal growth and serving women in the community in some aspect." Neighboring other lesbian lands, over

the years Womanshare has offered workshops, apprenticeships, concerts, and gatherings, plus a visitor cabin and camping for women. Four to six women live permanently on the land, each in their own cabin. The cabins all have electricity and woodstoves, but no running water. In addition, there is a communal main house with a living room, kitchen (for cooking meals from their large organic garden), dining room, and shower.

The majority of buildings and the garden have been in place since the mid-1970s, beginning with the Main House in 1974, which was the only livable space during the first year. The Coop, an abandoned chicken coop, was the first of the cabins. Both of these buildings were on the land when it was purchased, but the other structures were built from the ground up by collective members, apprentices, and visitors. Two early members, Shannon and Tori, taught the other women carpentry skills. One cabin, called Yarrow, was constructed by women who came to carpentry workshops at Womanshare during the summer of 1978. One of the builders, working with a broken heart, put the foundation blocks in the wrong places and the cabin had to be rebuilt! The last buildings to be constructed were the Cascade, a cabin built in 1990 at a cost of ten thousand dollars, and a composting outhouse added in 1991. "Many hours of love and care have gone into each building," the collective advertises.

Womanshare welcomes women and girl visitors by prior arrangement (phone: 503-862-2807) for stays of one to seven days.

OTHER SOUTHERN OREGON WOMEN'S LAND COLLECTIVES FROM THE 1970s

Cabbage Lane
Full Moon Rising (name soon changed to 1/2 and 1/2)
Oregon Women's Land (OWL)
Rootworks (see "Sunny Valley" below)

^   ^   ^

LEBANON

Ray Leonard grave
Lebanon Pioneer Cemetery
Buried in this cemetery are the remains of Ray Leonard (1849–1921), an Oregon pioneer who was, in fact, a passing woman. Leonard was a cobbler who immigrated to Oregon from the East with his family in 1889. Leonard had helped his father, also a cobbler, and with his father's apparent approval had taken to wearing men's clothing at a young age. When his father died in 1894, Leonard took over his local boot and shoemaking business. According to residents of Lebanon, Leonard "dressed in overalls, and was thought by most who knew her, including the census taker, to be a man."

In 1911, Leonard's "secret" was discovered by a frontier doctor, Mary Canaga Rowlands, when Leonard was committed to an asylum under Dr. Rowlands's care. On Leonard's medical chart the doctor noted that the patient experienced "hallucinations and illusions of . . . hearing people trying to get into [the] room." The medical records also listed Leonard as a "widower" but gave no information about his wife.

Dr. Rowlands died in 1966, and her autobiography was published in 1995 by her grandnephew. In it, she revealed how Leonard's birth gender was detected. "It is customary to strip each patient entering the hospital," she wrote, "and give them a bath before they are given quarters. The hospital immediately discovered that Ray Leonard . . . was a woman. After her secret was out, Ray made a rapid recovery and came back to Lebanon to live the rest of her life."

According to the doctor's account, "the authorities made her [*sic*] wear dresses, but she confided to her friends that she wore pants below her dress because her legs got cold." Leonard clearly identified as male, asking the doctor, who continued to treat him when he was ill, "Look at me . . . do you think I have one feminine feature?" Finally, Leonard died in 1921, and his newspaper obituary referred to him as a woman.

PORTLAND*

James Beard home
2223 SW Salmon Street

Now an apartment building, this site was once the home of culinary great James Beard (1903–1985). Beard was born and raised in Portland and studied at Reed College. In 1922, he was expelled from the school for homosexual liaisons with other students and with a professor. (Ironically, in 1974, he received an honorary degree from Reed, after he had become a celebrity.) After the scandal, Beard took voice lessons in London from Enrico Caruso's coach and later returned to Portland, where he pursued a career as an actor.

Eventually, Beard relocated to New York City, where he achieved fame as the author of numerous best-selling cookbooks. The well-known culinary institute, the James Beard Foundation, was named in his honor and is located at the site of the Greenwich Village home he shared with his lover, architect Gino Cofacci.

Marie Equi home
1423 SW Hall Street

Born in Massachusetts in 1872, Marie Equi migrated to Oregon when she was in her early twenties with a female "companion." In Portland, she began a study of medicine that led to her graduation from the University of Oregon Medical College in 1903. During her medical career, Equi became known as an ardent defender of women's reproductive rights, performing abortions long before it was legal to do so. Equi's life was dotted with arrests for various "seditious" activities, including demonstrating against American involvement in the First World War and assisting Margaret Sanger in her birth control crusade.

*For help in compiling the Portland listings, many thanks to Tom Cook, president of the Gay and Lesbian Archives of the Pacific Northwest. For more sites associated with gay Portland, see "From Silence to Celebration! A Guide to Portland's Historic Gay Sites," a publication of GLAPN.

A lesbian who was once described as "capturing every well-known woman who comes to Portland," Equi apparently felt more for Sanger than friendship. In 1916, she wrote to Sanger, "My sweet, sweet girl. I love you with an ecstasy and understanding of spirit that you alone have imparted to me through the very brightness and flow of your intellect. . . . I kiss your sweet mouth in absolute surrender." Equi also had well-known affairs with the Irish nationalist, Kathleen O'Brennan, and with labor organizer and ACLU founder, Elizabeth Gurley Flynn.

But it was Harriet Speckart, whom Equi hired as a medical assistant, who shared almost two decades of the radical doctor's life. They lived together for a number of years, raising the daughter whom Equi had adopted in 1915—an early instance of lesbian adoption. The girl, Mary, called Harriet and Marie her "ma and da." During Equi's relationship with her, Harriet married briefly, divorcing her husband after only two months. A friend of her husband later remembered the man complaining that "Doc stole his wife." Harriet died in 1927, and Equi lived until 1952.

Gay liberation sites

Portland's first Gay Community Center was housed at *256 SW Alder Street*, which is now a parking lot. The center opened its doors in May 1972 and remained in operation for about a year, when it relocated to the *Pythian Building, 918 SW Yamhill Street*. The Pythian Building was also the site of the first gay pride celebration in Oregon's history. On the night of June 28, 1971, in honor of the Stonewall Rebellion two years earlier, a public dance took place in the second-floor banquet hall, sponsored by the Second Foundation, Inc.

Another early meeting place for gay liberationists was the *Centenary Wilbur Methodist Church, 215 SE Ninth Street* (now LaLUNA disco), where in the late 1960s and early 1970s, Portland's Gay Liberation Front, the first gay political group in the city, and feminist groups such as the local chapter of the National Organization for Women and WITCH (Women's International Terrorist Conspiracy from Hell) used to meet. A historic marker from the Gay and Lesbian Archives of the Pacific Northwest commemorates the building's history.

Dr. J. Allen Gilbert office
610 SW Alder Street, 7th floor

In 1918, a young woman named Alberta Lucille Hart, who had graduated from both Albany College (now Lewis and Clark University) and the University of Oregon Medical College (*see below*), consulted a psychiatrist at this address about the possibility of surgery to become a man. She had already been in the habit of donning men's clothing and had pursued several lesbian affairs during her university career. In 1920, Dr. J. Allen Gilbert wrote a report of his treatment of "H" in a monograph in the *Journal of Nervous and Mental Disease*. After consultation with Gilbert, Hart underwent a hysterectomy, cut her hair, and began to live exclusively as a man. Amazingly, Gilbert concluded that "If society but leave her alone, she will find her niche in the world and leave it better for her bravery."

Hart (1890–1962) was a pioneering transgendered person, who not only assumed male garb and took on a male identity but legally married a woman "of decided physical attractions," according to Gilbert. "Women of normal sex life," wrote the psychiatrist, "felt themselves attracted to her because of her aggressive male characteristics." Dr. Alan Hart was a leading physician in the field of tuberculosis detection, who practiced in Oregon, Idaho, and Connecticut. In addition, Hart also wrote three novels, the best known of which is *Dr. Mallory* (1935), set on the Oregon coast.

Alberta Lucille Hart residence
3610 NE Hancock Street (formerly 1096 NE Hancock Street)

In 1916, while studying at the University of Oregon Medical College, Alberta Lucille Hart (1890–1962) (later Dr. Alan Hart; *see previous entry*) lived in a boardinghouse at this address, a building that is still standing. It was here that she met and wooed Isabelle (Maude) Dabney, who is referred to as "Mrs. D" in the account of their affair written in a monograph by psychiatrist Dr. J. Allen Gilbert (reprinted in Jonathan Ned Katz's *Gay American History*). Dabney was "a beautiful young woman, who was unhappily married" and had an infant son, according to Gilbert's chronicle. Hart pursued her, and Dabney "responded warmly." During the next months, the two embarked on an affair, "accompanied by the most passionate excitement and orgasms in each." Hart proposed relocating to the East, where they would live together and she would take care of Dabney and the baby. But Dabney got cold feet and broke off the relationship soon after she obtained a divorce from her husband. Instead of Hart, Dabney chose a man she didn't love for the financial security a traditional marriage would bring her. After her graduation from medical school in June 1917, Hart began seeking psychiatric help for her "problem"—desiring women.

Earlier boardinghouses where Alberta Lucille Hart lived during her medical school career are also still standing, though the street numbers have changed. They are *the Roselyn Apartments, 424 NW 21st Avenue (in Hart's day, 110 North 21st Street)* and *2265 NW Hoyt Street (formerly 745 Hoyt Street)*.

Pre-Stonewall hangouts

Bars, tearooms, bathhouses, and parks constituted the only public meeting places for queer people (primarily men) before the advent of the organized gay liberation movement in the late 1960s. Some of Portland's early queer hangouts include the following:

Aero-Vapor Bathhouse, 1237 SW Third Avenue: A city park called Terry Schrunk Plaza now stands on the site of one of Portland's most famous gay bathhouses. Schrunk, according to local gay activists, was the city's notoriously homophobic mayor. Across the street from the bathhouse was Mama Bernice's, a gay bar during the mid-1960s.

Derek's Tavern/Family Zoo, 820 SW Oak Street: This building was a gay bar from at least 1957 until the mid-1980s, when it became a social service agency. Derek Akerson, its owner during the 1960s, claims that it was serving a gay clientele as far back as World War II, since it was the closest bar to a bus stop used by GIs on leave. The Portland police tried unsuccessfully to close Derek's in 1964, but the bar's attorney argued that to do so would violate the constitutional rights of homosexuals to gather in public. Renamed the Family Zoo in the 1970s, the bar was featured in Edmund White's famous account of his travels through gay America, *States of Desire*.

Harbor Club, NE corner of First and Yamhill Streets: This was one of the best-known gay bars in the city from 1946 to 1965. The navy declared it off limits to sailors, the only bar in town to receive that dubious honor.

Lownsdale Square rest room, Fourth and Salmon Streets: Oregon's oldest tearoom was first mentioned as a "queer" meeting spot in 1909. The little square was originally known as Fourth Street Plaza. During the 1940s and 1950s, the tearoom in the park was the site of numerous police entrapments of gay men, whose names and addresses were subsequently printed in the local newspapers.

Milwaukee Tavern, 1535 West Burnside Street: A lesbian hangout in the early 1960s, authorities tried to close the tavern by denying it a liquor license. One police report noted that the patrons "dress like men, act like men, and are believed to be from areas outside Portland."

The Music Hall, 413 SW Tenth Street: Opened in 1937, the Music Hall was the city's well-known drag club, popular with both gay men and lesbians. It was closed by Mayor Dorothy McCullough Lee, who announced that "pansies" were not welcome in Portland.

The Rathskellar, 722 SW Taylor Street: Opened as a straight beer and vaudeville joint in 1936, this bar achieved its gay reputation during World War II, when soldiers began frequenting it, using it as a cruising place. City officials closed it in 1951.

YMCA residence, Sixth and Taylor Streets: As in other cities across the country, Portland's YMCA was a popular cruising spot during the first half of this century, particularly for soldiers and sailors. Two public "scandals" over homosexual activity occurred here, one in 1912 and the other in 1951. Across the street from the Y, the Greyhound Bus Depot was also a gay pickup place.

Turnverein Hall
Fourth and Yamhill Streets (northwest corner)
Now a parking lot, in 1915 this was the site of the Scandinavian Socialists'
Hall, where anarchist Emma Goldman delivered her famous and groundbreaking public lecture, "The Intermediate Sex: A Discussion of Homosexuality," on August 7. Goldman was touring the country speaking openly
on what were considered controversial topics, but meeting no police resistance until she hit Portland. Two days before her lecture there, Goldman
was arrested on trumped-up charges of distributing birth control literature.
Her arrest was really a ploy by the mayor's office to keep her from delivering her speech on homosexuality. But Goldman's attorney, Colonel C. E. S.
Wood, got her off with a brilliant defense that exposed the city officials' fla-
grant abuse of Goldman's First Amendment rights. (Her lecture on homosexuality was attended by medical student Alberta Lucille Hart—*see above*.)

   In her autobiography, *Living My Life*, Goldman reported that much of
the censorship she encountered on her lecture tour came from her own
anarchist comrades. "Anarchism was already enough misunderstood, and
anarchists considered depraved," Goldman wrote; "it was inadvisable to
add to the misconceptions by taking up perverted sex-forms, they argued."
To Goldman's credit, she ignored her censors and presented her talk as
planned. She noted that many isolated and anguished homosexuals came
to speak with her after her lecture, and they "were often of finer grain than
those who had cast them out." "To me," Goldman said in defense of her
decision to speak freely on homosexuality, "anarchism was not a mere theory for a distant future; it was a living influence to free us from inhibi-
tions . . . and from the destructive barriers that separate man from man."

SUNNY VALLEY

Rootworks
2000 King Mountain Trail
Southern Oregon has a rich history of lesbian and gay back-to-the-land
movements. One lesbian separatist community established in 1978 is still

going strong, run by Ruth and Jean Mountaingrove. "The philosophy was that we would live without men, separate from the patriarchal world," says Ruth. "That is still pretty much the idea."

At Rootworks, there were originally only two houses—the Moonhouse and the Kitchen cabin. At the beginning, there was no electricity or running water. In the years that followed, Ruth and Jean added the Sunhouse, a barn (called "Natalie Barney"), and the All Purpose crafts cabin. In the barn is a study and a feminist library. From 1974 to 1984, Ruth and Jean also published the magazine *WomanSpirit* from an office in the barn, and *The Blatant Image*, another feminist magazine, was published there from 1981 to 1983; back issues of both are stored in the barn. Ruth credits *WomanSpirit* with bringing a lot of women to the southern Oregon region, by encouraging their creativity and spirituality. Though the magazine folded, Jean says, "The main elements of *WomanSpirit* are still being lived in this community now—feminism, spirituality, all forms of creativity, sisterhood, nature, art, music, dance, literature, healing, and personal development."

Gardens that are nestled around some of the Rootworks buildings are filled with vegetables, beans, and berries. Solar energy provides heat and hot water and also powers the community's lights. Ruth notes that "it's not easy in the winter and that's when women usually leave."

Though men do occasionally come onto the land (tax accessors and hunters, for example), Ruth notes that "it is possible to live relatively freely . . . even to the extent of being able to walk out at midnight if you wish without being afraid." Feminist women are invited to come and spend a night, a week, or months at a time and be part of living herstory.

Utah

Salt Lake City

In a groundbreaking new book by D. Michael Quinn, *Same-Sex Dynamics among Nineteenth-Century Americans: A Mormon Example*, the author explores lesbian and gay relationships and community in Utah in the last century. His remarkable findings show that Mormon society a hundred years ago was much more accepting of homosocial and homoerotic experiences than it currently is. Quinn profiles many lesbian and gay individuals and couples, among whom are the following.

Ada Dwyer Russell home
166 W North Temple Street

Born in 1863, actress Ada Dwyer Russell was raised as a Mormon. Her father, James Dwyer, had come west in a covered wagon and opened the first bookstore in the far West. He also helped found the Latter Day Saints University. The Dwyers' residence is listed at this location on North Temple Street beginning in 1867, when Ada was age four.

Ada grew up to be an actress who first performed at the Salt Lake Theater (*corner of South First and State*) and later on the Broadway and London stages. She married once but separated from her husband, the British actor Harold Russell, after the birth of their only child, Lorna; the reasons for the split were never disclosed. In 1912, she met poet Amy Lowell, who was eleven years her junior, at a women's luncheon club in Boston. The two were instantly smitten; Lowell wrote that "between us lept a gold and scarlet flame." Two years later, after much coaxing on Lowell's part, Russell moved into the Lowell family estate, Sevenels (*see* Brookline, Massachusetts). Though she gave up her own career for Lowell's and was the subject of Lowell's lesborotic poetry for the next eleven years, Russell maintained until her death in 1952 that the two of them had only been "friends."

Evan Stephens home
1996 S State Street

Evan Stephens (1854–1930) was leader of the world famous Mormon Tabernacle Choir from 1890 until his retirement in 1916. Stephens came to Salt Lake City from a small Utah town as a teenaged boy to sing with the choir, and he eventually worked his way up to choirmaster. At school, Stephens was called "Queener," and at a tender age he began having passionate attachments to other boys.

D. Michael Quinn has found that Stephens had a number of what he called "boy chums" over the years that he was choirmaster, who lived with him at this location (a four-acre lot surrounded by a boating lake) and at an apartment in downtown Salt Lake City. All of these "chums" eventually married, though Stephens never did. At age sixty-five, he "came out" in an official magazine of the Mormons, talking freely about his relationships with other men and boys. That so prominent a figure was able to do so, Quinn concludes, shows that nineteenth-century Mormons were more tolerant than their twentieth-century counterparts.

ASIDE-STEP

Poet May Swenson (1913–1989) was born in Logan, Utah, the daughter of Swedish immigrants. During her childhood, only Swedish was spoken at home, and English was actually her second language.

WASHINGTON

PORT ANGELES

Elwah Acres
Lower Elwah Road (off Dry Creek Road)
In the late 1970s, there was a fifty-five-acre self-supporting "gay farm" called Elwah Acres just west of Port Angeles and located in the middle of the Clallam Indian Reservation (but on land not owned by the Clallams). Two lesbians made the initial donation that purchased the land, the title of which was held by the Gay Community Social Services, or GCSS, a non-profit consortium that included groups such as RFD, Sappho Survival School, Gertrude's Carpentry Collective, Women's Elwah Land Project, Lavender Country, and others.

Half of the land was farmable, and the other half was woods. Selling hay paid the taxes, and growing vegetables and fruit, as well as raising goats and chickens, supplied food for those (four women and four men in 1977) living on the land. There were separate women's and men's spaces, with the women's having no electricity or running water. On the women's land, the resident lesbians held workshops, gatherings, and seminars for women visitors.

In 1977, the board members of GCSS (all apparently white) voted to sell the land to the Clallams, because they found it "politically awkward . . . to have a gay farm in the middle of an Indian Community which seeks independence from an imposing society." The Clallam Indians had never owned the Elwah land, and it was "a strategic piece of land that would benefit their community immeasurably."

SEATTLE

The Double Header/The Casino
407 Second Avenue

By most accounts, this is one of the oldest continually operating gay bars in the country. The Double Header was opened as a straight bar in 1934 by a heterosexual couple, John and Mary Delevitti. But from its earliest days, gay men and lesbians were welcome and congregated primarily in the basement room called the Casino, which had two pool tables and a card room. Former patrons remember that the Casino had no decorations on the walls except for Coke and Pepsi signs and a picture of Franklin Roosevelt, in whose first term prohibition was repealed. The Double Header and the Casino were within a few blocks of Pioneer Square (*see below*), a popular gay cruising area.

Garden of Allah
1213 First Avenue

Seattle's first gay-owned bar (which was also one of the first in the country) was located at this downtown address from 1946 to 1956, in the basement of the 1890s-era Arlington Hotel. The hotel sat midway between a gambling and red-light district at one end of First Avenue and an upper-class commercial district at the other.

The Garden of Allah, as the club was called, was operated as a gay cabaret, occupying a fifty-by-one-hundred-foot space that had been a speakeasy in the 1920s. From First Avenue, a guest descended a white marble staircase and slipped a one-dollar bill through a peephole for admittance to the beer and wine club. Inside, blue and pink lightbulbs provided a sensual ambience, and palm trees and stars stenciled on the walls gave the place a "Casbah" atmosphere. Tables were tightly packed in front of a stage, the centerpiece of which was a 1924 Wurlitzer pipe organ that accompanied every cabaret show. The owners paid off the police to avoid raids, and an ever-present off-duty cop was stationed in the club to make sure that same-sex couples didn't touch each other.

Female impersonators were the highlight of the Garden of Allah shows, and gay men, lesbians, and straight people alike composed the boisterous audiences. On opening night in 1946, the featured attraction was the Jewel Box Revue, the famous drag show that had started touring clubs in 1939. Over the years, some of the Garden's female impersonators also performed striptease.

With a decline in interest in drag during the repressive 1950s, the Garden of Allah eventually closed. For a while, the space was used to store nuclear-attack rations. Later, it became a biracial rock club called House of Entertainment, where Jimi Hendrix once played. The building was razed in 1974.

Lesbian-feminist Seattle

Seattle boasted a variety of resources and organizations for lesbians, beginning in the early 1970s. Among them were the following:

Lesbian Resource Center, 4224 University Way, NE: This is the oldest independent social services agency in the country exclusively for lesbians. It was founded in March 1971 and is still growing. In its early years, the Center hosted a variety of meetings, including twelve-step groups, poetry readings, dances, and a weekly Toklas-Stein Memorial Salon Tea with speakers or entertainment. Now located at *1808 Bellevue Avenue, Suite 204*, LRC offers a drop-in center, a lending library, a referral service, support groups, a health program, and educational services. It also publishes a monthly newsletter, *LRC Community News,* and operates with a paid staff of five.

Out and About, 7031 Second Avenue, NW: This was the city's lesbian-feminist newsletter, founded in 1976. *OAA* included articles, a calendar of events, announcements, and interviews and profiles of celebrities such as Rita Mae Brown and Alix Dobkin.

It's About Time, 5241 University Way, NE: A women's bookstore carrying all the usual array of feminist publications and ephemera, It's About Time also housed the *Triple Moon Women's Coffeehouse* in its basement.

Pioneer Square
First Avenue

Along this "sinful" edge of First Avenue in the early twentieth century were restaurants, pool halls, Turkish baths, and bars, where both heterosexual and homosexual men went looking for liquor, sex, and gambling. The square itself—particularly the area around the totem pole—was a popular gay cruising spot. Pioneer Square also boasted an underground men's rest room, which saw considerable action.

Pre-Stonewall lesbian bars

A few local lesbian bars listed in *Vector* magazine in 1968 are the following:

The Madison, 922 Third Avenue: In the early 1960s, it appealed "principally to girls," but by the end of the decade had become a men's leather bar.

The Stage Door, 158 South Washington: A bar that "cater[ed] to the girls" but also had some gay male patrons.

Seattle lesbians also had a choice of several all-women's bars in the Vancouver, B.C., area.

Seal Press
533 Eleventh Avenue East

Barbara Wilson and Rachel Da Silva started Seal Press, a feminist publishing company, in Seattle in 1976, in a small wooden garage in the backyard of Rachel's mother's Victorian home at *2622 Franklin Avenue East.* There they installed a Chandler and Price letterpress and set the type for their first poetry chapbook, *Private Gallery* by Melinda Mueller, by hand. On the copyright page they listed the address of Barbara's one-bedroom apartment on Eleventh Avenue on Capitol Hill, which for the first five years functioned as the Seal Press office.

"All of my closets were full of books," Barbara remembers. "I was the office person, book packer, and bookkeeper. I typed everything on the old

Hermes typewriter I got from my dad when I was sixteen." Because Barbara worked part-time in the pediatric unit of a local hospital, all Seal's early book shipments went out in recycled boxes marked "Lactated Ringers" on the outside!

Seal's early list consisted mostly of books with a Northwest focus. The press got its first "real" office in 1981 at *310 South Washington* in Pioneer Square. There Seal shared space with a collective printshop called Work-Shop Printers (who provided the inspiration for Barbara's first mystery novel, *Murder in the Collective*). That was also the year that Ginny NiCarthy brought the manuscript of *Getting Free*, a groundbreaking self-help book on domestic violence, to Seal. NiCarthy's book became Seal's first best-seller and allowed the founders to start receiving salaries and exploring bigger dreams. Faith Conlon (the press's current publisher) arrived from New York the following year and began working with Seal.

"There was a wonderful fervor about what feminism could do," Barbara recalls of those early days, "what feminist and independent publishing could do to change the world. Almost all doors were closed to us—nobody was publishing books about domestic violence and lesbian writing and writing by women of color in New York—and there was a certain stubborn joy in trying to pry those doors open." In 1996, Seal celebrated its twentieth anniversary, with a backlist including such lesbian writers as Becky Birtha, Rebecca Brown, Terri de la Peña, Ellen Hart, Sarah Schulman, Barbara Wilson, and yours truly.

Alice B. Toklas home
1006 Ninth Avenue

Now the parking garage of the Sorrento Hotel, this was the location of the home of Alice B. Toklas's family for the six years they lived in Seattle. Toklas's father owned a series of successful clothing stores in Seattle and San Francisco, where Alice was born in 1877. When a 1889 fire destroyed his Seattle venture, *Toklas and Singerman (First Avenue and Columbia Street, southwest corner)*, as well as much of the downtown area, Alice's father decided to move to Seattle in order to rebuild his mercantile empire. While living at this location, Alice attended *Mt. Rainier Seminary*, a girls' school located at *922 Fifth Street*, and later studied music at the University of Washington. When Alice's mother became ill with cancer in 1895, the Toklas family returned to San Francisco so that she could receive treatment. After she died two years later, the Toklases moved back in with Alice's grandfather, so that Alice could run the household and act as the hostess. (*See also* San Francisco, California.)

After a trip to Paris in 1907, during which she met her life partner, Gertrude Stein, Alice never again resided in the United States. During Gertrude's life, Alice served principally as a scribe and "housewife" and made taking care of Gertrude her primary focus. But after Gertrude died in 1946, Alice authored a few of her own books, including a memoir and the famous *Alice B. Toklas Cookbook* (1954).

WYOMING

CASPER

Independence Rock National Monument
State 220

For years, Independence Rock's two-hundred-foot height served as a natural landmark for westward-bound immigrants. Today, it bears a plaque honoring Dr. Grace Raymond Hebard (1861–1936), a professor and department chair at the University of Wyoming who was a pioneer of coeducation in this country and a lesbian. (*See also* Laramie, Wyoming.)

LARAMIE

Grace Raymond Hebard home
318 South 10th Street

Grace Raymond Hebard (1861–1936) came to Wyoming from her home state of Iowa, where she had attended the University of Iowa, the first woman ever to earn a degree in civil engineering there—an occupation not befitting a "lady." Her first position after graduation in 1882 was a drafting job with the surveyor general's office in Cheyenne, where she was eventually promoted to deputy state engineer. At the same time, she was pursuing a master's degree in English via correspondence school. After nine years as a draftsperson, she changed careers, becoming trustee and secretary to the trustees at the new University of Wyoming. Within a few years, she had earned her Ph.D. in political science (also by mail) and joined the very small faculty of the university (nineteen total). A popular teacher and librarian, Hebard often received "fan" notes from students, such as from one young woman who wrote, "I just love you so much, it almost hurts."

Hebard's particular interest was in western history, and today a room at the university's American Heritage Center is named in her honor. Notable among Hebard's scholarly achievements was her definitive biography of Sacajawea, the Shoshone scout who traveled on the Lewis and Clark expedition.

A strident feminist, Hebard fought for professional treatment for herself and for other female faculty. She also spoke and wrote extensively on the issue of women's suffrage—glorifying the example of Wyoming, which had allowed women to vote since 1869—and included Carrie Chapman Catt among her close friends. On her seventieth birthday, one colleague said of her, "To speak of Dr. Hebard's work with women is to speak of her whole life."

Hebard had two successive intimate companions in Wyoming. Irene May Morse was a member of the university's history department. The home that Hebard and Morse shared was a popular gathering spot for both students and faculty, and they dubbed it "Old Maids' Paradise."

At this address on Tenth Street Hebard lived for twelve years with her life partner, Agnes Mathilde Wergeland, a poet and historian. Their home was nicknamed "The Doctors' Inn," in recognition of their advanced degrees. When Wergeland died in 1914, a grief-stricken Hebard endowed two scholarships in her partner's name. The couple is buried under one headstone at the *Green Hill Cemetery, Fifteenth Street*, in Laramie.

Sources and Bibliography

Primary

Lesbian Herstory Archives collection. Brooklyn, New York.

New York Public Library.

City Directories of the United States, 1861–1935 (microfilm).

Books and articles:

Anderson, Margaret. *My Thirty Years' War: The Autobiography.* Horizon Press, 1969.

Baldwin, James. "Fifth Avenue Uptown: A Letter from Harlem," in *Nobody Knows My Name: More Notes of a Native Son.* Dell, 1962.

Bishop, Elizabeth. *One Art: Letters.* Selected and Edited by Robert Giroux. Farrar Straus Giroux, 1994.

Bowles, Paul. *Without Stopping: An Autobiography.* Ecco Press, 1972.

Culley, Margo, ed. *A Day at a Time: The Diary Literature of American Women from 1764 to the Present.* The Feminist Press at CUNY, 1985.

Faderman, Lillian, ed. *Chloe Plus Olivia: An Anthology of Lesbian Literature from the Seventeenth Century to the Present.* Viking, 1994.

Flanner, Janet. *Darlinghissima: Letters to a Friend.* Edited and with Commentary by Natalia Danesi Murray. Random House, 1985.

Gidlow, Elsa. "Lesbianism as a Liberating Force." *Heresies: A Feminist Publication on Art and Politics,* Vol. I, no. 2 (May 1977), p. 94.

Graham, Martha. *Blood Memory.* Doubleday, 1991.

Hansberry, Lorraine. *To Be Young, Gifted and Black: An Informal Autobiography of Lorraine Hansberry.* Adapted by Robert Nemiroff. Signet Books, 1970.

Hudson, Rock, and Sara Davidson. *Rock Hudson: His Story.* William Morrow, 1986.

Hughes, Langston. *The Big Sea.* Pluto Press, 1986.

Jewett, Sarah Orne. *The Country of Pointed Firs and Other Stories.* Doubleday Anchor, 1956.

Larsen, Nella. *Quicksand and Passing.* Edited by Deborah E. McDowell. Rutgers University Press, 1986.

Lewis, David Levering, ed. *The Portable Harlem Renaissance Reader.* Viking, 1994.

Lorde, Audre. *Zami: A New Spelling of My Name.* Firebrand Books, 1982.

Martin, Mary. *My Heart Belongs.* William Morrow, 1976.

Melville, Herman. *Pierre, Israel Poffer, The Piazza Tales, The Confidence-Man, Uncollected Prose, Billy Budd.* Library of America, 1984.

———. *Billy Budd, Sailor and Other Stories.* Penguin Books, 1967.

Nichols, Charles H., ed. *Arna Bontemps–Langston Hughes Letters, 1925–1967.* Paragon House, 1990.

Rechy, John. *City of Night.* Grove Press, 1963.

Rowlands, May Canaga. *As Long as Life: The Memoirs of a Frontier Woman Doctor.* Edited by F. A. Loomis. Storm Peak Press, 1995.

Russell, Ina, ed. *Jeb and Dash: A Diary of Gay Life, 1918–1945.* Faber and Faber, 1993.

Shockley, Ann Allen. *Afro-American Women Writers, 1746–1933: An Anthology and Critical Guide.* New American Library, 1988.

Stein, Gertrude. *The Autobiography of Alice B. Toklas.* Vintage Books, 1933.

Williams, Tennessee. *The Glass Menagerie.* Signet Books, 1987.

———. *Memoirs.* Doubleday, 1975.

Windham, Donald, ed. *Tennessee Williams' Letters to Donald Windham, 1940–1965.* Holt, Rinehart and Winston, 1977.

SECONDARY

Adams, Michael Henry. "Homo Harlem." Slide lecture given at the Lesbian and Gay Community Services Center, New York, June 27, 1996.

Alexander, Paul. *Boulevard of Broken Dreams: The Life, Time, and Legend of James Dean.* Penguin, 1994.

Allen, Thomas B. "Berkshires Serenade." *National Geographic Traveler*, Vol. VIII, no. 4 (July/August 1991), pp. 43–49.

The Alyson Almanac, 1994–95: The Fact Book of the Lesbian and Gay Community. Alyson Publications, 1993.

Baker, Jean-Claude, and Chris Chase. *Josephine: The Hungry Heart*. Random House, 1993.

Bakerman, Jane, ed. *And Then There Were Nine . . . : More Women of Mystery*. Bowling Green State University Popular Press, 1985.

Barth, Jack. *Roadside Hollywood: The Movie Lovers State-by-State Guide to Film Locations, Celebrity Hangouts, Celluloid Tourist Attractions, and More*. Contemporary Books, 1991.

Beatty, Noelle Blackmer. *Literary Byways of Boston and Cambridge*. Starrhill Press, 1991.

Bedini, Silvio A. *The Life of Benjamin Banneker*. Scribner's, 1972.

Bérubé, Allan. *Coming Out Under Fire: The History of Gay Men and Women in World War II*. Plume, 1991.

Bird, Christiane. *The Jazz and Blues Lover's Guide to the U.S.* Addison-Wesley, 1994.

Blodgett, Geoffrey. "John Mercer Langston and the Case of Edmonia Lewis, Oberlin, 1862." *Journal of Negro History*, Vol. LIII, no. 3 (July 1968), pp. 201–218.

Boag, Peter. "'Peeping Toms' and Tearooms in 1920s Boise." *Northwest Gay and Lesbian Historian*, Vol. 1, No. 3 (Summer/Fall 1996), pp. 4–5.

Boston Gay and Lesbian Architects and Designers, and Boston Area Lesbian and Gay History Project. "Location: A Historical Map of Lesbian and Gay Boston," 1995.

Boutelle, Sara Holmes. *Julia Morgan, Architect*. Abbeville Press, 1988.

Brown, Arnold R. *Lizzie Borden: The Legend, the Truth, and the Final Chapter*. Rutledge Hill Press, 1991.

Brown E. K. *Willa Cather: A Critical Biography*. University of Nebraska Press, 1987 (reprint of 1953 ed.).

Campbell, Karlyn Kohrs. *Women Public Speakers in the United States, 1800–1925*. Greenwood Press, 1993.

Carpenter, Margaret Haley. *Sara Teasdale: A Biography*. Pentelic Press, 1977.

Cayleff, Susan E. *Babe: The Life and Legend of Babe Didrikson Zaharias.* University of Illinois Press, 1995.

Chapman, Mary Lewis. *Literary Landmarks: A Guide to Homes and Memorials of American Writers.* Literary Sketches Magazine, 1974.

Chaput, Don. *Nellie Cashman and the North American Mining Frontier.* Westernlore Press, 1995.

Chase, Henry. *In Their Footsteps: The American Visions Guide to African-American Heritage Sites.* Holt, 1994.

Chase, Stacy. "Honoring Jack Kerouac." *Poets & Writers Magazine* (May/June, 1989), pp. 11–13.

Chauncey, George. *Gay New York: Gender, Urban Culture, and the Making of the Gay Male World, 1890–1940.* BasicBooks, 1994.

Cheney, Anne. *Millay in Greenwich Village.* University of Alabama Press, 1975.

Cheney, Joyce, ed. *Lesbian Land.* Word Weavers, 1985.

Citron, Stephen. *Noel and Cole: The Sophisticates.* Oxford University Press, 1993.

Clarke, Donald. *Wishing on the Moon: The Life and Times of Billie Holiday.* Penguin, 1994.

Clifford, Geraldine Jonçich. *Lone Voyagers: Academic Women in Coeducational Universities, 1870–1937.* The Feminist Press at CUNY, 1989.

Coakley, Davis. *Oscar Wilde: The Importance of Being Irish.* Town House, 1994.

Collins, Andrew. *Fodor's Gay Guide to the USA.* Fodor's, 1996.

Collis, Rose. *Portraits to the Wall: Historic Lesbian Lives Unveiled.* Cassell, 1994.

Cook, Blanche Wiesen. *Eleanor Roosevelt, Volume One, 1884–1933.* Viking, 1992.

———. "Female Support Networks and Political Activism: Lillian Wald, Crystal Eastman and Emma Goldman." *Chrysalis,* Vol. 3 (1977), pp. 43–61.

Coss, Clare. *Lillian D. Wald: Progressive Activist.* The Feminist Press at CUNY, 1989.

Cowart, Jack, and Juan Hamilton. *Georgia O'Keeffe: Art and Letters*. National Gallery of Art, 1987.

Cummings, Joe. *Texas Handbook*. Moon Publications, 1995.

Curb, Rosemary. "Catalog of Feminist Theater—Part 2—The First Decade of Feminist Theater in America." *Chrysalis*, Vol. 10 (1980), pp. 63–75.

Curtin, Kaier. *"We Can Always Call Them Bulgarians": The Emergence of Lesbians and Gay Men on the American Stage*. Alyson Publications, 1987.

Dahl, Linda. *Stormy Weather: The Music and Lives of a Century of Jazz Women*. Limelight Editions, 1984.

Daniels, Doris Groshen. *Always a Sister: The Feminism of Lillian D. Wald*. The Feminist Press at CUNY, 1989.

Dean, Andrea Oppenheimer. "Reflections from a Glass House." *Preservation*, Vol. 48, no. 4 (July/August 1996), pp. 70–81.

Deedy, John. *Literary Places: A Guided Pilgrimage, New York and New England*. Sheed Andrews and McNeel, 1978.

D'Emilio, John. *Sexual Politics, Sexual Communities: The Making of a Homosexual Minority in the United States, 1940–1970*. University of Chicago Press, 1983.

Dillon, Millicent. *A Little Original Sin: The Life and Work of Jane Bowles*. Holt, Rinehart and Winston, 1981.

Duberman, Martin. *About Time: Exploring the Gay Past*. Gay Presses of New York, 1986.

———. *Black Mountain: An Exploration in Community*. Anchor Books, 1973.

Duberman, Martin, Martha Vicinus, and George Chauncey, Jr., eds. *Hidden from History: Reclaiming the Lesbian and Gay Past*. New American Library, 1989.

Duggan, Lisa. "The Trials of Alice Mitchell: Sensationalism, Sexology, and the Lesbian Subject in Turn-of-the-Century America." *Signs*, Vol. 18 (Summer 1993), pp. 791–814.

Dupont, Joan. "The Poet of Apprehension: Patricia Highsmith's Furtive Generosities." *Village Voice* (May 30, 1994), pp. 27–29.

————. "Criminal Pursuits." *New York Times Magazine* (June 12, 1988), pp. 60, 62, 64–66.

Edelman, Lee. "Tearooms and Sympathy: The Epistemology of the Water Closet," in *The Lesbian and Gay Studies Reader*, ed. Henry Abelove, Michele Aina Barale, and David M. Halperin (Routledge, 1993), pp. 553–574.

Edmiston, Susan, and Linda D. Cirino. *Literary New York: A History and Guide*. Houghton Mifflin, 1976.

Estell, Kenneth, ed. *The African-American Almanac*. Gale Research, 1994.

Faderman, Lillian. *Odd Girls and Twilight Lovers: A History of Lesbian Life in Twentieth-Century America*. Columbia University Press, 1991.

————. *Surpassing the Love of Men: Romantic Friendship and Love between Women from the Renaissance to the Present*. Morrow, 1981.

Farnan, Dorothy J. *Auden in Love*. New American Library, 1984.

Faas, Ekbert. *Young Robert Duncan: Portrait of the Poet as Homosexual in Society*. Black Sparrow Press, 1983.

Fitch, Noel Riley. *Sylvia Beach and the Lost Generation: A History of Literary Paris in the Twenties and Thirties*. Norton, 1983.

Foster, Marcia. "We in the Northwest Still Love You, Alice B. Toklas." *Guide Magazine* (June 1989), pp. 10–11.

Franzen, Trisha. *Spinsters and Lesbians: Independent Womanhood in the United States*. New York University Press, 1995.

————. "Differences and Identities: Feminism and the Albuquerque Lesbian Community." *Signs*, Vol. 18, no. 4 (Summer 1993), pp. 891–906.

Friedwald, Will. "Silent Partner." Review of *Lush Life: A Biography of Billy Strayhorn*, by David Hajdu. *New York Times Book Review* (July 14, 1996), p. 8.

Funnell, Bertha H. *Walt Whitman on Long Island*. Kennikat Press, 1971.

Garber, Eric. "Gladys Bentley: The Bulldagger Who Sang the Blues." *OUT/LOOK* (Spring 1988), pp. 52–61.

Gay and Lesbian Archives of the Pacific Northwest. "From Silence to Celebration! A Guide to Portland's Gay Historic Sites." N.d.

Gener, Randy. "Back to the Cino: Remembering the Cafe Where Gay Theater Came Out." *Village Voice*, Special Section on Gay Games and Cultural Festival (June 21, 1994), p. 5.

Giles, James R. *Claude McKay*. Twayne Publishers, 1976.

Gillette, Jane Brown. "Louisa's Reward." *Historic Preservation*, Vol. 47, no. 6 (November/December 1995), pp. 42, 44–45, 93–95.

Gould, Jean. *Amy: The World of Amy Lowell and the Imagist Movement*. Dodd, Mead, 1975.

Gould, Lois. "Creating a Women's World." *New York Times Magazine* (January 2, 1977), pp. 10–11, 34, 36–38.

Grahn, Judy. *Another Mother Tongue: Gay Words, Gay Worlds*. Updated and expanded edition. Beacon Press, 1990.

Grier, Barbara. "Proud, Disputed Names." *Sinister Wisdom* 14 (1980), pp. 64–67.

Grier, Barbara, and Coletta Reid. *Lesbian Lives: Biographies of Women from "The Ladder."* Diana Press, 1976.

Grimes, William. "Wit at the Round Table: Was It, Er, Um, Square?" *New York Times* (June 28, 1994), C15, C20.

Guest, Barbara. *Herself Defined: The Poet H. D. and Her World*. Doubleday, 1984.

Hadleigh, Boze. *Hollywood Lesbians*. Barricade Books, 1994.

Hajdu, David. *Lush Life: A Biography of Billy Strayhorn*. Farrar Straus Giroux, 1996.

Hansen, Karen V. "'No *Kisses* Is Like Youres': An Erotic Friendship between Two African-American Women during the Mid-Nineteenth Century." In *Lesbian Subjects: A Feminist Studies Reader*, ed. Martha Vicinus. Indiana University Press, 1996.

Harrison, Daphne Duval. *Black Pearls: Blues Queens of the 1920s*. Rutgers University Press, 1993.

Harrison, Gilbert. *The Enthusiast: A Life of Thornton Wilder*. Ticknor & Fields, 1983.

Hart, James D. *The Oxford Companion to American Literature*. Oxford University Press, 1983.

Harting, Emile C. *A Literary Tour Guide to the United States: Northeast*. William Morrow, 1978.

Haskell, Barbara. *Charles Demuth.* Harry N. Abrams, 1987.

Higham, Charles, and Roy Moseley. *Cary Grant: The Lonely Heart.* Harcourt Brace Jovanovich, 1989.

Hippler, Mike. *Matlovich: The Good Soldier.* Alyson Publications, 1989.

Hobhouse, Janet. *Everybody Who Was Anybody: A Biography of Gertrude Stein.* Weidenfeld & Nicolson, 1975.

House, Charles. *The Outrageous Life of Henry Faulkner: Portrait of an Appalachian Artist.* University of Tennessee Press, 1988.

Hull, Gloria T. "Alice Dunbar-Nelson: Delaware Writer and Woman of Affairs." *Delaware History* XVII (Fall–Winter 1976), pp. 87–103.

Hurewitz, Daniel. *In Their Footsteps: Six Walks Through New York's Gay and Lesbian History.* Footsteps Publishing, 1994.

Johnson, William Oscar, and Nancy P. Williamson. *"Whatta-Gal": The Babe Didrikson Story.* Little, Brown, 1975, 1977.

Jones, Adrienne Lash. *Jane Edna Hunter: A Case Study of Black Leadership, 1910–1950.* Carlson Publishing, 1990.

Katz, Jonathan Ned. *Gay/Lesbian Almanac: A New Documentary.* Carroll & Graf, 1994.

———. *Gay American History: Lesbians and Gay Men in the U.S.A., A Documentary History.* Revised edition. Meridian, 1992.

———. "We'wha Went to Washington." *The Advocate* (Sept. 12, 1989), pp. 40–41.

———. "The President's Sister and the Bishop's Wife." *The Advocate* (January 31, 1989), pp. 34–35.

———. "Miss Willson and Miss Brundage." *The Advocate* (Dec. 5, 1988), pp. 45–46.

———. "Abe and Josh, Mary and Mercy." *The Advocate* (Sep. 13, 1988), p. 47.

Keister, Kim. "A Place to Call Home." *Historic Preservation,* Vol. 44, no. 3 (May/June, 1992), pp. 26–31, 87.

Kellner, Bruce. *Carl Van Vechten and the Irreverent Decades.* University of Oklahoma Press, 1968.

Kelsey, John. "The Cleveland Bar Scene in the Forties," in *Lavender Culture,* edited by Karla Jay and Allen Young. Revised edition. New York University Press, 1994.

Kenan, Randall. *James Baldwin*. Chelsea House, 1994.

Kennedy, Elizabeth Lapovsky, and Madeline D. Davis. *Boots of Leather, Slippers of Gold: The History of a Lesbian Community*. Routledge, 1993.

Knight, Carleton, III. "Philip Johnson Sounds Off." *Historic Preservation* (September/October 1986).

Koskovich, Ray Gerard. "Coming to Terms: From Passionate Friendship to Gay Liberation at Stanford." Stanford Queer Resources web page, 1995.

Kraft, Stephanie. *No Castle on Main Street: American Authors and Their Homes*. Rand McNally, 1979.

Kurth, Peter. *American Cassandra: The Life of Dorothy Thompson*. Little, Brown, 1990.

LaGuardia, Robert. *Monty: A Biography of Montgomery Clift*. Donald I. Fine, 1977, 1988.

Leeming, David. *James Baldwin*. Knopf, 1994.

Leverich, Lyle. *Tom: The Unknown Tennessee Williams*. Crown Publishers, 1995.

Lewis, David Levering. *When Harlem Was in Vogue*. Knopf, 1981.

Lieb, Sandra. *Mother of the Blues: A Study of Ma Rainey*. University of Massachusetts Press, 1981.

Ludington, Townsend. *Marsden Hartley: The Biography of an American Artist*. Little, Brown, 1992.

Madsen, Axel. *The Sewing Circle: Hollywood's Greatest Secret: Female Stars Who Loved Other Women*. Birch Lane Press, 1995.

Mainiero, Lina, ed. *American Women Writers*. 4 vols. Frederick Ungar Publishing Co., 1982.

Marcus, Eric. *Making History: The Struggle for Gay and Lesbian Equal Rights, 1945–1990*. HarperCollins, 1992.

Matthesen, Elise. "Quatrefoil Library Celebrates a Decade of Community Service." *Lavender Lifestyles* (March 29, 1996), pp. 34–36.

Mayne, Judith. *Directed by Dorothy Arzner*. Indiana University Press, 1994.

McGilligan, Patrick. *George Cukor: A Double Life*. HarperPerennial, 1991.

Meyerowitz, Joanne. *Women Adrift: Independent Wage Earners in Chicago, 1880–1930*. University of Chicago Press, 1988.

———. "Sexual Geography and Gender Economy: The Furnished Room

Districts of Chicago, 1890–1930." *Gender & History*, Vol. 2, no. 3, pp. 274–296.

Miles, Barry. *William Burroughs: El Hombre Invisible.* Hyperion, 1993.

Miller, Luree. *Literary Hills of San Francisco.* Starrhill Press, 1992.

Miller, Neil. *Out of the Past: Gay and Lesbian History from 1869 to the Present.* Vintage, 1995.

Miller, Page Putnam, ed. *Reclaiming the Past: Landmarks of Women's History.* Indiana University Press, 1992.

Miller, Patricia McClelland. "Afterword" to *Islanders* by Helen R. Hull. The Feminist Press at CUNY, 1988.

Mosel, Tad. *Leading Lady: The World and Theatre of Katharine Cornell.* Little, Brown, 1978.

Murphy, Lawrence R. "The House on Pacific Street: Homosexuality, Intrigue and Politics during World War II." *Journal of Homosexuality*, Vol. 12, no. 1, pp. 27–49.

Murray, Raymond. *Images in the Dark: An Encyclopedia of Gay and Lesbian Film and Video.* TLA Publications, 1994.

National Directory of Lesbian and Gay Community Centers. Lesbian and Gay Community Services Center, New York, 1996.

National Museum and Archive of Lesbian and Gay History, comp. *The Lesbian Almanac.* Berkley Books, 1996.

————. *The Gay Almanac.* Berkley Books, 1996.

National Park Service. *National Register of Historic Places, 1966 to 1994.* Preservation Press, 1994.

Newton, Esther. *Cherry Grove, Fire Island: Sixty Years in America's First Gay and Lesbian Town.* Beacon Press, 1993.

Nicholson, Stuart. *Billie Holiday.* Northeastern University Press, 1995.

Noel, Thomas Jacob. "Gay Bars and the Emergence of the Denver Homosexual Community." *Social Science Journal* 15 (April 1978), pp. 59–74.

O'Brien, Sharon. *Willa Cather: The Emerging Voice.* Oxford University Press, 1987.

Olson, Kirstin. *Remember the Ladies: A Woman's Book of Days.* University of Oklahoma Press, 1988.

O'Neal, Hank. *"Life Is Painful, Nasty and Short . . . In My Case It Has Only*

Been Painful and Nasty": Djuna Barnes, 1978–1981. Paragon House, 1990.

Palmieri, Patricia Ann. *In Adamless Eden: The Community of Women Faculty at Wellesley.* Yale University Press, 1995.

Paris, Barry. *Garbo: A Biography.* Knopf, 1995.

Paulson, Don, with Roger Simpson. *An Evening at the Garden of Allah: A Gay Cabaret in Seattle.* Columbia University Press, 1996.

"Physician's Memoirs Reveal 19th Century Lesbian—Seventy Years after Her Death." *Northwest Gay and Lesbian Historian,* Vol. 1, no. 2, pp. 1–2.

Prater, Donald. *Thomas Mann: A Life.* Oxford University Press, 1995.

Quinn, D. Michael. *Same-Sex Dynamics among Nineteenth-Century Americans: A Mormon Example.* University of Illinois Press, 1996.

"Radical Politics, Radical Love: Marie Equi's Life in Early Twentieth-Century Portland." *Northwest Gay and Lesbian Historian,* Vol. 1, no. 3 (Summer/Fall 1996), pp. 1–2, 7.

Ragaza, Angelo. "Aikane Nation: Sovereignty and Sexuality in Hawaii." *Village Voice* (July 2, 1996), pp. 34–35.

Rampersad, Arnold. *The Life of Langston Hughes. Volume I: 1902–1941: I, Too, Sing America.* Oxford University Press, 1986.

Reed, Kenneth T. *Truman Capote.* Twayne Publishers, 1981.

Reid, Dorothy. *Edith Hamilton: An Intimate Portrait.* Norton, 1967.

Retter, Yolanda. "Lesbian Activist Los Angeles, 1970–1990: An Exploratory Ethnohistory." Unpublished paper, 1995.

Reynolds, David S. *Walt Whitman: A Cultural Biography.* Knopf, 1995.

Roberts, J. R. "'leude behauoir each with [the] other vpon a bed': The Case of Sarah Norman and Mary Hammond." *Sinister Wisdom* 14 (1980), pp. 57–62.

Robinson, Roxana. *Georgia O'Keeffe: A Life.* Harper & Row, 1989.

Rochlin, Harriet. "The Amazing Adventures of a Good Woman." *Journal of the West,* Vol. XII, no. 2 (April 1973), pp. 281–295.

Roscoe, Will. *The Zuni Man-Woman.* University of New Mexico Press, 1991.

———, ed. *Living the Spirit: A Gay American Indian Anthology.* St. Martin's Press, 1988.

Ruckstuhl, Irma. *Old Provincetown in Early Photographs*. Dover Publications, 1987.

Salem, Dorothy C. *African American Women: A Biographical Dictionary*. Garland Publishing, 1993.

Salley, Columbus. *The Black 100: A Ranking of the Most Influential African-Americans, Past and Present*. Citadel Press, 1993, 1994.

Savage, Beth L., ed. *African American Historic Places*. The Preservation Press, 1994.

Sawyer-Laucanno, Christopher. *An Invisible Spectator: A Biography of Paul Bowles*. Weidenfeld & Nicolson, 1989.

Schanke, Robert A., and Kim Marra, moderators. "Straight Acting: Closeted Stars of Theater." National Museum and Archive of Lesbian and Gay History INQUEERY! series panel discussion, Lesbian and Gay Community Services Center, New York, August 8, 1996.

Schwartz, Charles. *Cole Porter: A Biography*. Da Capo, 1977.

Schwartz, Judith. *Radical Feminists of Heterodoxy: Greenwich Village, 1912–1940*. Revised edition. New Victoria Publishers 1986.

———. *"Yellow Clover:* Katharine Lee Bates and Katharine Coman." *Frontiers*, Vol. 4, no. 1 (Spring 1979), pp. 59–67.

Shelton, Suzanne. *Divine Dancer: A Biography of Ruth St. Denis*. Doubleday, 1981.

Sherr, Lynn, and Jurate Kazickas. *Susan B. Anthony Slept Here: A Guide to American Women's Landmarks*. Times Books, 1976, 1994.

Sherwood, Dolly. *Harriet Hosmer, American Sculptor, 1830–1908*. University of Missouri Press, 1991.

Shilts, Randy. *Conduct Unbecoming: Gay and Lesbians in the U.S. Military*. St. Martin's Press, 1993.

———. *The Mayor of Castro Street: The Life and Times of Harvey Milk*. St. Martin's Press, 1982.

Shively, Charley. *Calamus Lovers: Walt Whitman's Working Class Camarados*. Gay Sunshine Press, 1987.

———. "Big Buck and Big Lick: Abe Lincoln and Walt Whitman," in *Gay Roots: Twenty Years of Gay Sunshine*, Vol. 1, ed. by Winston Leyland (Gay Sunshine, 1991), pp. 125–140.

Silverthorne, Elizabeth. *Sarah Orne Jewett: A Writer's Life*. Overlook Press, 1993.

Simon, Linda. *The Biography of Alice B. Toklas*. Doubleday, 1977.

Smith, Barbara. "Discovering African-American Lesbian and Gay History." The Mark E. Ouderkirk Lecture in Lesbian and Gay History, Museum of the City of New York, June 25, 1996.

Smith, Jane S. *Elsie de Wolfe: A Life in High Style*. Atheneum, 1982.

Smith-Rosenberg, Carroll. *Disorderly Conduct: Visions of Gender in Victorian America*. Oxford University Press, 1985.

Souhami, Diana. *Gertrude and Alice*. Pandora Books, 1991.

Spoto, Donald. *The Kindness of Strangers: The Life of Tennessee Williams*. Ballantine Books, 1985.

Stein, Rita. *A Literary Tour Guide to the United States: South and Southwest*. William Morrow, 1979.

Steitmatter, Rodger. *Unspeakable: The Rise of the Gay and Lesbian Press in America*. Faber & Faber, 1995.

Summers, Claude J., ed. *The Gay and Lesbian Literary Heritage*. Holt, 1995.

Swisher, Bob. "One Big Community." *Southern Exposure*, Vol. 16 (Fall 1988), p. 29.

Taylor, Frank. *Alberta Hunter: A Celebration in Blues*. McGraw-Hill, 1987.

Terry, Walter. *Ted Shawn: Father of American Dance*. Dial Press, 1976.

Thompson, Mark, ed. *Long Road to Freedom: The Advocate History of the Gay and Lesbian Movement*. St. Martin's Press, 1994.

Timmons, Stuart. *The Trouble with Harry Hay: Founder of the Modern Gay Movement*. Alyson Publication, 1990.

Tozer, Eliot. "Bewitching Salem." *National Geographic Traveler*, Vol. III, no. 3 (Autumn 1986), pp. 67–74.

Trager, James. *The Women's Chronology: A Year-by-Year Record, from Prehistory to the Present*. Holt, 1994.

Troester, Rosalie Ricgle. *Historic Women of Michigan*. Michigan Women's Studies Association, 1987.

Turner, Florence. *At the Chelsea*. Hamish Hamilton, 1986.

Turner, Frederick. *Spirit of Place: The Making of an American Literary Landscape*. Sierra Club Books, 1989.

Uglow, Jennifer S. *The Continuum Dictionary of Women's Biography*. Continuum, 1982, 1989.

Van Voris, Jacqueline. *Carrie Chapman Catt: A Public Life*. The Feminist Press at CUNY, 1987.

Wagner-Martin, Linda. *Telling Women's Lives: The New Biography*. Rutgers University Press, 1994.

Wall, Cheryl. *Women of the Harlem Renaissance*. Indiana University Press, 1995.

Washington, Mary Helen. "Nella Larsen: Mystery Woman of the Harlem Renaissance." *Ms.* (December 1980), pp. 44–50.

Watson, Steven. *The Harlem Renaissance: Hub of African-American Culture, 1920–1930*. Pantheon Books, 1995.

Weatherby, W. J. *James Baldwin: Artist on Fire*. Donald I. Fine, 1989.

Weightman, Barbara A. "Gay Bars as Private Places." *Landscape*, Vol. 1 (1980), pp. 9–16.

White, Edmund. *States of Desire: Travels in Gay America*. Dutton, 1980.

Wilchins, Rikki Ann. "The Menace in Michigan." *Village Voice* (Sept. 6, 1994).

Windham, Donald. *Lost Friendships: A Memoir of Truman Capote, Tennessee Williams, and Others*. Paragon House, 1989.

Wineapple, Brenda. *Genet: A Biography of Janet Flanner*. University of Nebraska Press, 1989.

Witt, Lynn, Sherry Thomas, and Eric Marcus, eds. *Out in All Directions: The Almanac of Gay and Lesbian America*. Warner Books, 1995.

Wolf, Deborah Goleman. *The Lesbian Community*. University of California Press, 1979, 1980.

Wolfe, Maxine. "Invisible Women in Invisible Places: Lesbians, Lesbian Bars, and the Social Production of People/Environment Relationships." Unpublished paper, 1992.

INDEX

Taylor, Elizabeth, 87
Teacutter, Henry, 199
"tearooms," 223, 292–93, 309
Teasdale, Sara, 222
    Missouri residence, 223–24
Ted Shawn Theater, 28–29
Tennessee, 171–74
Texas, 175–84
Therien, Alek, 25
Thomas, Linda Lee, 37
Thomas, M. Carey, 63
    Pennsylvania residence, 131–32
Thompson, Dorothy
    New York City residence, 120–21
    New York residence, 77–78
Thomson, Virgil, 100, 123
Thoreau, Henry David, 25
Three Sisters (bar), 287
Thurman, Wallace, 98, 99, 137
Thurmond, Strom, 265
Tocci, 190
Toklas, Alice B., 66, 121
    California residence, 278–79
    Washington residence, 318–19
Tombstone, Arizona, 245–46
Torrey, John, 106
Towne, Laura, 169–70
Trask, Katrina, 128
Traubel, Horace, 69
Traverse City, Michigan, 215
Turnverein Hall, 310
Two Seventeen, Cherry Street (bar), 79

Ubangi Club, 100
Union Hotel, 57
United, The (community center), 232
Up the Stairs Community Center, 232
Utah, 312–13

Vaid, Urvashi, 32
Vail, Arizona, 246
Valencia Street, 279
Val-kill Cottage, 83–84
Van Vechten, Carl, 121–22
Vaughan, Fred, 91
Vermont, 43–45

Vidal, Gore, 3, 29
Virginia, 185–87
Vivien, Renée, 235

Wald, Lillian D., 84
    Connecticut residence, 8
    New York City workplace, 111–12
    New York residence, 126–27
Walden Pond, 25
Walker, A'Lelia, 101
Walker, Nancy, 88
Wall, Cheryl, 137
Walsh, David, 90
Ward, Freda, 174
Warhol, Andy, 142
Washington, 314–19
Washington Square (Chicago), 197–98
Waters, Ethel, 99, 137
Watsonville, California, 284
Weatherby Lake, Missouri, 226
Weatherford, Texas, 183–84
Webb, Clifton, 258
Weddington, Sarah, 178
Welles, Sumner, 233
    D.C. residence, 57–58
    Maryland residence, 67
Wellesley, Massachusetts, 35–37
Wells, Maine, 12–13
Wergeland, Agnes Mathilde, 321
Westport, Connecticut, 8
We Want the Music Collective, 214–15
We'wha, 56–57
    New Mexico residence, 300–301
Whan, Del, 260
Wheatlands estate, 134
Wheeler, Eleanor, 10
Whistle Stop Cafe, 153–54
White, Dan, 275
White, Edmund, 309
Whitehall Inn, 9
White House, 58–59
White Oak, Maryland, 67–68
Whitman, Walt, 277
    D.C. haunts, 59–60
    gravesite, 70
    Louisiana workplace, 161–62

About the Author

Paula Martinac is a writer, editor, teacher, and activist. Born and raised in Pittsburgh, she has lived in New York City for the past fifteen years. She is the author of two critically acclaimed novels, *Out of Time*, winner of the 1990 Lambda Literary Award for Best Lesbian Fiction, and *Home Movies*, a Lambda Award finalist in 1993. Her third novel, *Chicken*, has just been published. She was also the editor of *The Lesbian Almanac* and *The Gay Almanac* (Berkley Books). Her young adult biography, *k. d. lang*, was published as part of Chelsea House's "Lives of Notable Gay Men and Lesbians" series and was named as one of the New York Public Library's "1997 Best Books for the Teen Age."